INDIA
AND HER
NEIGHBOURS

N. JAYAPALAN

PRIMEMAX
BOOKS

Published by

PRIMEMAX
BOOKS

F6, Sector A2, Trans Delhi Signature City,
Ghaziabad- 201102, U.P.

Reprint 2026

Printed & bound in India

Preface

It gives me great pleasure to place this book in the hands of the readers. The book is quite comprehensive and covers the entire syllabus prescribed by the several universities. I have narrated all the events chronologically from the beginning to the end. I have also made a serious attempt to present the matter in a simple manner.

There is a plethora of books on "India and Her Neighbours." Most of them are bulky. Hence, I have written this book in a sizeable volume *i.e.*, neither too small nor too big.

My experience of teaching the subject at the college level for several years has prompted me to write this book to meet the requirements of students of the various universities. I have drawn freely from a large number of standard works on the subject and tried to present the facts in a concise and lucid form. The book also meets the requirements of the examinees of Civil Services Examinations in History and Political Science. I hope that the present book will prove to be more useful to the students than any other book on the subject available in the market.

I am thankful to the M/S Primemax Books, New Delhi for readily agreeing to publish this book and bringing it out expeditiously and efficiently.

Suggestions, if any, for the improvement of the book in the next edition will be highly appreciated.

N. Jayapalan

Contents

1
Introduction

In the modern world, it is better and fitter to know about the relations between India and her neighbouring countries like China, Pakistan, Bangladesh, Sri Lanka, Nepal, Burma and Bhutan. Really it is an interesting and innovative to the students of history in particular and the common people in general.

Now let us trace the history of India and her neighbours in brief in the introductory chapter before we go into the details.

The Crusades compelled the Europeans to discover the new sea routes towards the East in order to procure the essential commodities. Many adventurous sailors undertook voyages in this direction. The Portuguese were the pioneers. Among them the voyage of Vasco-da-Gama was conspicuous. His arrival in Calicut on the West Coast of India in 1498 marked the beginning of a new era in the history of the Asian countries. Ever since that epoch-making incident, the Europeans sailed towards the East and ultimately monopolised the Eastern Seas. India, Ceylon, Burma, Malaya and other Islands came under the European influence very soon. Japan and China practically closed their doors for the foreigners whom they often described as 'the barbarians'. However, in the nineteenth century even these highly conservative countries of Asia were trapped into the European colonial network indirectly by 'unequal treaties'.

China was known for its feudal character from times immemorial. The people of this land for ages hated foreign contacts and lived in isolation. Agriculture was their main occupation. The society was constituted by the peasantry and the landed gentry. The latter practically governed China. It was from these families of the petty landlords that most of the civil servants were drawn. The Dragon throne of China was adorned by the Emperor. In him, he combined the political authority as well as that of the priest. The Chinese believed that the well-being of the people depended much upon the virtue of the Emperor. As observed by Professor Guy Wint "by performing the sacred rites of spring ploughing, the emperor could make the whole land fertile." Taoism and Confucianism influenced the life of the people.

Though the Chinese apprehended the foreign danger and closed their ports the Western navy often attacked them and forced them open their ports. The Portuguese merchants reached the shores of China from Malacca in 1514. But, they were not permitted to land on the China Coast. Later on Thomas Pires headed a Portuguese mission in 1517 to Canton and succeeded in setting up a trading port. It was destroyed in 1522. In 1557 the Portuguese obtained Macao to the south of Canton. But, they were controlled by the Chinese officials until 1849 when the Portuguese demanded exclusive jurisdiction. The Lisbon protocol of 1887 recognised Macao as Portuguese territory. The merchants were followed by the Catholic missions into China Francis Xavier introduced Christianity. He died in 1552 off the coast of Kwangtung. However, Catholicism gradually penetrated into the Chinese territory. The Portuguese were followed by the Spaniards, the Dutch and the English. The East India Company's first vessel was sent to Canton in 1635. The opium trade obtained for them vast wealth in the dazzling Chinese silver. Other European countries also joined these to secure the commercial treaties. Russia also took keen interest in the Chinese trade. Canton, Shangai, Hong-Kong and other cities came under these commercial treaties. The peculiarity of the Western impact on China was that they created their respective Zones of influence by mutual understanding among the different vested interests.

Ceylon, the island kingdom, to the South of India also came under the Western impact. Her first foreign contact was on 15th November, 1505, when the large sailing ships of Dom Loureno da Almeida, having been blown of course while bound for the Maldive islands, sailed to the shores of Ceylon. The king of the Kotte gave them shelter. Thereafter, the Portuguese traders established their roots in Ceylon. They were succeeded by the Dutch in 1658. The British coveted the attractive natural harbour at Trincomalee from the king of Kandy. In 1795, they took this harbour on 14th February, 1815. The British forces captured Kandy and, its King Sri Wickrama Rajasinha was deposed and exiled to Madras. The Sinhalese Kingdom came to an end. Thus, Ceylon was under the foreign rule for 450 years from 15th November, 1505 to 4th February, 1948, when she became independent.

The Indian sub-continent was under the Mughal Imperialism when the European merchants set their foot on the soil of this land. The Portuguese sailor, Vasco-da-Gama, arrived on the West coast in 1498. He appeared in the court of the Zamorin of Calicut on 27th May 1498. Gradually, the Malabar Coast was monopolised by them. The Dutch came in 1597. On 31st December, 1600 the English Queen Elizabeth granted a charter to a company of merchants which gave them the monopoly of Eastern trade and the East India Company came into existence in 1612. The French established their first Factory at Surat under Francis Caron in December, 1667. The Mughal emperors granted them imperial 'Firmans' for starting their trade centres. These European powers joined sides with the warring Indian princes in South India and in Bengal. The Carnatic wars and the battle of Plassey would be enough to point out their involvement in this land. The European political atmosphere often determined the political situation in India. Ultimately, the British became supreme and established their paramountcy. However, since it is not within the scope of this book, Indian affairs are not discussed. But suffice it to say that the British Raj certainly unified the Indian sub-continent under one political umbrella. India became westernised by the end of 19th century.

The Afghans did not attract the attention of the Europeans for a long time due to their geographical position and also due to the existence of independent Khanates in Central Asia as buffers. When Maharaja Ranjit Singh conquered the territory right up to the Hindukush between 1780 and 1839, the Hindukush formed the boundary between Punjab (India) and Afghanistan. Then the English East India Company developed interest in Afghanistan. But so long as Ranjit Singh was alive they could not penetrate, for they had entered into a treaty of friendship with him in 1831. When Dost Mohammed came to the throne of Afghanistan, became a subject of interest. Lord Palmerston inaugurated the British interests in Afghanistan. Russia also joined this game. She was very much concerned with the Ottoman empire, Iran and the Khanates of Central Asia. Shah Shuja, who was ousted out of Afghanistan was enjoying a pension from the East India Company. Palmerston employed this pensioner as a threat to pressurise the Ameer of Afghanistan to join the English camp instead of slipping into the rival camp of Russia. Lord Auckland, who came to India as Governor-General in 1836 was authorised to send a confidential agent to Dost Mohammed to negotiate a political and commercial treaty so as to prevent the Russian influence at Kabul. They also compelled the Shah of Iran, Shah Mohammed Shah, who succeeded Nadir Shah in 1834, to pressurise the Ameer. Thus, the triangular forces were operating around Afghanistan when Lord Auckland sent Col. Alexander Burnes to Kabul to open negotiations. At this juncture, the Ameer tactfully avoided the rupture by demanding the English to help him recover the province of Peshawar from Ranjit Singh. This could not be complied with by the English due to the Lahore Treaty obligations.

Therefore, the object of this book is the study of the relations between India and her neighbours in a detailed manner. As the history of the India's relations with her neighbours is imminent the readers are invited to go through the succeeding chapters to get a clear picture of such relations.

2

China

I. Background

Modern China covers the same area as the Chinese Empire at the end of the 19th century, except Outer Mongolia which has become an independent state. The old Chinese Empire consisted of the Chinese and non-Chinese people. The most important non-Chinese people were the Tibetans, Mongols and Turkish (now known as Uyghurs). The Chinese form over 93 per cent of the population and they predominate in areas of high population density. The non-Chinese people are found in low population density areas like mountains and deserts.

Three thousand years ago the Chinese occupied only the middle and lower basins of the Hwang-ho or the Yellow River. From this homeland they expanded in historical times in three directions. The main group expanded southward to the Yangtse-Kiang river, the South China coastlands, the West River basin and Yunnan. The second group expanded westward into the borderlands of Tibet and Turkestan. The third group expanded north eastward into Manchuria. In recent times the Chinese have migrated to several countries in Asia particularly in Malaya, Singapore, Korea, and Indonesia etc. These Overseas Chinese have retained their language and culture in the countries of their adoption.

The Yellow River basin is a region of low rainfall, hot summers and cold winters; Manchuria and the northwestern borderlands are even drier with greater extremes of temperature; the Yangtse-Kiang Valley and South China are regions of high rainfall, mild winters and humid summers. The climatic differences are reflected in the prevailing forms of agriculture. In the north wheat, millet and sorghum are the principal crops, whereas China south of the Hwang-ho and the Yangtse-Kiang is a region of wet rice cultivation.

The Chinese coast line on the looks out towards the Pacific Ocean but Japan, the Ryukyu Islands, Formosa (Taiwan) and the Philippines separate China from the Pacific. On the North, West and South-West there are great mountains and deserts which isolated China and prevented her from establishing contact with the civilisations of South Asia and Europe. In the North, there is the arid plateau of Mongolia consisting of the uninhabitable Gobi desert (Shamo or 'Sea of Sand') and short and long grass steppe lands. In the North-East there is Sinkiang or East Turkestan which has mountains and deserts. However, it has been in the past the main avenue of overland trade between China, and West Asia and India. The ancient 'Silk Road' ran through Sinkiang and Roman merchants used to go here to buy Chinese silk. South of Sinkiang lies Tibet, a plateau region of 4,000 to 5,000 metres above the sea level and uninhabitable because of its altitude and aridity. The lower slopes provide pasture for animals and in a few sheltered valleys, agriculture can be carried on. Tibet is separated from India by the mighty Himalayas. While the Tibetan plateau is treeless, the southern slopes of the Himalayas descending to the plains of India are covered with dense forests as they receive a heavy rainfall. Tibet is more accessible from China than from India—a fact which has helped to determine her history in modern times. (She has been conquered by China) In the South-West of China, there are mountains less high than the Himalayas, but forming natural frontiers with Burma, Laos and Vietnam. China's contact with her southern neighbours was only by sea.

II. History of Sino-Indian Relations

The relations between India and China have been cordial. When China was the victim of Japanese aggression, the people of India sympathised with her. In 1941, Chiang Kai-Shek and Madam Chiang came to India. After India became free in 1947, the first country which came forward to establish diplomatic relations with her was the Nationalist Government of China. However, when it was overthrown by the Communists in 1949, the Government of India recognised the Government of Red China on 30th December, 1949, many delegations have been exchanged between the two countries. India has left no stone unturned to bring Red China into the United Nations.

Chinese Hard-Line Policy and India: China, after 1949 decided to follow a 'hard-line policy' in its relations with non-Communist nations. Consequently, India was viewed by the Chinese as an appendage of western imperialism. It believed that Indian freedom was unreal, and Indian Non-alignment was a 'show', Nehru was described by the Chinese press as a "stooge of the imperialists with slavish and bourgeoisie reactionary character." In the era of 'hard-line policy' which continued till 1952, China showed little concern for India. Mao Tse Tung, in his letter to B.T. Randive, even expressed the hope that India would soon be liberated by the Communist Party from Anglo-American imperialism and its Indian 'lackeys'. Such Chinese negative and hostile attitude towards India prevented the growth of Sino-Indian relations during this period.

The most important issues with which both India and China were closely involved during 1950's were: (*i*) The Tibet issue, and (*ii*) the Korean crisis.

(*i*) *Tibet Issue*: After the establishment of Communist regime, People Republic of China decided to expand its frontiers and signify the minorities. China regarded Tibet as a part of China and made plans to secure annexation of Tibet. India had sympathies with the people of Tibet and wanted that their right to self-rule should be respected by China. It wanted that China should peacefully settle the question of its relationship with Tibet. India pleaded with China the need to hold negotiations with Dalai Lama, the temporal and spiritual head of Tibet, for maintaining the autonomy of Tibet in one form or the other. The Chinese not only ignored this suggestion but also attacked it as an interference in the internal affairs of China, and called India as the agent of Anglo-American imperialism. In October, 1950, China sent her troops into Tibet and established its military control over Tibet. This Chinese move shocked India. India had always maintained that Tibet was not a part of China. China had only nominal suzerainty over Tibet, and was bound to respect the autonomy of Tibet in one form or the other. The Chinese not only ignored this suggestion but also attacked it as an interference in the internal affairs of China, and called India as the agent of Anglo-American imperialism. In October, 1950, China sent her troops into Tibet and established its military control over Tibet. This Chinese move shocked India. India had always maintained that Tibet was not a part of China. China had only nominal suzerainty over Tibet and was bound to respect the autonomy of Tibet, India, therefore, decided to send a strong note to China. In a protest note dated 26th October, 1950 India declared, "In the present context of world events, the invasion by Chinese troops on Tibet cannot but be regarded as deplorable and in the considered judgment of the Government of India not in the interest of China or of peace." The note was strongly criticised by the Chinese. Peking reacted sharply and asked India to mind her own business. It further declared that Tibet was an integral part of China. In may 1951, China forced Dalai Lama's representative to sign a 17-point Agreement and under this Tibet became "The Tibet region of China", with a loose but unreal form of autonomy. Governed by the desire to secure friendly relations with China, India, after overcoming the initial shock of Chinese invasion of Tibet, decided to overlook and reconcile with Chinese action. As such when the Tibet issue came up for discussion at the United Nations, India took up the stand that the matter should be peacefully settled between China and Tibet.

In September, 1952, the Government of India and China announced their agreement that Indian mission in Lhasa should henceforth be designated as Consulate-General of India. This change in the status of Indian mission followed the change in the political set up in Lhasa itself whereby the Chinese government established its full control over the foreign relations of Tibet. Later on, in 1954, India entered into an agreement with China and formally recognised the Chinese sovereignty over Tibet. Thus, the friction in Sino-Indian relations that had come to develop since the Chinese march into Tibet in 1950, came to an end.

(*ii*) *Korean Crisis*: On the issue of the Korean crisis, Sino-Indian relations were governed by India's desire to develop friendship with China and to act as a mediator between China and the West. In 1950-53, India played a significant role as a mediator for achieving truce in Korea. From the very beginning of the Korean crisis, India realised the strategic importance of Korea to China and hence tried to use her influence to solve the Korean problem in co-operation with China. Although India had endorsed the UN resolutions condemning North Korea as the aggressor and had also supported the UN intervention for peace keeping in Korea, it opposed the decision of UN forces to cross the 38th parallel in Korea on the ground that it would lead to China's direct entry into war. When the UN forces did in fact cross the 38th parallel, India denounced the action as a dangerous Western move. When in November, 1950, China intervened directly and pushed back the UN forces, India, refused to vote in favour of the UN resolution which aimed at branding China as an aggressor. This action was heavily criticised by America and other Western 'friends' of India but was highly appreciated by China. India's independent, active and bold role in Korean crisis drew appreciation from China and the Chinese leadership began to realise the need for developing friendship with India.

Sino-Indian Relations Since 1951: Chairman Mao-Tse Tung graced the celebrations of the Republic Day of India on 26th January, 1951 by his presence at the Indian Embassy in Beijing, and toasted to the friendship of the peoples of China and India, India's whole-hearted support for the recognition of People's Republic of China (PRC) as the rightful representative of China and her decision to remain away from the Sanfrancisco Conference of 1951, which was called for signing a peace treaty with Japan—one of the reasons being that the PRC was not invited for it, received full appreciation from China, and this brightened the chances for the development of Sino-Indian friendly co-operation in post-1951 period. Chinese leaders began to understand Indian leaders better. They started recognising the fact that India was really independent and non-aligned.

In January, 1951, the Rice-Jute Barter Agreement was signed between India and China. In 1952, an Indian cultural delegation led by Mrs. Vijaya Laxmi Pandit visited China in 1952, on the invitation of PRC and observed on return that it had found in China a desire for friendship and understanding of India.

The Tibet-agreement and Panchsheel: The Sino-Indian friendly relations developed maturity, when on 29th April, 1954, an eight years agreement on trade and intercourse was signed. Under this agreement India gave up all the territorial rights enjoyed by the British government of India in Tibet, and recognised Tibet as a region of China. By this agreement, India and China pledged themselves to follow the Five Principles, called the Panchsheel, in their relations with each other. The five principles (Panchsheel) incorporated in the preamble of the agreement, were:

1. The mutual recognition of each other's territorial integrity and sovereignty.
2. Non-interference in each other's internal affairs.
3. Non-aggression.
4. Equality and mutual benefit.
5. Peaceful coexistence.

China gave a solemn undertaking to respect the territorial integrity and sovereignty of India. This agreement initiated a new era of Sino-India friendship and co-operation. The recognition of Chinese sovereignty over Tibet by India strengthened the Sino-Indian relations and the leaders of both the countries started taking similar stands on many world issues. Both voiced opposition to colonialism, military pacts and many other aspects of Western policies in Asia.

In June, 1954, Chinese Premier Chou-En-Lai visited India and he was given a rousing welcome. Both Nehru and Chou-En-Lai reaffirmed the five principles of Panchsheel in the joint communiqué issued at the end of the visit. "This, writes T.N. Kaul, gave Panchsheel added weight and respectability."

Hindi-Chini Bhai Bhai Spirit: "This was the honeymoon period of Sino-Indian relations when slogans like *Hindi-Chini Bhai Bhai* became popular in both the countries". Nehru's visit, later in the same year to Beijing, the close co-operation between India and China at the Bandung Conference of April, 1955, and

Chou En-Lai's second visit to India during November-December, 1956 went a long way in improving and stabilising the relations between the two countries. The signing of Lhasa Protocol on 1st April, 1955, India's full support to China over the issue of Taiwan, and for PRC's right to get admission to United Nations pleased China. It reciprocated by giving support to India over Goa. Both India and China joined hands in opposing SEATO, Baghdad Pact and other military alliances. The development of Sino-Indian relations came to be a common objective with the Indian and Chinese leaders.

Sino-Indian Differences over Maps: However, everything was not well even during this 'honeymoon period' of Sino-Indian relations. In 1954, some maps were published in China which showed large parts of Indian territories as Chinese territory. During his October 1954 visit to Beijing, Nehru brought this fact to the notice of Chou. He got the reply that these were the copies of old maps and were to be revised in the times to come. India accepted the Chinese explanation, but at the same time became apprehensive about Chinese intentions. Such Indian apprehensions proved to be correct when in June, 1955, Chinese troops set up a camp at Barahoti and came down to 10 miles South of the Niti Pass. In April, 1956, they entered the Nilag area of Uttar Pradesh. Six months later, they violated Indian territory through the Shipki Pass. In spite of these provocations, India took no action except the sending of some protest notes to China. During November, 1956 and January, 1957 visit of Chou En-Lai to New Delhi, it was decided "that while there were no disputes regarding the border, there were certain petty problems which should be settled amicably."

Chinese Movements along Borders with India: At about the same time, however, the Chinese started building the Sinkiang-Tibet Road — The road that crossed into eastern Ladakh. The Government of India did not become aware of it until the autumn of 1958. By 1957, Chinese intrusions into Indian territory had become a regular feature. India felt alarmed at the Chinese postures and started taking steps for strengthening Indian security positions all along the border with China. Relations with China started causing anxiety. The Barahoti and the Aksai Chin areas were intruded by the Chinese troops, and in July, 1958, they occupied India's Khurnak Fort. In the same month 'China Pictorial' an official Chinese monthly published certain maps of China showing large parts of India territory as Chinese. When the Indian Government draws the attention of Chinese government to this matter through a note, the latter replied that since China had not conducted surveys of the area and also had not consulted the countries concerned about the border issue, therefore, it could not change the maps. This reply showed a marked and definite departure from the previously held Chinese stand that 'the maps were old and would be revised in times to come.' The new stand meant that Chinese reserved the right to declare any time the territory shown as Chinese in her maps as disputed territory.

Chinese March into NEFA: Late in September, 1958, the Government of India received the information that a detachment of Chinese troops had crossed into Lohit Division of NEFA. In October, 1958, India came to know about the Aksai Chin road which Chinese had built up earlier and which crossed into the Indian territory. India sent a strong protest note to China and asked for an early reply to it. At about the same time, Indian Government received information that the Chinese had established out posts at Lapthal and Sangcho Malla along the Indo-Tibetan border. Consequently, another protest note was sent to China.

Trouble in Tibet: In 1959, the Tibet issue once again came to seriously affect Sino-Indian relations. On 9th March, 1959, demonstrations against China broke out in Lhasa and the Tibetan cabinet issued a proclamation declaring the Independence of Tibet. The PRC army, however, suppressed the revolt. Dalai Lama fled Tibet and along with his followers took shelter in India. Thereupon the Government of India granted political asylum to Dalai Lama and his followers. The Chinese sharply reacted against this Indian decision and showed their anger by leveling false charges against India and by increasing their intrusions into Indian territory. The news about the presence of an armed detachment in the western region of Pangora Lake and about the establishment of Chinese camp at Spanyggur gave big jolts to Sino-Indian relations. The increased frequency and intensity of Chinese intrusions into India made things worst. On 7th August,

1959, a Chinese patrol crossed into Indian border at Khinzemanne and on 25th August, 1959, a large Chinese detachment crossed the frontier in the Sabansiri Division of NEFA and occupied the Indian frontier post of Longju. This was followed up by a whole series of border incidents. All these incidents aroused strong anti-China feelings in India. Nehru himself felt greatly disturbed, and described the Chinese occupation of Longju as a 'clear case of aggression' against India. He affirmed the resolve to protect the territorial integrity of India, but at the same time expressed his faith in peaceful settlement of the dispute and declared: "the door is always open to accommodation." On the other hand, Chou-En-lai told Nehru that China did not recognise India's Northern frontiers. He stated: "The Sino-Indian boundary had never been formally delimited, that so-called MacMahon line was a product of British policy of aggression against the Tibet region of China" and therefore, "it cannot be considered legal." He further stated that Sino-Indian boundary question is a complicated question left over by history. Such a reply from Chou-En-Lai made it clear that China regarded her boundary with India as an open boundary which was yet to be demarcated. It was with shock that India received this intimation and herself faced with a serious Chinese threat. Sino-Indian boundary became a hot and disputed boundary. On 6th October, 1959 the Chinese ambushed a party of 19 Indians in Ladakh and killed 16 of them. On 9th November, 1959, Chou En-Lai proposed a withdrawal of troops by both sides to 12½ miles on each side of the positions held by them. This proposal was not accepted by India, because it meant indirect acceptance of Chinese view of the Sino-India boundary. On 18th December, 1959 China rejected the Indian proposal for the neutralisation of the whole disputed areas in Ladakh but accepted the proposal for the neutralisation of Longju. The Indian proposal was that China should withdraw its civil and military forces to the east of the Indian border in Ladakh and India in turn would withdraw to the west of the line claimed as international frontier in the Chinese maps of 1956. This proposal was rejected by China and it proposed the neutralisations of Khinzemanne, Lapthal Nilang, Shipki Pass, Demchok, Chura and Chuje. This proposal was rejected by India.

III. Border War

The initial Sino-Indian differences over issue of boundary between the two countries developed into a full-fledged boundary dispute in the late 1950s. By 1959, India and China came to develop highly tense and strained relations because of the border incidents and the rigid Chinese approach towards the situation. Replying to a debate in Rajya Sabha, on 9th December, 1959, Nehru observed: "The whole picture of the world is changing so far as India is concerned and India's borders are concerned. Here is a historical change of greatest magnitude. For the first time, two major powers of Asia face each other on an armed border. For the first time, a world power or a would be world power sits near our borders and frontiers." Indeed, India felt greatly disturbed by the Chinese illegal occupation of a large part of Indian territory and by the continued hostile postures of China. By the end of the fifties, India came to realise that her attempts to develop friendly co-operation with China has failed and the Chinese menace had come to develop all along here northern and eastern borders. "What originated in early 1950s as the Chinese game of mapmanship came to develop in the late fifties into the Chinese game of annexing a large part of Indian territory." From the categorical statement that "there was no boundary dispute between China and India" there came to be a stand that "Sino-India boundary was never delimited and that the so-called MacMahon line was a product of British policy of aggression against the Tibet region of China and, therefore, unacceptable to China." This change in Chinese stand on boundary issue was received as a great shock, and India found herself face to face with a serious threat to its northern borders with China. Increased presence of Chinese troops on the borders and their frequent intrusions into Indian territory became a source of big tension and strain for India. The border incidents started multiplying. Between 1955-62 there were more than 30 clear cases of the violation of Indian frontiers by Chinese troops, and these made the Sino-Indian boundary a hot boundary. The relations between the two countries became specially bitter after the Tibetan uprising in 1959, and a political asylum that India granted to Dalai Lama and his followers.

Even in the face of this Chinese threat to its frontiers, India was not prepared to miss the opportunity to work for securing Chinese friendship. Nehru still advocated: "We should avoid doing or saying anything which might give the Chinese the impression of their national prestige and honour being hurt." India still wanted to settle the boundary question with China through peaceful negotiations and in the spirit of Panchsheel. However, the various attempts made at a peace-fully negotiated settlement proved to be utter failures. In early 1960, Nehru invited Chou-En-Lai to visit India for holding talks on the question of boundary between India and China. Consequently, in April, 1960, Chou visited India for six days and held discussions with Nehru and other Indian leaders. It was a serious attempt to settle the border issue but, unfortunately, both the sides could reach neither an agreement nor an understanding about the nature and scope of the boundary problem. During the discussions, it was found that a wide gap existed between the positions adopted by the two countries. While speaking before Indian Lok Sabha, Nehru observed: "India and China always came up against the hard rock of different sets of facts." Nehru stuck to the legal claims of India to the boundary areas and refused to negotiate any settlement based on political or military consideration. Chou En-Lai on the other hand, stuck to the Chinese position in Aksai Chin area and the north-west where Chinese had already built a road and were in physical control of the territory. Consequently, the Nehru-Chau talks of 1960 failed to produce any result. After the failure, both sides accused each other of adopting a rigid stand.

The Differences over the Boundary Issue: The strong differences in respect of the boundary between the two countries were further reflected, when in December, 1960, after several weeks of fruitless talk between Indian and Chinese representatives, two divergent reports were published by the two sides. The Indian team furnished at the talk between Indian and Chinese representatives, two divergent reports were published by the two sides. The Indian team furnished at the talks evidence of 630 documents, of which 49 supported the legal and 516 supported the administrative and traditional basis of India's case. China produced evidence of only 245 documents, of which 47 supported legal and 198 supported the administrative and traditional basis. The talks revealed that China was already in unlawful occupation of 12,000 sq. miles of Indian territory.

During and after the talks of the officials, the Chinese continued to intrude into Indian territory both for establishing new areas of control and for consolidating the positions already occupied by them. In September, 1960, they intruded into Taktsang Gompa in the eastern sectors and into Sikkim. In October, 1960, they went up to the hot spring in Ladakh.

In 1961, war clouds began to gather over Ladakh and NEFA. The Chinese intruded in April, 1961 into-Sikkim, in May into Chushul area of Ladakh, in July into Kameng Division of NEFA and in August they established three new check-posts in Ladakh. These Chinese intrusions along with the threat to patrol the entire Sino-Indian border, as given in April 1960, made India highly conscious of the need to strengthen the security of its borders with China and it started building new out-posts in its territory. These Indian moves were highly resented by the Chinese. The situation seemed to be heading for a direct confrontation.

The Chinese Invasion of 1962: In January 1962, the Chinese crossed Longju in NEFA and in June, 1962, they had entered the Chi-Chap and Spanyggur areas of Ladakh. In July, 1962, they encircled the Galwan Valley. On 8th September, 1962, the Chinese crossed the Thagla Ridge and intruded further into NEFA. After this date, they kept on exchanging fire with Indian troops as a preparation for the massive attack that finally came on the early hours of 20th October, 1962. On this day, the Chinese launched a very big offensive on both the eastern and western sectors. They pushed back the Indian troops, who were smaller in number and poorer in equipment. The Chinese know that we were not prepared for a massive attack, and the massive Chinese attack surprised us. Our forces were routed in NEFA. But in spite of strategic disadvantages Indian troops were able to give a good account of themselves in Ladakh. In NEFA, within 3 weeks of the attack, China was in a position to move over all mountain passes and to threaten the plains of Assam. India became highly worried at the Chinese threat of full scale invasion and consequently decided to seek the help of some of the friendly nations. However, on 21st November, 1962, China announced a unilateral ceasefire and the decision to withdraw 20 kilometres behind the line of actual control which existed between India and China on, 7th November 1952. "Thus, the threatened invasions," writes N.D. Palmer, "turned out to be no more than a border war: but India had suffered severe reverses, militarily, diplomatically, and psychologically." Even Nehru admitted: "We have been living in an artificial atmosphere of our own creation.,. India had been shocked into reality by the Chinese actions."

The Watershed on Sino-Indian Relations: Chinese invasion gave a big blow not only to Sino-Indian relations but also to India's prestige at international level. Many Western observers felt that the crisis with China, was a watershed in the history of India's foreign relations and orientations. The defeat lowered Indian prestige in the eyes of Afro-Asian nations. It even encouraged Pakistan to thinking in terms of forcing a military solution of Kashmir on India. It was this thinking which led to Pakistani aggression against India in 1965. Economically, this war with China gave a set-back to the Indian plans for growth and development. India was forced to increase its defence spending. However, this invasion made India security conscious, and more united and determined towards its national interests. India woke up to the need to improve its defences, unite the people and harness the resources.

Analysing the results of 1962 war, T.N. Kaul observes: "The lesson of our dealings with China was that as a Non-aligned country we had to depend on ourselves and make the most of our resources. We had to become self-reliant in the economic, defence and political field, to the maximum extent possible in the minimum time. We had to look for reliable friends, who had a mutuality of interests with us and on whom we could rely in times of difficulty. The Chinese invasion of 1962, was the first serious threat to our policy of Non-alignment. But it increased our faith in this policy which helped us to forge better and more enduring friendships that stood us in good stead in later years."

Sino-Indian Relations after the War: In the post 1962 period, Sino-Indian relations continued to be characterised by lack of contacts and remained almost frozen till 1970-71. Even the diplomatic relations came to be downgraded to Charge-d' affairs level as after the war neither of the two countries appointed its ambassador to the other. China became more and more hostile towards India. It tried to isolate India by reaching border agreements with other small countries apparently for showing to the world that China was compromising and reasonable in settling border disputes with its neighbours, while India was rigid and uncompromising. China stepped up its hostile propaganda against India. One again, it started describing India as a stooge of imperialism and as a pawn on the hands of imperialists who were using it in the international anti-China campaign. It also started charging India of having imperialist designs towards Sikkim and Bhutan. Not on this, China started be friending India's enemy-Pakistan, by giving it full support on Kashmir and by pumping economic and military aid into Rawalpindi. It signed a border agreement with Pakistan in respect of the boundary which formed part of the Pakistani occupied Kashmir. During 1965 Indo-Pak War, China gave full moral, political, psychological and even military (supply of weapons) support to Pakistan. When Indian was engaged in repelling the Pakistani invasion, China made an attempt to increase tensions on the Sino-Indian borders. It threatened India with 'dire consequences' with a view to pressurise India and to support Pakistan. However, it refrained from any military intervention at the time of Indo-Pak War of 1965. After 1965, both China and Pakistan started strengthening the anti-India axis in South Asia. The danger of Sino-Pakistan collusion started haunting India.

The growing Beijing-Pindi axis, the rapidly increasing military power of China, particularly since 1964 when China exploded its first atomic bomb, the rigid Chinese attitude towards the border dispute with India, the continued border incidents between Chinese and Indian troops and the Chinese support to anti-India elements like extremist Nagas, Mizos, the Naxalities etc., all combined to create further strains and tensions in the bilateral relations between India and China. Chinese rigid attitude towards relations with India can be judged by the fact that it even cold-shouldered the offer made by Mrs. Indira Gandhi in 1968, to have unconditional talks over border issue. Till 1970, China maintained a policy of ignoring India and building relations with anti-India elements. Sino-Indian relations in the sixties remained bogged down in the Himalayans snow. The emergence of Sino-Soviet rift and the corresponding development of Indo-Soviet friendship further hardened the Chinese attitude towards India. The 1971 Indo-Soviet Treaty of Peace, Friendship and Co-operation was regarded by China as an Indo-Soviet collusion against China. It has been well-observed by Prof. Ram Mohan: "The Sino-Indian relations continued to deteriorate almost in the same proportion to the improvement of Indo-Soviet relations, which indeed had its impact on the Sino-Indian border dispute giving it an ideological dimension." Consequently, China became more critical of India and kept up its policy of helping, supporting and building Pakistan against India. During the Indo-Pak War of 1971, China once again gave full support to Pakistan. It strongly criticised the Indian role in Bangladesh crisis and accused India of having imperialist designs in South Asia.

IV. Normalisation Period

After having lived in an era of mutual distrust, fear, hostility or at least in an environment surcharged with animated tensions in which feelings and emotions, rather than reason, reigned supreme, both India and China started realising, since early seventies, the need for ending the deadlock in bilateral relations. The changed situation in Asia and the newly-emerging international scenario; the emergence of India as major power in South Asia as a result of its victory in the 1971 Indo-Pak War; the increased role in India as an important leader of the Third World; the realisation on the part of China of the need for mending relations with the Third World countries; and above all the mutual feeling for ending the stalemate in bilateral relations, provided strong ground for initiating the process of normalising the Sino-Indian relations.

After 1962, India was in a position to build up her strength. In 1965 War with Pakistan India gave a good account of herself. In 1971, her victory in the war with Pakistan demonstrated the big and effectively increased Indian power in South Asia. The Indian success in developing relations with both the super powers and the breakthrough in relations with Pakistan that came after the Simla-Agreement of July 1972, further proved the ability of India to successfully conduct her foreign relations. The important role which India had started playing as an important leader of the Third World and of the Non-aligned Movement, further improved India's image in international relations of the seventies, and this made China accept the need for normalisation of relations with India. The growing Indo-Soviet friendship and co-operation, particularly after the signing of Indo-Soviet Treaty of 1971, made China realise the danger of its India policy. It realised that 'strained relations with India' has been a major input of Indo-Soviet friendship. The fear of growing Soviet power and the continued Sino-Soviet rift again made China conscious of the need to do something positive about relations with India. All these factors influenced China and India to have a fresh look upon their relations. The beginning of 1970's therefore, came with a welcome change in the Sino-Indian relations. The rise of new leadership in China, in mid-seventies as a result of the deaths of Mao Tse tung and Chou En-lai, within a short span of time, was accompanied by the emergence of some liberalisation in Chinese foreign policy. This further gave strength to progress of normalisation between India and China. However, till today the chances of full normalisation and real detente still appear to be few. But before we answer the question: Why is it so, let us examine the history of Sino-Indian normalisation since 1971.

The first signs of change in the Chinese attitude towards India came in 1969, when the Chinese started attending the functions organised by Indian diplomatic missions and inviting Indian diplomats to the Chinese functions. The 'big sign', however, came in 1980 when at Beijing's May Day Reception, Chairman Mao Tse tung warmly greeted the Indian Charge-d' affairs and observed, "India a great country and China were friends for long. They should be friends again." This event came to be known as "Mao Smile', and was followed by increased contacts between Indian and Chinese diplomats during the course of their activities in the capitals of other countries. In May, 1971, Chinese ambassador at Moscow had three meetings with Indian Ambassador, Mr. D.P. Dhar. Similar contacts were established between Indian and Chinese Ambassadors at Cairo, Paris, Warsaw and Berne. As a result of these increased contacts there appeared good chances for some 'opening' between India and China. In October, 1971, Indian Foreign Secretary headed a team of officials which attended the Chinese National Day reception at New Delhi. In December 1971, the Government of India ordered the removal of the police post that was established in 1967 outside the Chinese Embassy at New Delhi. The exchange of smiles and handshakes between Indian and Chinese diplomats became more frequent. In November, 1971, China invited the Indian Table Tennis team to participate in the Afro-Asian Friendship Table Tennis Championship. The invitation was accepted by India and this led to emergence of Ping-Pong Diplomacy between the two countries.

In December, 1971 Indo-Pak War, the Chinese stand was opposed to the Indian role, yet it was not as hostile as it was in 1965. However, along with these positive developments, Chinese intrusions into Indian territory and border incidents between the Indian and Chinese troops continued to be there as before. Chinese press continued to be hostile towards India, and China continued to support Pakistan against India. In January, 1972, on the eve of Bhutto's visit to Peking, the Peking Daily editorially criticised both India and the Soviet Union for their roles in Bangladesh War and predicted that "India could expect more troubles on the sub-continent." During the early months of 1972, many Chinese leaders made many aggressive statements against India but at the same time China continued to show her willingness to enter into a process of normalisation with India. On the one hand, China voiced its open and full support for Pakistan on the Kashmir issue and on the other hand, welcomed the moves for a peaceful settlement between India and Pakistan. During Mrs. Indira Gandhi's visit to Czechoslovakia and Hungary, the Chinese diplomats attended all function and expressed to the Indian journalists the need for improvement of relations between India and China. Chinese policy towards India at this time of course, was characterised by many fluctuations but these were considered to be better than the rigid attitude of the sixties and the post-1962 stalemate in Sino-Indian relations. In mid-1972, the unofficial and indirect contacts between

Indian and Chinese officials were revived and increased. The Indian and Chinese ambassadors at Warsaw held important meetings and there appeared strong indications that there was to be some improvement in the Sino-Indian relations in the near future. Both the Indian and Chinese leaders too started talking of the possible gains that both countries can register by resuming their trade relations. Reviewing the Sino-India relations during 1972, Indian Foreign Minister, Mr. Swaran Singh observed in Rajya Sabha in 15th December, 1972 that Government was not happy over the state of relations existing between the two countries. "India was prepared to 'let bygones be bygones' and was ready to start a new relationship with China." He said, "Geography has placed us as neighbours of this country, we can't wish away with China any more than China can wish away from India. Border problems have existed between many countries throughout the ages and were settled peacefully. As such we see no reason why India and China should not be able to do the same." This statement clearly shows that by 1972, India had become willing to open a new chapter in her relations with China. However, in 1972 Chinese failed to fully reciprocate this desire. They still thought it good to "be soft in words but tense in actions."

The Change in Chinese Perceptions: In the next three years (1973 to 75) this see saw game continued. Both Indian and Chinese officials continued to maintain and develop contacts and to express the desire to build up Sino-Indian friendship and co-operation but nothing more was tried and achieved. Throughout this period, Chinese gave the impression that they were keen to have a rapprochement with India. This impression was distinctly recorded by the famous French author Mr. Andre Malraux, who in April, 1973 and Prof. John Galbraith, a former US Ambassador to India and a noted economist who visited Beijing in June 1973. Mr. Galbraith conveyed this impression to New Delhi that Chinese Foreign Minister had told him that "despite the continuing Sino-Indian differences, China had great regard and respect for Indian Prime Minister and that Peking was genuinely interested in improving its relations with India as part of its general desire for mutually beneficial contacts with all the three countries of the sub-continent"— The Government of India, however, regarded this as platitude without much significance because there was no direct and positive response from the Chinese Government towards Indian initiatives for normalisation. Subsequently, however, when China stepped down, the loud-speaker propaganda was going on since 1963 on the Sino-Indian frontiers. India accepted the possibility of a positive change in relations with China. This impression was given by Indian Minister of State for External Affairs, Mr. Surendra Pal Singh in the Rajya Sabha on August, 1973. The Chinese participation in Indian official level functions and the exchange of non-official private visits registered a big increase after August, 1973. The leaders of the two countries started exchanging greetings on the eve of their National Days.

The Stalemate in Relations: However in the main, the relations remained, as Mr. Swaran Singh remarked, in an interview given to a Cairo Newspaper, "in a dormant state neither better nor worst as compared to previous years." But he also expressed the hope that the relations may improve next year. In 1974, India's Peaceful Nuclear Explosion and in 1975, Sikkim's accession to India became the object of strong Chinese criticism and the Sino-Indian relations remained 'confined to only contacts'. The strong Chinese reaction against Sikkim's accession to India, the continued Chinese propaganda against India, the increased strength of Beijing-Pindi axis and the continued Chinese trouble at the Indian borders kept Sino-Indian relations cool. As such, like previous years, it was also a period in which expression of faith in the desire to develop friendly co-operation between India and China was maintained but no attempt was made to take any concrete step towards its realisation.

The Start of Normalisation: A real big change for the good, however came in the spring of 1976 when on 15th April, 1976, the Government of India announced its decision to restore full diplomatic relations with People's Republic of China and designated Mr. K.R. Narayanan as its ambassador to Peking. This was a bold Indian move for giving a sound opening to the process of Sino-Indian normalisation. This Indian move was welcomed by China and its government declared that "China would also reciprocate and restore ambassador level relations with India." However, it took nearly five months for the Chinese government to appoint Mr, Chen Chao Yuan as the Chinese ambassador to India. The restoration of full diplomatic relation in 1976, gave the much-needed strength to the cause of Sino-Indian normalisation. In the post-1976 period there came to be restored some trade and cultural links between the two countries.

Welcoming the restoration of full diplomatic relations between India and China Mr. Prem Bhatia, Editor-in-Chief of *The Tribune*, described it as the first step towards normalcy and observed in his editorial on 20th April 1976, "The New Delhi-Peking diplomatic link at the higher level.... may gradually help to promote friendly ties...... It will not by itself resolve the Sino-Indian differences and misunderstandings, but given good will and determination on both sides to ensure peace and amity, there is no reason why the traditional friendship between the two countries should not be speedily restored. India, on her part, may be relied upon to spare no effort to achieve that end."

At the time of restoration of the full diplomatic relations both the countries expressed their hopes and determination for the development of Sino-Indian friendly co-operation. The Indian ambassador, Mr. K.R. Narayanan expressed his determination to explore all avenues for improving and enlarging friendship between the peoples and the governments of the two countries. The Chinese ambassador Mr. Chen Chao Yuan too promised all positive efforts towards complete Sino-Indian normalisation. The year 1976, as such, opened a new era in Sino-Indian relations in which both sides decided to work for a complete detente between them. Indeed, this development turned the signs into a thaw in Sino-Indian relations.

Janata-Lok Dal Rule: In 1977, the Janata Party came to power in India, and the Janata leaders expressed their desire to follow "Proper Non-alignment'. This was interpreted by China as a move to check or balance India's relations with Soviet Union. It, therefore, decided to encourage the Janata leaders towards a possible greater normalisation in Sino-Indian relations. China wanted to draw India somewhat away from the Soviet Union, and as such was willing to show more love and accommodation for India ruled by the Janata Party. The Janata Government too declared its keenness to normalise relations with China.

Consequently, in the Janata period (March 1977-79) Sino-Indian contacts and trade links were increased. In April 1977, both India and China entered into a trade agreement involving a total value of ₹13.2 crores. The exchange of sports and cultural teams between the two countries also became frequent and China expressed her desire to develop Sino-Indian co-operation in Science and Technology, and to establish industrial co-operation with India in such fields as steel production. Throughout 1978, India and China kept up their increased contacts. The trade links were strengthened between them. In February 1978, a sixteen-member strong Chinese trade delegation visited India and discussed the chances of increased trade between the two countries. Similarly, a four-member trade mission of the Association of Indian Engineering Industry visited the Canton Fair organised by China. In March 1978, a Chinese goodwill mission led by Mr. Wang Pin-nan visited India. Mr. Wang had a 90-minute meeting with Mr. A.B. Vajpayee, the then Indian Foreign Minister. On behalf of the Chinese Foreign Minister, Huang Hua, the delegation extended an invitation to Mr. Vajpayee for visiting Beijing. This invitation was accepted in principle.

Vajpayee's Beijing Visit: In the autumn of 1978, Mr. A.B. Vajpayee and Mr. Huang Hua, the Chinese Foreign Minister had an incidental 45 minutes meeting at the U.N. Headquarters. Mr. Hua told Mr. Vajpayee that people of China were looking forward to his visit to China. "This visit", he observed, "would provide a bigger and closer opportunity for the exchange of views and discussing the problems left by history." Mr. Vajpayee also expressed the hope that his proposed visit to China towards the end of October would create a better climate for co-operation between the two countries. However due to a sudden illness, Mr. Vajpayee could not undertake his visit to China in October. It was only in February, 1979, that he could visit Beijing and hold direct talks with the Chinese leadership. It was after a lapse of 30 years that a high-level dignitary from India went on a visit to China. The visit opened an optimistic note with the expression of the desire for consolidation of relations and the holding of frank talks between the leaders and officials of the two sides. This visit after having progressed on an optimistic level, however, came to an abrupt and unfortunate and when Mr. Vajpayee, in order to show India's displeasure at the Chinese aggression against Vietnam, decided to terminate the visit and return to India. During these talks, a basic difference in approach between the two countries came to light. Whereas India regarded the settlement of boundary dispute on a first priority for securing full Sino-Indian normalisation, China advocated the view that development of relations in other spheres should be attempted first for creating the ideal conditions for the settlement of boundary dispute. This difference in approach made the progress of Sino-Indian normalisation slow and limited. The visit as such failed to secure any improvement in Sino-Indian relations.

The sudden political change in the Indian political scene in late 1979 gave a final end to process of Sino-Indian normalisation in the Janata era.

V. Sino-Indian Relations Since 1980

In January, 1980, Mrs. Indira Gandhi and her Congress-I Party returned to power in India. This change, once again brought with it the possibility of a return to the era of special Indo-Soviet relations and more cautious and restrained approach towards relations with China. However, Mrs. Indira Gandhi lost no time in assuring China that India would continue to work for the normalisation of relations with China, and for the development of Sino-Indian friendship and co-operation. Since, 1980, India and China started maintaining and even increasing their trade and cultural relations. But their political relations, till today continue to lack understanding and maturity because of the differences in respect of their policies towards Afghanistan, Pakistan, and Vietnam, and the continued dispute over the boundary. China strongly criticised. Indian recognition of the new regime of Kampuchea and India's support for Vietnam. India's refusal to outrightly condemn the Soviet presence in Afghanistan is disliked by China. Chinese pro-Pakistani policy in general and the opening of Karakoram and other highways between Pakistan and China, which pass through PoK, are looked with apprehensions and fear by India. The reports about the Chinese help for Pakistan's nuclear programme too are a source of disturbance for India. Biggest of all the irritants, however, continues to be the boundary dispute between the two countries. The complicated nature of the dispute and the wide gap that exists between the views of India and China make the border issue a big hindrance in the way of Sino-Indian normalisation. The two countries have been conducting official level negotiations but are finding it difficult to resolve the tangle. On 2nd February, 1983, the third round of India and China official level talks was concluded without any success. Like the earlier two rounds which were held at Beijing in December, 1981 and at Delhi in July 1982, at the third round of talks at Beijing, in January, 1983, also both sides failed to narrow down the differences. Major differences between India and China continued to persist over the issue of boundary dispute.

Commenting upon the stalemate in relations with China the Editorial in *The Tribune* dated February 3, 1983 observed, "The trickiest issue standing in the way of normal neighbourly relations is demarcation of the 4,200-km. long border at the foot of Himalayas. There have been favourable noises from Beijing and Delhi about quickly improving cultural, educational, scientific and commercial relations. The border problem, however, is likely to defy solution for years to come." The Editorial then referred to the wide gap that existed between the Chinese thesis for a package deal and the Indian desire to settle the issue through sector by sector adjustment based on the internationally accepted watershed principles. "The 'package deal' if agreed by Indian will vest China with control over Aksai Chin and an additional 5,000 sq. km. of Indian territory it occupied in 1962. Conversely, if India's watershed principle is accepted, China has to withdraw to the border that existed before 1959." Neither of the two countries is, as such, prepared to accept the view of the other. China is having border disputes with the Soviet Union, Vietnam, Mangolia and other countries and as such a settlement with India can have important implication for it. China has yet to formulate its border policy and as such is not much interested in settling the border dispute with India.

Moreover, after 1962, it has been occupying a pretty comfortable position in respect of control over a large part of disputed territory and as such appears to be in no hurry to settle the issue. India on the other hand, is keen to settle the border dispute with China but finds her position helpless in the face of Chinese policy. The border dispute as such continues to check the progress of Sino-Indian detente. Both sides are now conscious of the need for developing more friendly and mutually beneficial co-operation in the changed international scenario, but are finding the border disputes a big hindrance. Both now realise that border issue is the central issue in the process of normalisation of relations and are willing to settle it amicably. This brightens the chances of continuity in their attempts to iron out the differences. But the limited scope of possible solutions and their commitments to their peoples in respect of various disputed border areas constituted complicated hindrances in the way of such attempts.

The decision taken by Mr. Rajiv Gandhi to open out a major drive to secure an improvement in friendship and co-operation with the neighbours, has produced a welcome change in outlook and in the course of India's relations with her neighbours. "There is a whiff of fresh air in our relationship with many countries particularly with our neighbours." However, unfortunately, relations with China continue to be almost the same — slow and steady attempts at normalisation without any meaningful progress towards the settlement of the boundary dispute. Prime Minister Rajiv Gandhi has been repeatedly stating India's strong desire to go in for full normalisation with China including the settlement of the boundary dispute. While the leaders of the two countries stand committed to cultivate further the existing environment of goodwill and cordiality, yet are finding it difficult to find a solution to the boundary dispute. While speaking at a function to make the 35th anniversary of the diplomatic relations between India and China. Mr. Khursheed Alam Khan, then Minister of State for External Affairs, commenting upon the continued dialogue with China observed that the current dialogue with China was based on India's sincere desire to resolve the border issue. "Notwithstanding this (the tragic setback of 1962) development, we in India continue to look towards the future with firm determination to try and resolve the differences which had arisen between us." He reiterated India's commitment to achieve this end. Prime Minister Rajiv Gandhi in a message to the Chinese

Premier, Mr. Zhao Ziyang also expressed the hope that through joint efforts all outstanding problems between India and China would be solved. The five principles of peaceful co-existence would enable the two people to resume and consolidate their long-standing and historical ties."

However, despite such a thinking and commitment, India is finding China committed to its old policy of "normalisation before settling the boundary dispute through a package deal." Chinese proposal (July 1985) that India should reopen its mission at Lhasa with a reciprocal facility for opening a Chinese mission at Calcutta or elsewhere, was rejected as unacceptable to India on the ground that this constituted a Chinese attempt to normalise relations without coming to grips with the real problem of the border dispute. A top Government source, as quoted by Kuldip Nayar in *The Tribune* (13th, July 1985) observed; "We have no objection to the reopening of our mission at Lhasa or taking other steps which will help restore the position as prevailed before the Chinese attack in 1962, but we must first restore the status quo ante. China must return occupied Indian territory." Several rounds of Sino Indian talks over the normalisation of relations have produced little progress on the boundary issue. When the talks began, India had hoped that a step by step approach would generate so much goodwill between the two countries that a solution of the border dispute might become easier. But this has not happened even marginally. Cultural and other delegations which have toured China have come back with the impression that there is a pronounced change in the attitude of the people and that they are friendlier than before. But they take the same rehearsed line on the border issue from one end to the other.

The border dispute continues to be a major road-block in the way of the development of Sino-Indian relations. Beijing maintained that it is willing to recognise MacMahon line in exchange for India's acceptance of its position in the Ladakh region and the Chumbi Valley in the central sector. New Delhi on the other hand, felt that its hands are tied by a unanimous resolution of both houses of Parliament and at best, a sector by sector adjustment of border can, alone be attempted for an amicable solution of the problem. The boundary dispute has kept Sino-Indian relations strained.

Sino-Indian Talks: The meeting between Prime Minister Rajiv Gandhi and the Chinese Prime Minister Zhiao Ziang at New York in October, 1985 provided a good background to the Sixth Round of Sino-Indian Talks (New Delhi November 11, 1985). But it could make little substantive headway. Both sides discussed the boundary issues and reviewed the eastern sector. It was agreed to review the western sector boundary in the next round. A free and frank discussion on the progress of bilateral relations also took place. The two sides agreed to exchange delegations in the field of agricultural education, computer industry, plasma physics and bio-technology. It was also agreed to hold a joint seminar in China on socio-economic planning. However, the failure to make a headway over the boundary issue kept the talks limited.

In June 1986, China committed a big intrusion into Indian territory, 6 to 7-km. South of the MacMahon line into the pasture land in Thongdrong area of Arunachal Pradesh's Kameng division. India lodged a strong protest with China about the intrusion and took up the issue at the Seventh Round of Sino-India border talks held in Beijing between July 21-22, 1986. The Chinese, however, asserted that the area was north of the line of actual control and in their territory and re-asserted their position that the whole of Arunachal Pradesh (formerly known as NEFA) as their territory. India saw in it an attempt on the part of China to reactivate the dispute over the eastern boundary. The border talks, held under the shadow of this latest Chinese intrusion into India, naturally made no headway.

As such the relations between India and China continued to adrift throughout 1986. However, both the countries were successful in overcoming the strains caused by the unresolved border dispute and the Sino-Indian trade turn over came to be to the tune of $140 millions in 1986. But the balance was heavily in China's favour with India's share being as little as $21 millions.

On May 27, 1987 India and China signed their second trade protocol envisaging a total trade volume of between $150 to 200 millions between January 1987 and March 1988. The protocol is called for an increased export of Indian iron ore to China.

In order to secure a break throw in the stalemate in Sino-Indian relations and the boundary talks, India decided to change the level of Sino-Indian official talks to a political dialogue. Accordingly, India's External Affairs Minister, Mr. N.D. Tiwari, on his way back from Pyongyang NAM conference decided to have a stop-over at Beijing and use the opportunity or holding talks with the Chinese counterpart. Mr. Tiwari observed that the purpose of the visit was "to review our assurances that we want a full normalisation of our friendly relations with China, that we want to settle all our outstanding differences, including the boundary dispute, through negotiations, and that there is no need or any conflict or anything like that. You can settle the whole thing by negotiations, even though it may take time." He had talks with Chinese Prime Minister, Mr. Wan Li and the Vice Foreign Minister Mr. Lin Shuging. Mr. Tiwari was successful in impressing upon the Chinese the need for determined efforts towards the full normalisation of friendly co-operation between the two countries.

In a press conference held on June 29, 1987 Prime Minister Rajiv Gandhi observed that both Indian and China now had a positive view on the border issue and shared the desire to find a solution.

November 1987: This round of Sino-Indian talks was held in atmosphere of hope and goodwill generated by the political contacts made at the highest level. The Chinese made a conscious effort to dispel the fear of new strains in the bilateral relations. Both the sides informally agreed not to let the border issue cloud the other positive aspects of their relations. India also demonstrated fully her willingness to reconstruct its relations with China for building a climate of trust and co-operation. Both agreed to continue efforts towards a peaceful and negotiated settlement of the boundary question.

They expressed their resolve to keep peace and tranquility all along the borders. Talks also covered the issue of reopening consulates in each other's territories.

Eighth round of talks involved a refreshing attempt on the part of the two Asian giants to qualitatively improve the atmosphere of Sino-Indian Relations. For the first time the boundary issue was discussed in a substantive manner. Summing up the discussions which were held, Prime Minister Rajiv Gandhi, while addressing the Parliamentary Consultative Committee on External Affairs on December 2, 1987 observed that India welcomes the intention to upgrade the talks by supplementing the official level talks with political level talks. He stressed that any solution to the India-China boundary issue should be equitable not only to the two governments but also to the people of the two countries. Both sides should, therefore, strive to see that the right atmosphere was created for working towards a just solution to the border problem. It is, indeed, a welcome development.

3
Pakistan

I. Issues between India and Pakistan Resulting from Partition

Our relations with Pakistan have been particularly unhappy. There have been constant threats of war. Between the two countries there are some major problems and disputes from partition.

The following major issues and problems determined the nature of Indo-Pak relations during the period 1947-65:

1. Transfer of Population and Problem of Religious Minorities.
2. Problem of Recovery or Compensation for Abandoned Property of Refugees in India and Pakistan.
3. Division of State Assets at the Time of Partition.
4. Canal-water Disputes.
5. Boundary Disputes.
6. Issue of Integration of Princely States.

1. Transfer of Population and Problem of Religious Minorities: One of the most tragic and serious problems that emerged as the side effect of the partition was the transfer of population. Beginning with months before 1947, the migration was the transfer of population. Beginning with months before 1947, the migration was the largest in modern history, involving perhaps 12 millions persons flowing both ways. In spite of such migration the problem of religious minorities was not solved in either state: about 40 millions Muslims remained in India and 10 millions Hindus in East Pakistan. The fever of religious communalism was heightened by the unfortunate happenings of 1947. The legacy of the communalism of partition still sometimes leads to the occasional out-break of communal riots.

After Independence, while India sought to solve its minority problems by establishing a secular state, Pakistan decided to be an Islamic republic. The reports of maltreatment of minorities in either side started causing serious strains on bilateral relations of India and Pakistan. It was to arrive at a consensus regarding the treatment of minorities in the two states, that Prime Minister Nehru and Prime Minister Liaquat Ali Khan held talks in April 1950 and the Nehru-Liaquat Pact was concluded. This pact gave constitutional guarantees for minorities and promised the return/transfer of refugee and recovery of abducted women. It also assured freedom of movement and protection in travel to the migrants. It provided for the setting up of minorities commissions in East Bengal and West Bengal for carrying out the arrangements made in respect of the migrants. After the conclusion of this pact the refugee migration suddenly dropped. However, it erupted again in 1951 in particular; the influx of Hindus from East Pakistan to West Bengal registered a big increase. The migration problem became very acute but both the countries, having adopted different and opposed positions on many international issues, failed to implement even the Nehru-Liaquat Pact fully. Throughout the late fifties and early sixties the influx of refugees from Pakistan to India continued to be a source of trouble for Indo-Pak relations. Even in 1971, a large number of Hindus and Muslim refugees crossed over to India after a military crackdown and massacre was let loose in East Pakistan by the Government of Pakistan. The influx of refugees became an important reason for the outbreak of war between India and Pakistan in December, 1971. Thus, after partition the refugee problem came to be a source of big strain of Indo-Pak relations. Even after 39 years of partition, the problem of illegal migration of refugees from Sindh (Pakistan) into India continues to be there.

2. Problem of Recovery or Compensation for Abandoned Properties of Refugees in India and Pakistan: Related to the problem of population migration was the complex problem of the recovery or compensation for the abandoned properties of the refugees. As a result of partition nearly a million non-Muslims migrated from Pakistan and nearly 75 millions Muslims from India to Pakistan. The communal riots compelled the migrants to abandon their immovable properties in their parent countries. The non-Muslim refugees left property worth ₹5,000 millions in Pakistan and the Muslim refugees from India left only ₹1,000 millions worth of property in India. The negotiations to solve the problem of evacuee property were initiated on 29th August, 1947, but because of the complicated nature of the problem and the differences in approach of the two governments, these negotiations failed to produce any result. India wanted that the Governments of both the countries should take over the evacuee property and then settle the compensations on the basis of the claims filed by the refugees. This proposal was rejected by Pakistan. Pakistan on the other hand, suggested that the issue should be taken up on the basis of case by case and the evacuee property should be either transferred or sold. This view was not accepted by India. When the stalemate continued till 1954, the Government of India decided to utilise the evacuee property for the benefit of refugees, who had come to India. This was accomplished by the Displaced Persons Act which was passed by the Indian Parliament in October, 1954. In April 1955, an agreement was signed at Karachi between India and Pakistan and the dispute relating to immovable property was resolved. In January, 1956, the two Governments agreed for the transfer of evacuee Bank Accounts, Lockers and Safe Deposits. This issue, as such was resolved by the loss suffered by the refugees kept the environment governing the Indo-Pak relations tense and strained till late fifties.

3. Division of State Assets at the Time of Partition: The problem of division of assets of India between Pakistan and India too kept Indo-Pak relations tense and strained during the initial years of their relations. On 14th August 1947, the cash balance of India were about ₹4,000 millions out of which Pakistan wanted ₹1,000 millions. India was not willing to give such a big share to Pakistan. The issue was, therefore, referred to an Arbitral Tribunal which decided that ₹750 millions should be paid to Pakistan as its share. After initial hesitation India decided to implement the agreement. However, Pakistan refused to pay to India, ₹55 crores which it was to pay as its share of the pre-1947 foreign debt of India. At the time of partition, it was decided that India would take the entire responsibility of paying the foreign debts and Pakistan would pay its share to India to three equal installments. The refusal of Pakistan to pay its share led the development of bad blood between the two countries. Similarly, the problem of division of military stores and delinking of Banking services too acted as irritants in Indo-Pak relations. The problem of establishing trade and economic relations also caused tensions. Areas that formed part of Pakistan were rich wheat and cotton producing areas which used to supply these commodities to other parts of India likewise, India after partition came to be the inheritor of rich sugarcane, coal and iron ore producing areas. The partition upset the complementarities of economic and trade relations. In 1947, both the countries signed a 'Stand Still Agreement' which permitted free flow of goods between the two countries. However, this arrangement failed to work smoothly because there arose disputes over the issue of sharing the export duty on Jute and other taxes levied and collected on such goods. Consequently, a new trade agreement was signed in May 1948. But this agreement too failed to resolve the trade tangle. The third agreement was signed on 24th June 1949, but the devaluation of Indian rupee and Pakistan's refusal to do the same made the implementation of this agreement impossible. Thus, the differences over trade relations too kept the Indo-Pak relations tense and strained during the period under review.

4. Canal-water Disputes: The division of Punjab into West Punjab, which came to be a part of Pakistan and East Punjab which remained with India, brought with it the problem of distribution of canal waters. This problem arose out of the unnatural partition of Punjab.

The problem of canal waters could be simply stated: East Punjab in India was relatively under-developed in irrigation works, while West Punjab in Pakistan included most of the canal systems of the pre-partition Indus basin; but most of the Pakistani canals originated in rivers and head works located in and controlled by India. In 1947, both the countries agreed to maintain status quo; Pakistan agreed to pay for the continued flow of water from Sutlej and Ravi rivers which flow through India. After the expiry of this agreement in April 1948, the East Punjab Government cut off the supply of water to Pakistan. The farmers of Pakistan strongly reacted against the failure of their Government to settle the question of supply of waters. This gave rise to a big pressure on the Pakistani Government and on May 4, 1948, after ministerial level talks, India and Pakistan signed a new agreement. Under this agreement India agreed to supply waters to Pakistan but the later was called upon to build its own irrigation resources. It was agreed that India would gradually reduce and ultimately stop the supply of water to Pakistan. However, later on this agreement was repudiated by Pakistan and it asserted the right to get an uninterrupted supply of waters from Indian rivers. It started challenging the Indian plans for the construction of new dams and canals which were to provide irrigation facilities to the dry lands of East Punjab and Rajasthan. Pakistan wanted to maintain the status quo and desired that the dispute should be referred to the International Court of Justice. This demand was rejected by India.

In March 1952, Mr. Eugene Black, President of the World Bank offered mediation between India and Pakistan for settling the canal water dispute. After six years of hard negotiations the two countries accepted a draft treaty in 1959. However, it took sixteen more months for finalising the Indus Water Treaty, which was ultimately signed by Nehru and Ayub at Karachi on 11th September, 1960. The Treaty gave India the full right to utilise the waters of three rivers Sutlej, Beas and Ravi, and accepted the right of Pakistan to use the waters of Jhelum, Chinab and Indus. The Treaty also provided for the establishment of a Permanent Indus Commission and Indus Basin Development fund. The fund agreed to pay most of the cost of building 400 miles of canals in Pakistan and two large storage dams. India too obtained financial assistance from the World Bank and the U.S. for the construction of the Beas Dam. The canal water dispute was as such amicably resolved and the Indus Treaty now stands fully implemented. But the dispute over resources involving Farakka Barrage remains unresolved. The Farakka Barrage dispute has since 1971, come to be a dispute between India and Bangladesh.

5. Boundary Disputes: After Partition both the countries started in the right earnest the process of demarcating, on the basis of Radcliff Award, the boundaries between them. Through rational compromises, reached through mutual negotiations both the countries accomplished the gigantic task in approximately 25 years. The demarcation of East Punjab-Pakistan boundary was completed in June, 1960 and the Rajasthan-Pakistan boundary; in 1963.

However, the two sides failed to demarcate the Kutch-Sindh boundary. India was of the view that the Government of Bombay's resolution of February 1914, had settled the matter finally. Pakistan did not accept the view and asserted that the issue was still in dispute and that Kutch-Sindh boundary had never been demarcated. In early 1964, Pakistan sent some of its troops to occupy Chhad Bet area of north Rann of Kutch. But these troops withdrew when Indian troops moved into the area. However, in April 1965 there developed a war between India and Pakistan over the issue of ownership of Rann of Kutch. In June 1965, both India and Pakistan agreed to a cease-fire which was to be effective from 1st July 1965. Afterwards, it was agreed to refer the dispute to a three-Judge Arbitration Tribunal gave its award in February 1968 and decided against the Pakistani case that the International boundary of the Rann passed through its middle. Nevertheless, it awarded to Pakistan some 350 sq. miles of the disputed area. India, though did not regard the decision as just, decided to accept it unconditionally because of the terms of the June, 1965, agreement. The Pakistani invasion of Kutch was however, really designed to test its army and guns for the future aggression against India, which came in September 1965.

6. Issue of Integration of Princely States: As a part of partition settlement it was agreed that after 15th August 1947, the British Paramountcy over the Princely States would lapse and these states would be free to accede either to India or Pakistan or to remain independent. Gradually, all the Princely States decided their future except the rulers of Junagadh, Hyderabad and Kashmir, who decided to avoid a decision. The issue of accession of these three states led to the development of tensions and strains in Indo-Pak relations.

(*i*) *Junagadh*: The Princely State of Junagadh was a Hindu majority state (80 per cent) ruled by a Muslim ruler Sir Mahabat Khan Hussain. It had no land link with Pakistan. However, the Muslim ruler, on 15th August 1947, announced his decision to accede to Pakistan. This decision led to serious internal disturbances in Junagadh which forced the Dewan of Junagadh, Mr. Shah Nawaj Bhutto to invite the Indian Government to take over the administration of Junagadh on 9th November 1947. India took over the administration of Junagadh. Pakistan strongly protested against the Indian action and wanted the reinstatement of the Nawab. On 20th, February 1948, a plebiscite was held in Junagadh for settling its future. The verdict of the people came in favour of India. Only 91 persons voted in favour of Pakistan. After this verdict, Junagadh became a part of India. Nevertheless, Pakistan took the complaint to the Security Council where it still stands buried.

(*ii*) *Hyderabad*: The Princely State of Hyderabad too was a Hindu majority state ruled by a Muslim. It also had all its borders with Indian states. The Nizam of Hyderabad decided to remain independent and issued a 'Farmaan' in this connection. In November 1947, he signed a 'Standstill Agreement' with India. The internal situation in Hyderabad however deteriorated as a result of the atrocities which the Razakars, a Pro-Nizam Muslim group, started committing against the Hindus. The situation became so deteriorated that Indian Government was compelled to take 'Police Action' against the Nizam. After the Indian Police action the Nizam decided to accede to India and consequently, on 23rd September 1948, sent a cable to the Security Council withdrawing Hyderabad's complaint against the Indian action. Thereafter, Hyderabad became a part of India. Pakistan was shocked by this development and it tried hard to use this development both for maligning India and for winning favour for its views on Kashmir.

(*iii*) *Kashmir Issue*: Right from the initial years of Indo-Pak relations, Kashmir issue continues to be a crucial and the most irritating issue. After the Partition and the lapse of British Paramountcy, the Maharaja of Kashmir, Mr. Hari Singh decided to postpone the decision regarding issue of accession to India or to Pakistan. Pakistan, there upon conceived of a plan to secure Kashmir with the help of tribal's raiders. It engineered a tribal invasion of Kashmir with a view to create disturbances in Kashmir. The tribal invaders were fully supported and backed by the Pakistani army. The Pakistani move, however, misfired when on 26th, October 1947, the Maharaja of Kashmir decided to accede to India for securing Indian help in repelling the invaders. This decision of the Maharaj was supported by the National Conference—the political party of the people of Kashmir. Indian government further gave an assurance to the people of Kashmir that after the full restoration of law and order in Kashmir and the eviction of invaders, a plebiscite would be held for determining the Kashmir issue. The Pakistani government however, rejected the accession of Kashmir to India and this led to the emergence of the Kashmir dispute between India and Pakistan.

In November 1947, Lord Mountbatten tried to settle the Indo-Pak controversy over Kashmir and for this purpose held discussions with the leaders of Pakistan. His efforts yielded no result and in December 1947, it became clear that a negotiated settlement of the problem was practically not possible. Consequently, on 1st January 1948, India took the issue to the Security Council of the United Nations. Since that time Kashmir issue has been lying with the Security Council.

Initially, the Security Council established a 5-member United Nations Commission for India and Pakistan (UNCIP) for solving the Kashmir dispute. This commission was, in December 1948, successful in securing a cease-fire in Kashmir operative *w.e.f.* 1st January 1949. It also submitted 3 interim reports. On its recommendations the Security Council appointed M.C. Naughton as mediator on Kashmir. He, however, failed to resolve the tangle. In April 1950, Security Council appointed Owen Dixon for implementing M.C. Naughton's proposals. He too failed to achieve any success. He, in his report suggested a partition of Kashmir between India and Pakistan. This proposal was rejected by both the countries. Afterwards, the Security Council appointed

F.P. Graham as U.N. Representative for India and Pakistan and he suggested direct negotiations between the two countries for resolving the Kashmir issue. Between 1953-56 both India and Pakistan conducted bilateral negotiations for Kashmir but failed to reach any agreement.

Meanwhile, the situation underwent a big change. The people of Kashmir through the National Conference, their Constituent Assembly, the elections and through the resolutions passed by the J&K Legislature, gave full approval to Kashmir's accession to India. This development encouraged India to reject the Pakistani demand for holding a Plebiscite in Kashmir. In 1954, Pakistan became a member of U.S.-led security alliance system and started using its aligned position for securing settlement of Kashmir issue through Western pressures on India. This Pakistani move was met by strong Indian stand and the Soviet support for India in the Security Council of the United Nations. Consequently, the Security Council failed to settle the dispute. By 1960, the inability of the Security Council failed to settle the Kashmir issue became very clear. Pakistan then decided to use U.S. and British pressures for forcing India to hold talks with Pakistan over the Kashmir issue. Particularly after the 1962 Chinese invasion of India—Pakistan became quite eager to secure a settlement of Kashmir issue. India by this time had taken up the stand that Kashmir was an integral part of India and a symbol of Indian secularism. However, in the post-1962 period India accepted the proposal to discuss Kashmir with Pakistan. Six rounds of talks over Kashmir were held between the two countries. These talks failed to produce any result. In 1965, Pakistan attempted a military solution of Kashmir. Through a band of trained infiltrators it tried to create disturbances in Kashmir with a view to prepare ground for the subsequent conquest of Kashmir. In September, 1965, it attacked India for securing its objective. However, India gave a befitting reply and instead captured certain new areas of Kashmir which were under the illegal occupation of Pakistan.

In 1966, both countries signed the Tashkent Declaration and agreed to settle all their issues and problems through bilateral negotiations. But this agreement too failed to secure good neighbourly relations between them. It also kept the Kashmir issue unresolved. Towards the ending years of the seventh decade India and Pakistan once again came to develop highly tense and strained relations due to the emergence of Bangladesh crisis. In December, 1971, there broke out the third war between them. But this time India achieved a decisive victory over Pakistan. Pakistan suffered a military defeat in East Pakistan (now Bangladesh). India was in a position to capture some vitally important and strategic areas of Pakistan and a large number of Pakistan POW. However, for securing normalisation in Indo-Pak relations India decided to hold the Simla Summit with Pakistan and to sign the Simla Agreement of 1972. This Agreement constituted a bold bilateral attempt to normalise Indo-Pak relations. Since 1972, this agreement has been guiding the course of Indo-Pak detente.

In the post-1972 period, both the countries have been attempting to normalise their relations and establish trade, social and cultural links between the two countries. Pakistan has now expressed its desire to sign a 'No-War Pact' with India. India has expressed her pleasure over the Pakistani desire for normalisation of Indo-Pak relation, but has shown its preference for signing a comprehensive of Peace, Friendship and Co-operation with Pakistan. The negotiations are still going on and both sides are trying to narrow down their differences. They have now, for the first time, agreed to institutionalize their relations through the establishment of a Joint Commission for promoting trade and cultural co-operation between the two countries. Two meetings of the Joint Commission have been held so far and important steps have been initiated towards the development of Indo-Pak relations.

Nevertheless, Pakistan still continues to harp on the Kashmir issue and advocating the need to settle outstanding dispute India does not accept that the question of Kashmir's accession is still open for negotiations. There exists a big gap between the stands of the two countries over this issue. Meanwhile, Kashmir continues to be a divided state between India and Pakistan with the line of actual control as determined after the 1971 Indo-Pak war, as the boundary. For India, Kashmir's accession to India and its political unity with Indian Union is complete and irrevocable. For it the Kashmir problem means the problem of securing the liberation of POK. Pakistan thinks otherwise and still demands a plebiscite and a final settlement of the status of Kashmir. It has even illegally entered into boundary agreements with China involving a surrender of some parts of POK to China. India has strongly opposed these clandestine agreements. Kashmir thus continues to be an important issue in Indo-Pak relations. Despite the difficulties and strains inflicted by the problems and disputes generated by partition, India and Pakistan have now come to reach settlements in respect of all issues except the issue of Kashmir. The present detente, which has been going on since July, 1972, has produced a welcome change in the environment. Yet one cannot predict a very bright future. Indo-Pak relations have always been like a see-saw game. Ups are suddenly followed by downs. The existence of differences over Afghanistan, the supply of highly sophisticated US weapons to Pakistan, Indian apprehensions about Pindi-Beijing collusion, Pakistan's Nuclear Policy. Pakistan's stand over some of the internal issues and problems of India, the existence of strong anti-India elements in Pakistan and the Pakistani apprehensions about Indo-Soviet friendship and India's growing power in world politics, force us to keep our fingers crossed and refrain from striking an optimistic prediction in favour of increased Indo-Pak friendship and co-operation in the years to come. Pakistan is now a Non-aligned state. Its present leadership appears to be willing to open a new era of friendship with India. Indian leadership is also eager to develop friendly co-operation with Pakistan. Prime Minister Rajiv Gandhi has set into motion an important, major and active drive for improvement of relations with Pakistan. Let us hope that it would result into good understanding and mature Indo-Pak relations.

II. Kashmir Problem

Kashmir has been the most major issue and a bone of contention between India and Pakistan. The partition gave rise to many disputes and problems. All of these disputes, except the dispute over Kashmir were solved gradually through mutual negotiations—one through the mediation of World Bank and another through Arbitration. The issue of Kashmir, however, continues to remain unsettles. Despite a series of lengthy, tiring and patient attempts by many individuals, nations and organisations, a solution to the Kashmir issue acceptable to both India and Pakistan has yet to emerge. Since 1947, it has been a major irritant in Indo-Pak relations. It has been pending with the Security Council of the United Nations and there appears to be almost no chance for a settlement through the Council. In 1965, it led to a war between the two countries. The Tashkent meeting of 1966, and the Simla meeting of 1972 failed to fill the gap between the positions adopted by the two countries in respect of Kashmir. India, since mid-fifties, has been maintaining that Kashmir is an integral part of Indian Union, and its accession to India is full and final. For India, Kashmir problem means the issue of securing the liberation of Pakistani occupied Kashmir (PoK). Pakistan, however, still advocates that the future of Kashmir is yet to be settled in accordance with the wishes of the people of Kashmir. As such there are present strong Indo-Pak differences over the issue and Kashmir still constitutes a determinant of the bilateral relations between these two South-Asian countries. A review of Indo-Pak relations since 1947 can be complete only by reviewing the nature of history of Kashmir dispute between the two countries.

Origin of the Problem: Jammu and Kashmir constitute one state of Indian Union with an area of 86,023 sq. miles and include besides the valley of Kashmir, the area of Jammu and Ladakh, the Hill Districts and the Tribal areas. (Baltistan, Gilgit, Hunza and Nagar), Under the present *de facto* position of the state, Jammu, the valley and Ladakh are in India. The Tribal areas are in Pakistan, and Hill Districts (mainly Poonch) stand divided between India and Pakistan. Because of its strategic situation and geographical position Kashmir is intimately connected with the security of India.

In August, 1947, when the paramountcy of the British crown lapsed Kashmir, became an independent state and under the partition settlement it had the option to accede either to India or Pakistan or to remain independent. The Maharaja of Kashmir, Mr. Hari Singh decided to maintain the independence of Kashmir and as such did not accept either of the two instruments of accession that were forwarded to him by the Governments of India and Pakistan. Three days before the partition (August 12, 1947) the Maharaja proposed a 'Standstill Agreement' with India and Pakistan for maintaining a *status quo* in economic and communication services. Pakistan accepted the Agreement but India did not commit herself and invited the Maharaja for talks.

The Pakistani acceptance of the 'Standstill Agreement' was only superficial and surficial as within a month of the agreement it started harassing the people of Kashmir by stopping economic activities, food and fuel supplies from the Pakistani side to Kashmir. This economic boycott appeared to be designed to force Kashmir's accession to Pakistan. The Maharaja, however, did not show any inclination to accede to Pakistan and his reluctance made Pakistan eager to put military pressure for securing its desire-accession of Kashmir to Pakistan. It was inconceivable to Pakistan that Kashmir should not become a part of the new Muslim State. It consequently, engineered a tribal invasion of Kashmir. In October 1947, armed tribesmen started invading Kashmir. On October 15, 1947, nearly 5,000 raiders began the siege of Fort Owen inside Kashmir, and by October 22, infiltration and raids were transformed into frill scale military attack upon Kashmir. These raiders were openly supported by Pakistan and were in fact Pakistani soldiers in tribal clothes. Kashmir came under the imminent danger of falling to invaders. The Maharaja of Kashmir requested India for help, but the latter refused to comply until a decision in favour of Kashmir's accession to India was made.

Kashmir Accession to India: On October 23, Maharaja Hari Singh decided to accede to India. On 26th October, 1947, he signed the Instrument of Accession and made Kashmir a part of India. By this act of the lawfully constituted Government of Kashmir, of which the Maharaja was the head and with whom Pakistan had earlier entered into the 'Standstill Agreement', Kashmir became a part of India. India immediately flew its troops into Kashmir and the Indian army went into action against the invaders. Through a quick and efficient military operation India was successful in saving Srinagar and in driving out the invaders to Uri.

Kashmir as a Dispute between India and Pakistan: While accepting the Instruments of Accession, India voluntarily pledged that "as soon as law and order have been restored in Kashmir and her soil cleared of the invaders, the question of the state's accession should be retained by the people. Pakistan, however, refused to accept the accession of Kashmir to India and described it as a 'fraud perpetrated on the people of Kashmir by its cowardly rulers with the aggressive help of the Government of India.' On October 27, 1947, M.A, Jinnah, the Governor-General of Pakistan ordered the Pakistani troops to enter Kashmir. This order was later on withdrawn when the Commander-in-Chief of the Pakistani army pointed out that such a direct invasion would involve the withdrawal of British officers' serving with the Pakistani army. Consequently, Pakistan decided to increase its un-official and underground help to the invaders. The Government of India, through its Governor-General Mr. Mountbatten started negotiations for securing an end to Pakistan's help to the invaders. Pakistan first denied its role in the Kashmir war and then challenged the accession of Kashmir to India. After two rounds of talks in November and December 1947, Mountbatten became convinced that Kashmir issue could not be resolved through negotiations. Realising this India decided to refer the Kashmir issue to the United Nations.

Kashmir Issue in the Security Council: On 1st January, 1948, India under Article 35 of the U.N. Charter, referred the Kashmir question to the Security Council of the United Nations and requested the Council to ask the Government of Pakistan:

(*i*) to prevent the Pakistani Government personnel, military, and civil, from participating in or assisting the invasion of J&K state;

(*ii*) to call upon Pakistani nationals to desist from taking part in the fighting in J&K state, and

(*iii*) to deny to the invaders;

(*a*) access to and use of its territory for operations against Kashmir;

(*b*) military and other supplier, and

(*c*) all other kinds of aid that might tend to prolong the present struggle.

During the first few U.N. debates over Kashmir. India justified Kashmir's accession to India but accepted that for a final settlement it was essential that Pakistan should withdraw all the invaders from Kashmir. India agreed that after the Pakistani withdrawal, it would reduce the number of its forces in Kashmir to a minimum that would be essential for maintaining the security and administration of the entire state and that after the normalisation of conditions, a plebiscite under the control of the popular government of the State and the supervision of U.N. representatives would be held to settle the question of Kashmir's accession. Pakistan's representative at the U.N., Mr, Zafarullah Khan, however, argued that Kashmir dispute was merely a tragic aspect of the deep conflict between Hindus and Muslims of the sub-continent which could be solved only by a peaceful separation of the two communities with Kashmir becoming part of Pakistan. He observed that India has achieved Kashmir's accession by fraud. He described Kashmir issue as an Indo-Pak dispute but denied Pakistan's involvement in the tribal attack.

In the discussions of the Security Council, Indian view did not receive much support. The central issue, according to India, was Pakistan's complicity in the invasion of Kashmir. The Security Council on the contrary, emphasised the right of self-determination by the people of Kashmir and thus questioned the state's accession to India, which it said, gave Pakistan a *locus standi* in the case. India on her part agreed to carry out the promise to the people of Kashmir, provided Pakistan withdraws its armed forces, tribesmen and other nationals from Kashmir.

The Security Council's Resolutions on Kashmir: The Security Council passed a resolution and appointed a Commission for investigating the Kashmir dispute. The Commission—The United Nation Commission on India and Pakistan (UNCIP) began its work in June 1948. When it reached the sub-continent in July, the Pakistani government informed it that two months earlier Pakistani regular troops had been sent to Kashmir for meeting the increased Indian military operations. The Commission after investigating the matter and after holding talks with the government of India and Pakistan submitted its first resolution on 3rd August 1948. This resolution was accepted by India but rejected by Pakistan. Therefore, the Commission held further negotiations and issued fresh proposals on 11th December 1948. These proposals were accepted by both India and Pakistan and under it both the countries effected a cease-fire between them *w.e.f.* 1st January, 1949.

The proposed settlement plan was:

(*i*) That Pakistan shall withdraw from Kashmir its troops and shall try its best to secure the withdrawal of tribesmen and the Pakistani nationals, who were not the normal residents.

(*ii*) That pending a final solution, the territory vacated by the Pakistani troops shall be administered by local authorities under the supervision of the U.N. Commission.

(*iii*) That after the completion of the first step, the Commission shall notify the Government of India and thereafter India shall withdraw gradually the bulk of its troops from Kashmir.

(*iv*) That Government of India would maintain, within those areas of Kashmir which are under its control at the movement of cease-fire, that minimum strength of its forces as shall be necessary for maintaining law and order, and

(*v*) That the future status of J&K shall be determined in accordance with the wishes of the people of the state.

The Security Council passed a resolution on 5th January, 1949 by which it proposed: (*i*) a plebiscite under the auspices of the Government of Jammu and Kashmir; (*ii*) affirmed the right of the Indian army to defend the state, and (*iii*) called for the withdrawal of the Pakistani forces and other elements from Kashmir.

The Failure to Implement the S.C. Resolutions: But both India and Pakistan failed to implement this settlement. Pakistan persistently refused to withdraw its forces from Kashmir and thus, according to India made the resolution inoperative and ineffective. Pakistan wanted a synchronised withdrawal of troops of both the countries; and India insisted on the demilitarisation of the PoK as a condition proceeding to plebiscite. The UNCIP failed to resolve the tangle. In August 1949, it suggested that the points of difference be submitted to arbitration. This proposal was accepted by Pakistan but rejected by India. By the end of 1949, the UNCIP accepted its failure and in its final report of 9th December, 1949 suggested the appointment of a single mediator for replacing the Commission.

U.N. Commissions on Kashmir: On the recommendation of the Commission, the Security Council appointed its President, General M.C. Noughton as a mediator. He forwarded certain proposals to India and Pakistan, but failed to secure an agreement from them. On 12th April 1950, the Security Council appointed Mr. Owen Dixon of Australia for securing a demilitarisation of Kashmir but he too failed to carry out his mission. On 15th September 1950, Dixon submitted his report and suggested the holding of plebiscite on region by region basis. Alternatively he suggested that Kashmir should be partitioned without holding a plebiscite. The proposals were rejected by both India and Pakistan. India rejected the proposal because it did not name Pakistan as the aggressor and equated India and Pakistan. Pakistan rejected it because it did not support the holding of a full plebiscite in Kashmir. The Western opinion, though shared Dixon's pragmatic view, did not agree with him in ruling out a full plebiscite on political grounds. Dixon, thereupon, suggested that the dispute should be returned to the parties for negotiations. But the Security Council thought otherwise and appointed another mediator Frank P. Graham, an American.

The Graham Mission lasted for two years and it coincided with many important events in the sub-continent *e.g.*, the movement of Indian troops to the borders with Pakistan in July 1951, the assassination of Prime Minister Liaquat Ali Khan of Pakistan and the convening of the Kashmir's Constituent Assembly. Nevertheless, working with great patience Graham succeeded in reducing the areas of disagreement between India and Pakistan. But his five reports and the two Security Council resolutions made during this period, did not meet all the vital demands of either side and hence were rejected by both India and Pakistan. Thus, under the circumstances the Graham Mission also failed to solve the Kashmir dispute. Graham suggested that bilateral Indo-Pak negotiation should be held for settling the dispute.

Bilateral Indo-Pak Negotiations over Kashmir: In the summer of 1953 India and Pakistan initiated bilateral talks for settling the Kashmir dispute. The bilateral talks, first held at the Queen's Coronation in June 1953, continued in Karachi and Delhi in July and August. The talks began in an atmosphere of goodwill but soon these became clouded because of certain negative developments. On August, 9, 1953, Sheikh Abdullah was dismissed and detained by the Government of India on charges of anti-national activities. In February 1954, Kashmir's Constituent Assembly unanimously ratified the state's accession to India. Both these developments made the atmosphere heavy and suspicious. Further damage was done to the talks when the American decision to provide large quantities of military aid and the Pakistani decision to join the Western Military Alliances were announced in 1954. Despite the efforts made by the Pakistani Governor General, Gulam Muhammad and the decision of India reciprocate the goodwill, no progress could be registered toward an agreement over Kashmir. The Pakistani decision to join American sponsored military alliances was interpreted by India as a device for pressurising India. Consequently, Indian stand over Kashmir came to be stated as "the inviolability of Kashmir's accession to India". The change of Government in Pakistan in 1956 and Prime Minister Choudhri Mohammad Ali's decision to resume the struggle at the United Nations, obviously with the help of Pakistan's new allies, gave an end to the era of bilateral talks. The Indian stand on Kashmir now rejected the demand for plebiscite on the ground that the Constituent Assembly of Kashmir already has ratified Kashmir's accession to India and the Constitution of Kashmir under Article III stated: 'The state of J&K is and shall be an integral part of the Union of India'. This further hardened the Pakistani attitude. Consequently, India and Pakistan once again became engaged in sharp interactions over Kashmir in the Security Council.

Revival of Kashmir Issue at the United Nations: The beginning of 1957 came with sharp Indo-Pak exchanges in the

Security Council over the question of Kashmir's accession to India. Pakistan, through its Foreign Minister Feroze Khan Noor, challenged the J&K Constituent Assembly's ratification and the Constitution of J&K, as illegal acts Mr. Noor argued. "Since the future of Kashmir was still to be settled and a plebiscite was still to be held, there could be no legal justification for such acts". He further questioned Indian role in Kashmir and called upon the Security Council to direct India to implement the 1948 and 1949 Security Council resolutions. He even demanded the induction of a U.N. Force into Kashmir. India on the other hand, strongly refuted the allegations levelled and the points raised by Pakistan. It strongly defended the accession of Kashmir to India and its ratification by the Constituent Assembly of J&K and by Article III of the Constitution. India's representative, Mr. Krishna Menon argued that the constitution of J&K was only a declaratory act and that it only restated the fact of Kashmir's accession to India.

The Proposal for Arbitration over Kashmir and its Rejection: The Security Council, after the famous Four Power Resolution (Moved by Australia, Cuba, U.K. and U.S.A.) had been vetoed by the Soviet Union, adopted an amended resolution and called upon its President Gunnar Jarring of Sweden to discuss with the Indian and the Pakistani governments, any proposal which they deemed fit for the settlement of Kashmir issue having regard to the previous resolutions of the U.N. In his report submitted on 29th April, 1957, Gunnar Jarring observed that if a plebiscite would be held "grave problems might arise". He seemed to favour status quo but proposed that through arbitration it should be determined whether the two sides had met the terms of the first resolution, which specified preliminary steps to a truce and a plebiscite. India rejected the suggestion for arbitration and thus ended the Jarring mission.

Second Graham Mission: Pressed by Pakistan, the Western powers in September 1957, requested the Security Council to reappoint Frank P. Graham as its representative and entrust him the task of making recommendation to the parties for further appropriate action for the implementation of the U.N. resolutions on Kashmir. After holding discussions with the Governments of India and Pakistan, Graham submitted his report in March, 1958.

He favoured an Indo-Pak conference on Kashmir at Prime Minister's level and the stationing of U.N. troops on the Pakistani side of Kashmir borders. The suggestion was accepted by Pakistan but rejected by India. The United Nations took no action on it and in fact did not take up the Kashmir issue again until 1962.

The Indo-Pak Efforts: In 1958, Field Marshal Ayub Khan became the military dictator and later on the President of Pakistan. He met Prime Minister Nehru twice in 1960 and discussed the Kashmir issue. In 1960, the signing of Canal Water Treaty between India and Pakistan gave rise to the expectations that an attempt to settle the Kashmir would also be made by the Governments of the two countries. However, the march of history after September 1961 produced no progress in this direction.

Renewed Pakistani Attempts to Secure Security Council's Action over Kashmir: In January, 1962, Pakistan once again requested the Security Council to take up the Kashmir issue on the ground that a new and grave situation seems to be emerging in Kashmir. This Pakistani request was not entertained by the Security Council because of India's plea for postponement due to the coming General Elections in India. Upon a second request made by Pakistan, the Security Council once again took up the Kashmir issue and debated it from 27th April to 4th May and from 15th June to 22nd June 1962. On the last day, a resolution sponsored by Ireland was moved. It called for the resumption of bilateral talks between India and Pakistan over the Kashmir. This resolution was vetoed by the Soviet Union.

Chinese Aggression and its Impact on Indo-Pak Relations: The Sino-Indian War of 1962 further strained the relations between India and Pakistan. Pakistan's open support for China emergence of Sino-Pak ties and the Pakistani displeasure over the emergence of warmth and understanding between India and America, which involved the agreement for the supply of American arms to India, made the nature of Indo-Pak relations complicated and more cloudier. U.S.A. and Britain however, decided to use the changed situation in South Asia, which had developed as a result of the Chinese menace over the Himalayan Borders and its aggression against democratic India, for securing a breakthrough in Indo-Pak dispute over Kashmir through their representatives Duncan

Sandy and Averall Harriman, they were successful, in November, 1962, in securing an agreement from the Governments of India and Pakistan for holding ministerial level talks over Kashmir.

Failure of Indo-Pak Talks on Kashmir: Consequently, on 27th December 1962, Indo-Pak talk on Kashmir began in Rawalpindi. But the question of good faith arose as the first issue at the meeting when the Pakistani Government announced that it had signed a joint communiqué with China on the alignment of borders between Sinkiang and Pakistan. The Government of India strongly condemned and rejected as illegal the Sino-Pak border agreement of 2nd March 1963. It was described by India as a mischievous agreement signed by Pakistan for pressurising India and for securing Chinese support for the Pakistani stand on Kashmir. Pakistan on the other hand, defended the agreement and challenged Indian stand over Kashmir. Under the circumstances the six rounds of Indo-Pak talks failed to produce any result except that the Indo-Pak differences and all the possible solutions of Kashmir issue became more widely known.

1964 Security Council's Resolution Calling upon India and Pakistan to Resolve Kashmir Dispute through Mutual Negotiations: In 1964, Pakistan once again appealed to the Security Council for discussing the Kashmir issue. After two fruitless debates the Security Council, on 18th May 1964, passed a resolution proposing that Kashmir dispute should be solved through mutual negotiations between India and Pakistan. This can be described as the last resolution passed by the Security Council over the Kashmir issue. Commenting upon the Security Council debates on Kashmir, Charles Heimsath has well-observed, "The debates provided both Indian and Pakistani Government with opportunities to publicise their uncompromising positions, to test the responses of the great powers and to dramatise to their own peoples their skill and persistence in furthering national interest. Nothing more was expected or accomplished".

Pakistan's 1965 Invasion and its Attempt to Secure Kashmir by Force: By mid-1964, Pakistan came to realise the futility of raising Kashmir issue in the Security Council. The failure to encash the alliance relationship with the West for securing Kashmir, the disgust over the failure of its attempts in the Security Council, the strong dissatisfaction with the new role of Sheikh Abdullah in India, the feeling that Indian leadership after Nehru's death was weak, the growing military power of India after October, 1962 Sino-Indian war, the friendship with India's enemy—China, the belief in superior military power of Pakistan and the Chinese assurance of help against India, impelled the Pakistani rulers to attempt a forcible annexation of Kashmir. They initiated the process of creating tensions along the Indian borders, particularly along the cease-fire line in Kashmir. A military probing operation was launched in March-April 1965 in the Rann of Kutch and a scheme was prepared for creating trouble in Kashmir by sending armed Pakistani infiltrators into Kashmir. They directed to create trouble through acts of sabotage in the Indian side of Kashmir. The attempt for the implementation of this scheme on the part of Pakistan led to the outbreak of a war between India and Pakistan in August-September 4, 1965.

In August, 1965, Pakistan sent a large number of infiltrators into the Indian side of Kashmir for instigating Kashmiris against India and for fomenting trouble in J&K through acts of sabotage. Through them Pakistan was able to create some problems but the quick and efficient Indian action let to the capturing of a large number of infiltrators and the sealing of the borders of Kashmir. Disturbed by this development, the Pakistani troops launched an attack on the Indian posts in the Chhamb sector. India appealed to the Security Council for directing Pakistan to withdraw the aggression but got disgusted with the partial attitude of the Security Council which under Western pressures refused to name Pakistan as the aggressor.

Irritated by this partial attitude, India decided to take military action against the aggressor. On 15th August 1965, after crossing the cease-fire line in Kashmir, Indian forces went into action and captured the strategically important posts in Kargil, Tithwal, Hajipir and Uri-Punch from where Pakistani infiltrators were being sent. On September, 1, Pakistan launched a massive attack on India across the international frontier in the Chhamb Sector of South-West J&K towards Akhnoor. Indian forces met the attack but felt that for relieving the Pakistani pressure on Chhamb, it was essential to open the Western front against Pakistan. On

September, 5, India therefore launched a three-pronged attack in the Lahore Sector and a day later in the Sialkot sector. This produced the desired effect and the Pakistani pressure on Chhamb and its strength in positions in POK got reduced. The result, however, was the outbreak of a full but undeclared war between India and Pakistan. The war continued till 23rd September 1965, when on the basis of the Security Council resolution as supplemented by the peace mediation done by U.N. Secretary-General, U. Thant, both the countries agreed to a cease-fire. India accepted the Security Council resolution for cease-fire but expressly rejected the resolution relating to Kashmir. The failure to achieve success, the failure to secure Chinese involvement, the stoppage of American and British arms sales to both India and Pakistan and the heavy losses it suffered compelled Pakistan to accept the cease-fire. India accepted the cease-fire also because war was seriously taxing its economic resources and was considered to be highly harmful to future security interests of India *vis-a-vis* China. Thus, the 18 days war came to an end on 23rd September 1965, through the agreement to observe cease-fire.

Tashkent Meeting between India and Pakistan: The cease-fire effected since the mid-night of 22nd and 23rd September ended the war but the atmosphere governing Indo-Pak relations remained surcharged with emotions and tensions. The violations of cease-fire and the continued Pakistani hatred against India kept the possibility of war alive. To help India and Pakistan get out of this explosive situation, the Soviet Premier Kosygin offered his good offices. He proposed a meeting between India and Pakistan leaders in the Soviet Union (at Tashkent) for holding negotiations for settling peacefully the differences that had arisen between them. This Soviet move was designed to secure rapproachment between India and Pakistan. The Soviet leadership felt that Indo-Pak differences were, on the one hand, strengthening China and on the other hand, helping the Western powers to maintain and increase their influence in South Asia. To check this, the Soviet Union invited India and Pakistan to meet at Tashkent for settling their bilateral problems.

The Soviet offer was accepted by India immediately but Pakistan took nearly two months to accept the offer. It was on 25th November, 1965, that the Foreign Minister of Pakistan, Mr. Z.A. Bhutto declared at a press conference in Moscow that President Ayub Khan would be willing to discuss with the Indian Prime Minister Lal Bahadur Shastri, "the whole gamut of Indo-Pak relations."

The Tashkent Declaration: The Tashkent conference between India and Pakistan was held from 4th to 10th January 1966. It was after a series of meetings, involving protracted and hard negotiations that the leaders of the two countries were in a position to agree upon certain issues which together formed the Tashkent Declaration. "Pakistan writes T.N. Kaul, was being deliberately difficult in order to pressurise India. But, Shastri was a tough negotiator". The conference experienced the greatest difficulty while negotiating for the return of territories captured by both the sides, particularly on the issue of return of Hajipur in exchange for Chhamb. India expressed willingness for the return of Hajipur to Pakistan in exchange of Chhamb, but at the same time wanted Pakistan to renounce the use of force. Prime Minister Shastri compromised his stand on No-War Pact and the return of areas captured in Kashmir and President Ayub Khan, over ruling Bhutto compromised the Pakistani stand and agreed to Shastri's proposal. The result was the signing of the Tashkent Declaration in the afternoon of 10th January, in an atmosphere of goodwill and with the hope that India and Pakistan would begin to talk directly and resolve the problems bilaterally. The death of Shastri at about 1 a.m. on 11th January came as a sad and unfortunate anti-climax. The death of Shastri, who was fast getting recognised as the builder of post-Nehru India came as a big blow and serious loss to India and it dampened the spirit of Tashkent. Moreover, sharp criticism of Tashkent Declaration by the Pakistani press and certain sections of Indian public opinion, as well as the failure of the Government of both India and Pakistan to implement provisions, other than the military provisions, made the Tashkent Declaration a weak basis for the post-1965 Indo-Pak relations. Further it failed to induce any change in the respective stands of India and Pakistan over the Kashmir issue.

Indo-Pak Relations after Tashkent Declaration: After Tashkent declaration, there appeared possibilities of Indo-Pak bilateral talks over Kashmir and other issues. On 15th August, 1968, Mrs. Indira Gandhi offered a No-War Pact to Pakistan, and on January 1st, 1969, supplemented this offer by a proposal for setting up a joint machinery for examining all disputes with Pakistan. But before these proposals could get articulated, the march of events in late sixties and early seventies made it difficult for India and Pakistan to make efforts in this direction. The development of crisis in East Pakistan and the subsequent issue of the liberation of Bangladesh made things worst and in December 1971 both the countries got involved in another war. However, in this war the Kashmir issue never came to the forefront. It was kept alive by the Pakistani Press and leaders for securing popular support and for enhancing their legitimacy but in actual practice no serious attempt was made to raise the issue at the U.N. Bangladesh crisis kept the Pakistani rulers engaged in issues other than Kashmir and the defeat of Pakistan in December 1971 was totally demoralised them.

Simla Agreement 1972 and Kashmir Issue: In the Simla Conference of 1972, Prime Minister Bhutto did raise the Kashmir question but purely at the surficial level. The Simla Agreement included a sub-clause of clause IX and it said, "In Jammu and Kashmir, the line of control resulting from the cease-fire of December 17, 1971, shall be respected by both sides without prejudice to the recognised position of either side. Neither side shall seek to alter in unilaterally, irrespective of mutual differences and legal interpretations. Both sides further undertake to refrain from threat or the use of force in violation of this line".

After the Simla Agreement, the line of control as stood on December 17, 1971, came to be the new cease-fire line. India got better placed that what its position was after Tashkent agreement. It has control-over certain highly strategic positions like Hajipur, Tithwal, Uri-Poonch, Bulge and Kargil. The line of actual control has now come to be the *de-facto* boundary between India and Pakistan. Pakistan, even today keeps on harping upon Kashmir and the right of self-determination of the people of Kashmir. Its rulers keep on talking about the necessity of resolving the

Kashmir issue. Even while negotiating for a No-War Pact—A Treaty of Peace and Friendship with India or while addressing any international forum, the Pakistani spokesmen always make it a point to refer to Kashmir dispute and stress the need to settle it. President Zia-ul-Haque has often remarked that a No-War Pact with India will not change his country's stand on Kashmir (*Indian Express* 10th August, 1982). Pakistan has entered into certain agreements with China which relate to the territory of Kashmir under its occupation. The opening of the Karakoram Highway and the signing of protocol regarding the opening of Khunjerab Pass have been effected by Pakistan, which according to India are illegal and clandestine agreements since these make China an interested party in Kashmir from the side of Pakistan and these involve territories which are under the illegal occupation of Pakistan. Pakistan has now claimed that Gilgit, Hunza, Nagar, Yasion, Ponial, Chitral and Skarda have never been part of the state of J&K—India has strongly criticised the Pakistani moves. Presently, Pakistan is desperately, trying to secure control over the Siachen Glacier in Ladakh. It has been attacking Indian security forces which are determinedly controlling the area. India has totally rejected Pakistani claims regarding Siachen. Pakistan wants to strengthen its position by forcibly occupying Siachen. However, India is determined to keep the Pakistani desire unfulfilled. It stands fully committed to the full and final accession of Kashmir to India and regards Kashmir as a symbol of Indian secularism. Speaking before the F.P. Association in New York during her visit to America, Mrs. Indira Gandhi categorically stated, while answering a question regarding Kashmir that "we do not see any problem at all". For India the issue of Kashmir simply means the issue of securing the liberation of POK, but for this India is not willing to use force, nor even threat of force against Pakistan. The people of Kashmir like the people of other states of India have accepted fully Kashmir's status as a part of the Indian Union. They are participating as equal partners in the national democratic process and the march towards socio-economic development. They are successfully rejecting pro-Pakistani and anti-Indian elements in Kashmir.

After the death of Sheikh Abdullah, his son Dr. Farooq Abdullah emerged as the new leader of Kashmir. He too categorically stated that the accession of Kashmir to India is full and final. The Chief Minister of Kashmir, Mr. G.M. Shah has repeatedly declared that Kashmir's accession to India is full and final and Kashmir continues to be and will always remain an integral part of Indian Union. The people of Kashmir have accepted their position as a part of India. They fully accept Kashmir accession to India is full and final. The grave situation in POK contrasted with the growing prosperity on the Indian side of Kashmir make them fully aware of the goodness of their decision.

Kashmir issue as such, at present remains an issue/dispute in discussions and speeches only. In actual practice history seems to have settled in the form of a division along the line of actual control as stands determined after the December 1971 war. Both the sides now appear to be more interested in normalising their relations through a Treaty of Peace and Friendship/No-War Pact, and through the institutionalisation of their relations by means of such institutions like the Joint Commission for Economic and Cultural Co-operation. Both are now willing to keep aside Kashmir and normalise the relations. The attempt is to make the environment of Indo-Pak relations congenial and then initiate suitable steps for settling all outstanding issues and disputes on the basis of a new faith on peace, friendship and mutual goodwill. Yet, the Pakistani rulers do not hesitate to talk of "Kashmir dispute" on almost every occasion. It is regarded by them as a useful means to increase their legitimacy in Pakistan. For India "Kashmir Speeches" by the Pakistani leaders carry neither any weight nor conviction.

III. Tashkent Declaration

The August-September 1965 Indo-Pak war came to an end on 23rd September, 1965, when both the countries agreed to cease-fire on the basis of the Security Council resolution. But the peace that the cease-fire brought was tense, unstable and risky. Even after the cease-fire the armies of the two countries continued to face each other in the battle fields. There continued to be a large number of air violations and exchanges of fire across some of the border posts. Both India and Pakistan found themselves placed in a situation that needed careful handling. Realising the danger and gravity of the situation, the leaders of both the countries agreed to accept the Soviet offer of good offices to meet at Tashkent in January 1966 for discussing "the whole gamut of Indo-Pak relations" and to resolve their outstanding disputes and issues through peaceful negotiations. Kosygin's offer of 4th September 1965, stated: "Acting in the spirit of the U.N. Charter and the Bandung principles the parties should enter into negotiations for the peaceful settlement of differences that have arisen between them".

India accepted the Soviet offer because it was an offer made by a valued friend and because it was based upon the fundamental ideological foundation of Indian Foreign Policy. Pakistan, though initially hesitated, accepted the offer because it felt: (*i*) that it involved the possibility of neutralising the Soviet support for India over Kashmir; (*ii*) that development of Soviet-Pak relations would make China and Western powers realise better the need for helping and supporting Pakistan; (*iii*) that after the failure to secure Kashmir, first through UN and then through force the only way left open was to hold negotiations with India, and (*iv*) that there was the need to get back the territories lost in Kashmir and secure a reopening of Kashmir issue.

The Tashkent Conference: It was on 4th January 1966, that the Tashkent conference opened on an optimistic note. In the opening speech Mr. Kosygin expressed the Soviet desire to see India and Pakistan living in friendship and peace. Prime Minister Shastri called upon Pakistan to accept the principle of peaceful co-existence and repudiate war as a means for settling issues between the two countries. President Ayub Khan also expressed the desire that both countries should live in peace and devote all their energy and use resources for liquidating the dismal legacies of colonialism. He however, expressed opposition to No-War Pact and instead advocated the need for settling the problems through negotiations.

The Tashkent Conference experienced difficulties on the very second day of negotiations when there appeared strong differences over the question of formal agenda of the conference. Pakistan wanted Kashmir and troops withdrawal as the first priorities whereas India wanted a thorough discussion over the question of peaceful means and wanted to negotiate Pakistan's assurance against the sending of infiltrators into Kashmir. It was only on the fourth day of conference that some really important negotiations were held between the two countries. On 7th January 1966 Pakistan declared that it would not agree to a 'No-War Pact' but would agree 'not to use force in future, On 8th January, a real crisis over the question of troops withdrawal from the new posts captured by them during 1965 war without itself withdrawing from Chhamb. India on the other hand, advocated its right to retain the areas captured in Kashmir and to get back Chhamb. Later on, as a reconciliation and goodwill gesture India agreed to return those areas of POK that came under Indian occupation during the war in return for Chhamb and a Pakistani assurance to renounce the use of force. The Ayub-Shastri meeting of 8th afternoon made things better. The draft declaration was negotiated, finalised and exchanged by the morning of January, 10. The signing ceremony was held in the afternoon and the celebrations took place in the evening and at night.

Tashkent Declaration: The nine-point Tashkent Declaration was described by Prime Minister Shastri as "a unique international diplomacy between a Socialist Government and a Government aligned with two military blocs." President Ayub hailed it as a victory for common people. The Soviet Premier Mr. Kosygin remarked: "It makes a new stage in the development of relations between India and Pakistan."

The salient provisions of the Tashkent Declaration are as under:

1. The Prime Minister of India and the President of Pakistan agree that both sides will exert all efforts to create good neighbourly relations and reaffirm their obligation under the U.N. charter not to have recourse to force and to settle their disputes through peaceful means.
2. That all armed personnel of the two countries shall be withdrawn not later than 25th February 1986 to positions

they—held prior to 5th August, 1965 and both sides shall observe cease-fire terms on cease-fire line.

3. That bilateral relations between the two countries shall be based upon the principle of non-interference in the internal affairs of each other.
4. That each side shall discourage any propaganda directed against the other country.
5. That the High Commissioners of both the countries shall return their posts and restore the normal diplomatic relations between the two countries.
6. That the two countries shall consider measures for the restoration of economic and trade relations, communications and cultural and exchanges shall implement the existing agreements.
7. That instructions shall be issued to the respective authorities for carrying out the exchange of the Prisoners of War.
8. That both sides shall take steps to prevent the exodus of people and shall continue to hold discussions on the problem of refugees and eviction of illegal immigrants. They would further discuss the return of property and assets taken over by either side in connection with the conflict.
9. That both sides agree that they will continue to meet both at the highest and other levels on matters of direct concern to each other.

Along with these provisions both the sides recorded their feelings of deep appreciation and gratitude to the leaders and government of the Soviet Union.

Reactions

The Tashkent Declaration was warmly welcomed by various countries. China was the only country which refrained from hailing it. It was hailed by many others as "an important landmark in the relations of India and Pakistan."

Reactions in India: In India the declaration was welcomed by the majority of people and by all the leaders of Congress Party.

However, it was criticised by the leaders of Janasangh and PSP mainly because it involved the provision for the withdrawal of Indian troops from Hajipur and TithwaL Mr. A.B. Vajpayee even declared that Indian leaders had lost in peace what the Jawans had won on the battle field. Rajagopalachari observed that "a beginning has been made by way of relaxation of rigidities on both sides". Government of India strongly defended the declaration in the Indian Parliament. It was commended as an important step towards the securing a peace and acceptance of peaceful means against the use of war. However, it was criticised by the critics as being "far away from a no-war declaration."

Reactions in Pakistan: In Pakistan there was a sharp reaction against the declaration. The general feeling was that it constituted 'a sellout'. The students at Lahore described it as 'the great betrayal'. The Bar Association of Pakistan described it as disappointing. Miss Fatima Jinnah declared, "The Tashkent Declaration betrays lack of sagacity, wisdom, forbearance and vision in the minds of those who accepted, signed, sealed and delivered it on behalf of Pakistan." The exception was The National Awami Party whose General Secretary, Mr. Mohmood-ul-Haq Usmani described it as a "triumph of sanity, reason and forces of peace." The Government of Pakistan defended it. But President Ayub had to clarify that Pakistan would not accept it as a No-War Pact and would continue to support "the inalienable right of the people of Kashmir to decide their own future." To pacify the public opinion in Pakistan, he added that "the basic cause is the dispute concerning J&K and unless this is settled there can be no peace between India and Pakistan." Gradually, the Pakistani rulers and press started expressing doubts about the implementation of Tashkent Declaration in practice. In an interview on 15th November 1966, President Ayub Khan observed, "It settled nothing. All it did was to enable the two countries to disengage their armies from each other".

The Implementation of Tashkent Declaration: In reality also only those parts of the declaration which related to troops withdrawal, exchange of POW's and restoration of diplomatic links were implemented. These provisions were speedily implemented and these tasks were completed by 25th February 1966. The rest of the provisions were kept non-operative. The strong reaction in Pakistan against the Tashkent Declaration, the refusal of Pakistan to accept it as a no war declaration, the lack of clear cut and specific provisions regarding its implementation, the absence of provisions regarding a machinery for settling the controversies and differences in respect of the interpretation of the provisions, and the failure to effect any change in regard to the respective views of India and Pakistan over the Kashmir issue, made the implementation of the Tashkent Declaration difficult. The death of Prime Minister Shastri soon after the signing of the declaration, the failure of Pakistan to reciprocate the offers of No-War Pact and a joint machinery for the peaceful settlement of disputes as were made by Prime Minister Mrs. Indira Gandhi in 1966 and 1968, further impeded the attempts at normalisations that could have been made in the post-Tashkent period of Indo-Pak relations. The Indian opposition to the supply of Soviet arms to Pakistan and to the resumption of anti-India propaganda by the Pakistani press further reduced the chances of implementation of Tashkent Declaration. Renewed Pakistani attempts to raise the Kashmir issue at the UN and the failure to accept the responsibility towards the infiltrators made it difficult to operationalise the normalisation provisions of the Tashkent Declaration. Even the first ministerial level conference held on 1st and 2nd March 1966, failed to make any headway. India's unilateral decision to end the trade restrictions too failed to get positive response from Pakistan. In July 1966, India announced its decision to release all non-military Pakistani cargo seized during war. This time, Pakistan also reciprocated and ordered the release of India-bound goods seized by it during the 1963 war. In 1967 and 1968 some limited progress was achieved towards the restoration of telecommunication links between the two countries. The Army Chiefs of India and Pakistan met in Rawalpindi on 24th October 1967, and agreed to take steps for preventing border violations. In July 1969, India released 16,000 tonnes out of 21,530 tonnes of Pakistani cargo of all types.

It took several steps to secure an implementation of the Declaration but failed due to the negative and cold attitude of

Pakistan. Mrs. Indira Gandhi's offer of 15th August 1968 to sign a No-War Pact with Pakistan was ridiculed and described as an exercise in hypocrisy by the Pakistani Press. (The same Pakistani Press now strongly advocated the hypocrisy of No-War Pact as the necessary and ideal condition of good-neighbourly relations between India and Pakistan!) Similarly, Mrs. Indira Gandhi's proposal to Pakistan, for the creation of a joint machinery for going into various Indo-Pak issues was rejected by Pakistan. "As nothing but a new propaganda campaign." Against India's desire for implementing the Tashkent Declaration, Pakistan preferred to criticise the declaration and to observe an anti-Tashkent day on the occasion of its first anniversary. Even President Ayub Khan in his message to Premier Kosygin on this eve observed "without the solution of Kashmir problem the Declaration could not be implemented." This was much against the message sent by Prime Minister Indira Gandhi in which she affirmed her faith in the Declaration. Thus, by 1967 Pakistan had started questioning the utility of the Declaration and in the 1968 it felt no hesitation in ignoring it all other. Soon afterwards a change in Pakistani leadership took place. Anti-Ayub propaganda and movement made it essential for President Ayub to quit and handover the regime to General Yahya Khan. Though President Yahya Khan lost no time in expressing the desire to live in peace and happiness with India, yet he took little interest in initiating steps for normalising the ties with India.

The March of events in 1970 once again brought with them war clouds over India and Pakistan. The emergence of a crisis in East Pakistan brought with it serious constraints and tensions for Indo-Pak relations. A big deterioration in India-Pak relations came in January, 1971 because of the failure of Pakistani Government to return or compensate the loss of Indian Airlines civil aircraft which was first hijacked and then set on fire at the Lahore airport. This incident was retaliated by India and it banned the over-flights of Pakistani planes across Indian territory. This incident and the outbreak of civil war in East Pakistan in March 1971, made the environment in South Asia highly tense and which ultimately led to the outbreak of December 1971 Indo-Pak war. Thus, within six years of the signing of Tashkent Declaration, which involved the agreement to avoid the use of force, both India and Pakistan again got involved into a big war. The Tashkent Declaration and the spirit in which it was signed had an in glorious burial effected by the emergence of Bangladesh crisis. Indeed, the Tashkent Declaration failed to provide a useful basis for the conduct of Indo-Pak relations even for a short period.

IV. Indo-Pak Relations Since 1966

"Almost since the day of British withdraw from the South Asian sub-continent", writes Mohammad Ayub, "the major countries of the region India and Pakistan have been in a state of perpetual cold war." The problem and disputes that arose out of the partition of country, the emergence of dispute over Kashmir, the China factor, and differences in foreign policy perceptions of the two countries were some of the key factors responsible for this cold war between them. On three different occasions *i.e.*, 1947, 1965 and 1971 this cold war led to the outbreak of armed conflict. The third one was a short, roughly two-week was but its results were far-reaching and its impact on the power structure and politics in the sub-continent was indeed very big. It gave India a decisive victory over Pakistan. It cut Pakistan to size. It led to the emergence of an independent Bangladesh. It made Pakistan realise the futility of attempting a power equilibrium with India. It made India and Pakistan more conscious towards their bilateral relations and both concluded the famous Simla Agreement which was designed to serve as the basis for Indo-Pak detente in the post-1971 period.

Circumstances that Led to the War in 1971: After the 1965 war, both India and Pakistan, acting under the good offices of Soviet Union, agreed at Tashkent to settle the disputes peacefully and to live as good and friendly neighbours. However, the Tashkent Declaration, because of its inherent weakness as well as because of the unhealthy environment in which it was sought to be implemented, failed to provide a sound and viable basis to Indo-Pak normalisation and friendship. After the speedy completion of the provisions which provided for military disengagement and exchange of territories and POWs, no major attempt was made, particularly by Pakistan, to work for operationalising the Tashkent spirit in practice. The negative and hot reaction with which the Pakistani press and public received the declaration, made it very difficult for the Pakistani rulers to accept it as the basis for cultivating good neighbourly relations with India. They even failed to respond favourably towards Indian offers for a No-War Pact and for the setting up of joint machinery for the peaceful settlement of Indo-Pak issues and disputes.

The hostile propaganda campaign as maintained by the Pakistani Press, continued differences over Kashmir, the fall out of the Agartala Conspiracy Case, the dispute over Farakka, the expulsions of diplomats, the auctioning of Indian property by Pakistan, and the growing strength of anti-India Sino-Pak Axis made the conditions of the 1966-71 period unhealthy for the development of good Indo-Pak relations on the basis of Tashkent principles. The change of regime in Pakistan on 31st March 1969, which came is a result of President Ayub's resignation under the pressure of hostile public opinion and the rise of General Yahya Khan to power in Pakistan, further prevented Pakistan from following the principles contained in the Tashkent Declaration. Though immediately after this change of regime, the Pakistani foreign office did show more interest in developing good relations with India, yet certain negative developments and the desire of a new regime to strengthen its legitimacy through a bold stand against India prevented any progress in this directly.

On 30th January 1971, an Indian Airlines plane was hijacked to Lahore. The hijackers were given asylum by Pakistan because they described themselves as supporters of Kashmir Liberation Front. The Government of Pakistan did not give any consideration to the Indian demand for the arrest and extradition of hijackers and the return of the plane to India. On 2nd February 1971, the hijackers, in the presence of the Pakistani authorities, Press and Television, set the plane on fire. This incident gave a big blow to the cause of Indo-Pak relations. India held Pakistan responsible for the hi-jack drama and as a retaliatory action it decided to ban the over-flights of the Pakistani planes on Indian territory. This incidents once again made the environment of Indo-Pak relations tense and strained. The emergence of a crises in East-Pakistan in March 1971, and the pressure it put on India made the things worst. The Tashkent spirit was forgotten. Pakistan once again started talking of war with India. Its press came up with a call for 'Crush India'. But in the process it was Pakistan which got crushed under a humiliating defeat coupled with the loss of East Pakistan.

The Domestic Environment of Pakistan in 1970: The December 1970 Elections in Pakistan were held for the noble and high purpose of transferring power from military to the elected representatives of the people. The election results, however created a political and constitutional crisis invoking a direct conflict between Bhutto's PPP dominated West Pakistan and Mujib's Awami League dominated East Pakistan. The crisis in turn led to an outbreak of a civil war in East Pakistan.

Under the decision of the Yahya Administration, elections to the National Assembly of Pakistan and the Provincial Assemblies were held in December 1970. The election results gave the East-Pakistan-based Mujib's Awami Party a land-slide victory. In the National Assembly it won 167 seats against the 84 seats won by West Pakistan-based Bhutto's Peoples Party of Pakistan (PPP). In the East-Pakistan Provincial Assembly too, the Awami League scored a massive victory while in West-Pakistan Bhutto's PPP scored an impressive win. The results were not well-received by the persons in power as well as by Mr. Bhutto and his party. The Election shattered the dream of Mr. Bhutto to become the Prime Minister of Pakistan. The West-Pak dominated administration could not relish the coming of an administration run by men from East Pakistan. They were not prepared to accept an end of the era of domination and exploitation of East Pakistan by the West Pakistan. They looked with suspicion and distrust Mujib's six-point programme, which had been the central core of Awami League's Election Manifesto. They regarded it as a charter of sedition and tension against Pakistan. Consequently, steps designed, at first for delaying and then for denying the possibility of transfer of power to Mujib-led Awami League (AL) were initiated. After the Elections, the President of PPP declared that his party would boycott the session of the National Assembly (NA) which was scheduled to be held at Dacca on 3rd March 1971. Mr. Bhutto demanded a postponement of the session of

NA. He held consultations with President Yahya, and the latter agreed to postpone the session for an indefinite period. This decision was prompted by the desire to deny AL the opportunity to determine the future constitution of Pakistan. The Awami League which was at this time committed to uphold the integrity of Pakistan took this decision as a deliberate move to deny to it the legitimate opportunity of ruling Pakistan and hence, it gave a call for strike in East-Pakistan. On 3rd March 1971, the strike was total. Afterwards, it was followed by regular general strikes in East-Pakistan. The administration used force, including the military force to suppress the strikes but failed to make a dent in the morale of the people. This forced Yahya Khan to announce on 6th March 1971 that the NA session would be held on 25th March 1971, but the place was not announced.

The people of East-Pakistan led by Mujib accepted the new date but demanded the fulfillment of certain conditions mainly for normalising the situation that had developed after 3rd March. On 8th March, civil disobedience was launched by Awami League in East-Pakistan. This movement was strongly supported by all sections of Bengalese (East-Pakistan *i.e.*, East Bengal and its inhabitants were mostly, Bengalese). The Martial Law Administrator of East Pakistan, General Tikka Khan's attempt to suppress the popular uprising by the imposition of curfew and through the use of force had no effect. On 15th March Mujib declared the independence of Bangladesh and took over the reins of administration. President Yahya Khan also initiated negotiations with Mujib but these were merely designed to camouflage the decision to let loose terror and naked force for suppressing the Bengalese. On the night of 25th March, Mujib was arrested and transported to West Pakistan and West Pakistani forces started executing a planned genocide of the Bengalese. The conditions in East Pakistan became so bad and inhumane that thousands of Bengalese started entering India and taking shelter in the Indian territory. Within a short span of time their number rose to over 10 millions. The burden of providing shelter and food to these refugees became so big that Government of India urged General Yahya Khan to solve the problem of East-Pakistan and to create normal conditions which would lead to the return of refugees to their home. The inability of the Pakistani Government to take effective steps and the continued opposition to it by the Bengalese made the conditions worst and compelled India to raise her voice in sympathy with the Bengalese. Mrs. Indira Gandhi issued several appeals to world leaders and called upon them to condemn the atrocities being committed by the Pakistani army on the Bengalese. The world leaders, with the exception of Soviet Leadership, however failed to respond favourably. Meanwhile, the Bangladesh liberation struggle gained momentum when many Bengali diplomats announced their decisions to renounce their allegiance to Pakistan and declared themselves to be the diplomats of Bangladesh. On 17th April 1971, the birth of the Republic of Bangladesh was announced. This brought into focus the question of recognition of Bangladesh. The people of India voiced strong demand for the grant of recognition, at least a *de facto* recognition to Bangladesh but the Government of India decided to wait and show restraint. It did not want to do anything to antagonise Pakistan. As such, it simply expressed sympathy with the people of East-Bengal, who were struggling hard for securing their human rights.

Meanwhile, Pakistan acting with the assurance of help and support from America and China, kept up its drive against the Bengalese. It termed the happenings of East Pakistan as a revolt engineered and backed by India. It linked the event to Agartala Conspiracy Case and accused India of interfering in the internal affairs of Pakistan. It gave threats of war and serious consequences to India. Feeling the pressure on her security and the near isolation from the Western Powers, America and China, India decided to strengthen her interests by entering into a Treaty of Peace, Friendship and Co-operation with the Soviet Union. This treaty gave India sense of security and assurance of dependable friendship. However, Pakistan interpreted this treaty as a device to pressurise and blackmail Pakistan. President Yahya Khan once again took the opportunity to malign and threaten India. He gave a call to the people of Pakistan to be prepared for a war with Hindu India. The environment in the South Asian sub-continent as such became tense with a distinct possibility of another Indo-Pak War.

In October 1971, the uprising in East-Bengal gained further strength and momentum due to the organisation of the Bengalese into a Guerrilla force-Muktibahini. The guerrilla attacks made by Muktibahini became a major source of tension and loss to the Pakistani forces stationed in East-Pakistan. Pakistan decided to concentrate its forces all along the borders with India because it felt that Muktibahini was actually being backed and guided by India. War between India and Pakistan appeared to be a certainty. Mrs. Indira Gandhi decided to make a new big effort to resolve the crisis peacefully and with the help of world leaders. She undertook a tour of a number of Western nations and brought to the notice of their leaders the grave situation that was developing in South Asia. Her efforts, however, did not produce any fruitful result.

The War of 1971: By November 1971 the condition became still more grave. The forces of Pakistan started committing border violations and the situation became explosive when on 22nd November, four Pakistani Sabre Jets violated the Indian air space to the tune of 5 miles. On 25th November, General Yahya Khan boastfully declared that he shall attack India within 10 days, and in reality on the 9th day after this declaration *i.e.*, on 3rd December 1971 at about 6 p.m. the planes of Pakistani Air force commenced an attack upon several Indian Air-fields. This pre emptive attack was designed to paralyse Indian Air Force. Indian vigilance prevented this and by mid-night, IAF went into action against Pakistan by launching a counter-attack on Pakistani air fields. On 4th December 1971, the gazette of Pakistan notified that Pakistan was in a state of war with India. Thus, the internal civil war of Pakistan forced a war upon India in December 1971. But within a short span of 14 days India was in a position to: (*i*) Liberate Bangladesh with the help of Muktibahini; (*ii*) To secure the surrender of Pakistani forces in Bangladesh and (*iii*) To score major victories on the Western front also.

Impact of 1971 War: It was on 16th December 1971 that General Niazi, the Commander of Pakistani forces in Bangladesh surrendered to Lt. General J.S. Arora of India. The same night India announced its decision to observe a cease-fire *w.e.f.* from mid-night. This Indian offer was accepted by Pakistan and thus ended the war of 1971. It was indeed a short but a decisive war that produced far-reaching impact on the scene and power structure in the South Asian sub-continent.

"The 1971 conflict", writes Kalim Bahadur, "radically changed the sub-continental structure created in 1947. It cut Pakistan to size and doomed its efforts to claim and attain parity with India forever". Pakistan lost a big part of its territory. In place of two, there emerged three independent sovereign states on the sub-continent. It gave a serious blow to the two-nation theory and to the principle of religion as the key factor of a nation. Politically, Pakistan got the opportunity to come under a civilian rule after a lapse of nearly 14 years. Economically its position stood at a low ebb. Militarily it stood defeated with nearly, 95,000 of its army-men in India as POWs. Such a bad situation was accompanied by certain indirect advantages for it. Pakistan became geographically more compact and economically close-knit state with Urdu as its national language. Pakistan was forced to concentrate more on its domestic affairs and the threat from India came to be regarded as a secondary factor. Under the circumstances Mr. Z.A. Bhutto, a new Prime Minister of Pakistan, found his tasks difficult, but the popular support-base that came to be developed around him as a result of the thorough disappointment and disgust with military rulers, made him formulate and successfully execute certain radical economic and military measures for getting Pakistan out of a very bad situation. In respect of foreign relations, he retained the old line of maintaining good and very friendly relations with America and China, but at the same time he also came forward to accept the new realities of the situation after the war and therefore did not hesitate to enter into the Simla Agreement with India, and through it to initiate the process of the Indo-Pak detente. Of course, along with it Mr. Bhutto kept up his usual 'blow-hot blow-cold policy towards India. On the one hand, he talked of a durable and honourable peace in the sub-continent, and on the other hand, he kept on harping on Kashmir and the threat from India.

India, though emerged stronger and victorious from the war yet never showed any inclination to unnecessarily punish or humiliate Pakistan. It did not want to utilise its position as a major power of South Asia for securing certain ends. In fact, the day Bangladesh was liberated, it offered the cease-fire to Pakistan and on 31st December 1971, the Indian Prime Minister declared that direct negotiation with Pakistan was the only way to solve the existing problems between the two countries. Pakistan at this stage was trying to keep alive the issue of Bangladesh along with the issue Kashmir. Bhutto was engaged in the process of visiting America, China and other Muslim countries for projecting Pakistan as a sufferer of foreign aggression which deserved full sympathy and huge military and economic aid. However, at home, under the pressure of the demand for getting the release of the Pakistani POWs, he on many occasions, in January 1972, expressed his willingness to go to India for talks with Mrs. Indira Gandhi over the question of POWs. India, through third countries, also conveyed to Pakistan its readiness for bilateral talks on issues of mutual concern. President Bhutto, on the one hand, talked of peace and the desire to have talks with India and on the other hand repeated: "We cannot forget Kashmir" and that he would not accept any humiliating solution. At the same time, the increasing pressure for securing the release of the Pakistani POWs, the withdrawal of Indian troops from Bangladesh, the recognition of Bangladesh by a number of other countries and the Indian offer for peace and good relations through bilateral talks, brought home to him the fact that the best way was to conduct direct talks with Prime Minister Indira Gandhi. On 4th April 1972, Mrs. Indira Gandhi declared that India and Pakistan were in direct touch. She wrote a letter to President Bhutto and proposed direct talks as the means for securing durable peace and for these emissary level talks for paving the way.

The emissary level talks were held at Murree in April 1972, and it was agreed that Prime Minister Mrs. Indira Gandhi and President Bhutto should meet in June 1972 and discuss matters relating to mutual relations between the two countries.

V. The Simla Conference and the Simla Agreement

The Simla summit between Prime Minister Indira Gandhi and President Bhutto commenced on 28th June 1972 and after negotiations extending over five days, produced on 3rd July 1972, the Simla Agreement between India and Pakistan.

In the Simla Agreement it was stated that the Governments of India and Pakistan have resolved to put an end to the conflict and confrontation that had hitherto marked their relations and to establish durable peace in the sub-continent so that both the countries may henceforth be able to devote fully their energies to the pressing need of promoting the welfare of their people. The agreement affirmed faith in the principles and purposes of the U.N. Charter and declared that the two countries have resolved to settle their differences by peaceful means through bilateral negotiations. Further, that pending final settlement of any of the problem between them. Neither side shall unilaterally alter the situation and both sides shall prevent and discourage all such acts as may be detrimental to the maintenance of peace and harmonious relations. Both the countries accepted the principles of peaceful coexistence, respect for each other's territorial integrity and sovereignty and non-interference in each other's internal affairs. Both sides agreed to take steps for preventing hostile propaganda against each other and for exchanging all such information as would promote the cause of friendly relations between them. It was also agreed to normalise, step by step, social, cultural, trade and economic relation between the two countries. Both countries agreed to withdraw their forces was to their respective sides of the International Border. The withdrawal of forces was to be completed within 30 days. In J&K, the line of actual control as resulted from the cease-fire of 17th December 1971, was to be respected by both sides.

The Simla Agreement postulated a momentous transformation of relationships in the sub-continent from confrontation to co-operation. It was designed to give a sound foundation and healthy beginning to the process of Indo-Pak normalisation on the basis of beneficial bilateralism. It solemnly upheld the principles of peaceful coexistence, mutual respect for territorial integrity, non-interference, good neighbourliness and normalisation of relations for peace and progress. Though it was criticised by Mr. Vajpayee for its failure to secure a package deal with Pakistan yet it was accepted by the people and press both at home and abroad, as a wise act of statesmanship which had the firm potential to give a new and positive direction to the course of Indo-Pak relations. India never wanted to exploit the weak position of Pakistan as resulted after the war for its own advantage. It wanted to see a stable Pakistan ruled by the people of Pakistan in accordance with their wishes. It was in a spirit of reconciliation, mutual adjustment and good-will that India signed the Simla Agreement with Pakistan on the principles of equality and honour.

The Simla Agreement constituted a big distinctive improvement over the Tashkent Declaration of 1966. It was the first big agreement signed through bilateral negotiations and thus opened the era of bilateralism in Indo-Pak relations. It reduced the dependence of both India and Pakistan upon other nations for getting their issues and problems resolved. The spirit in which the Simla Agreement was signed was indeed much more important than even the specific provisions that it contained. The speeches made by the two sides, and particularly the views expressed by Mr. Bhutto, clearly reflected a big positive change in the outlook of Pakistan towards Indo-Pak relations. It appeared certain that after the Simla Summit and on the basis of Simla Agreement the relations between India and Pakistan would be maturer in future.

After the Simla Agreement: The Simla Agreement was accepted by both India and Pakistan as the basis for the conduct of their mutual relations. It was ratified by the two countries and the process of normalisation commenced in August, 1972. To begin with, task of troops withdrawal was undertaken and completed smooth, except for the emergence of a dispute over the issue of control over Thaku Chak. Even this hurdle was cleared on 7th December 1972. Four days later, the new maps showing the actual line of control in J&K, as stood determined on 17th December 1972, were signed and exchanged. This new line of control distinctly improved the position of Indian forces in the J&K. It also made the U.N. cease-fire observers redundant because they had nothing to do with the new line of control.

The Delhi Agreement: In 1973, the two countries were successful in resolving the issue of repatriation of POWs and the problem of repatriation of Bengalese from Pakistan to Bangladesh and Bihari Muslims from Bangladesh to Pakistan. The issue of trial of 195 Pakistani POWs on charges of war crimes and genocide was also amicably resolved. The beginning in this direction was made by the Delhi Agreement of 28th August 1973, between India and Pakistan which was subsequently accepted by Bangladesh. According to this agreement the repatriation of Pakistani POWs and civilian internees was to commence with the utmost dispatch as soon as the logistic agreements were completed and from a date that was to be settled by mutual agreement. Simultaneously, the repatriation of all Bengalese in Pakistan and all Pakistanis in Bangladesh to their respective countries was to commence. The Government of Pakistan agreed to receive a substantial number of non-Bengalese from Bangladesh, who had opted for repatriation. Bangladesh agreed that no trial of the 195 POWs would take place during the entire period of repatriation and pending the settlement, such POWs would continue to remain in India. The issue of trial was to be subsequently discussed and settled at a later date. At this stage Bangladesh declared that it would participate in such future talks only on the basis of sovereign equality.

In February 1974, during the course of the Islamic Summit meet at Lahore, Pakistan accepted the advice of the Islamic nations and accorded recognition to Bangladesh on 22nd February 1974. This development made the task of holding talks for settling the issue of trial of 195 Pakistani POWs possible. In April 1974, tripartite talks between India, Pakistan and Bangladesh were held at New Delhi and a pact was signed under which Bangladesh agreed to abandon the move to try these POWs in charges of genocide and to repatriate them to Pakistan. The task of repatriation was thereafter, completed by 30th April 1974, and thus ended a critical irritant of the post-1971 relations between India, Pakistan and Bangladesh.

It was hoped that it shall be followed by immediate steps for normalising relations in other spheres. A negative development prevented a beginning and this was the strong and uncalled for Pakistani reaction against the peaceful nuclear explosion conducted by India on 18th May 1974. India made it clear that the conducting of PNE was simply a technological development which was conducted for purely non-military development purposes. Pakistan thought otherwise and on 1st June 1974, sent a communication to India postponing the June meeting between the Indian and Pakistani delegations, which was to discuss the resumption to postal and telecommunication links and travel facilities between the two countries.

It was only in September 1974, that these talks were held at Islamabad and agreements were reached for the exchange of postal articles, telecommunications, visa facilities and visits to religious places. On 30th November 1974, a bilateral Trade Agreement was concluded and on 7th December, the 9 years old trade embargo was lifted. It was followed by the signing of a new and comprehensive Trade Agreement on 23rd January 1975. On 14th January 1976, Pakistan agreed to purchase 5,000 tonnes of pig iron and 250 tonnes of bidi leaves from India. In May, 1976, Indian foreign secretary visited Islamabad and held important talks with his counterpart. This further paved the way for fresh attempts at normalisation of Indo-Pak relations.

Around 1975, Pakistan initiated moves for securing a political integration of 'Azad Kashmir' (PPP) with Pakistan PPP was encouraged to fan out into POK and a co-ordination council of 14 members was set up with Pakistani Prime Minister as the head, and President of POK as the ex-officio vice-chairman. This move was designed to secure a veiled integration of POK with Pakistan. Mrs. Indira Gandhi on her part deemed it fit to have an accord with Sheikh Abdullah and to take the sting out of thc Kashmir issue. The Indira-Sheikh Accord of February 1975, was designed to end to 20 years old stalemate. It was indeed a bold and wise act on the part of Mrs. Indira Gandhi as Sheikh's open and direct commitment to Kashmir's accession to India as full and final accession made Pakistani stand on J&K futile, Pakistani reaction to this accord was obviously hostile but inwardly, it gave Pakistan the much-needed ground to work for securing an integration of POK with Pakistan.

The Indo-Pak normalisation kept up its slow but steady pace during the period 1972-77. Nevertheless, ups and downs continued to mark the course. In February 1975, the U.S. decision to lift the arms embargo against India and Pakistan, once again gave rise to the possibility of big U.S. arms sale to Pakistan. It was regarded by India as a dangerous development. The continued strengthening of anti-India Sino-Pak axis further made the course of Indo-Pak relations tense. The strong Sino-Pak reaction against the accession of Sikkim to India, the renewed Pakistani search for more and more arms, Bhutto's talk of Islamic Bomb, the August 1975 coup in Bangladesh resulting into the assassination of Sheikh Mujib and the Pakistani fears of growing Indo-Soviet co-operations kept the course of Indo-Pak detente slow and uneven.

Indo-Pak Relations During 1977-80 (Janata Era): In 1977 there took place certain far-reaching changes in the domestic political environments of India and Pakistan, which in the initial stages appeared to be capable of further slowing down or producing a negative trend in Indo-Pak relations. In January 1977 General Elections were announced in Pakistan. The election campaign that took place exhibited that Bhutto's regime had eroded much of its support base in Pakistan. But the election results gave a massive victory to Bhutto's PPP. The opposition alleged a mass scale rigging of the elections. This made Bhutto's victory a matter of sharp controversy and conflict and the result came to be political instability in Pakistan. To end that, on 5th July 1977, General Zia-ul-Haq staged a coup and once again put an end to the era of civilian rule in Pakistan. The re-emergence of military dictatorship in Pakistan was viewed as a source of tension by India. The Indian leadership, however, took the development calmly and accepted it without comment as the change involved the domestic affairs of Pakistan.

In India, General Elections were held in March 1977 and the result saw the end of the 30 years domination of the Indian political scene by the Congress. The Janata Party came to replace the Congress as the ruling party in India. Before 1977, some of the Janata leaders particularly Mr. Atal Behari Vajpayee, who became the Foreign Minister in the Janata government, had seriously challenged some of the basic features of Indian foreign policy of the Congress era and as such it was hoped that the change in political leadership shall involve a change in Indian foreign policy and more particularly a change in relations with

Pakistan. However, shortly afterward, it became evident that Janata government was committed to follow almost the same foreign policy principles and objectives as were there in the past.

Towards Pakistan, Janata government decided to open out more activity on the basis of its policy to concentrate on the task of improving relations with India's immediate neighbours, particularly with Pakistan. General Zia too expressed his desire to secure Indo-Pak normalisation at a faster rate. In August 1977, General Zia announced the release of nearly 200 Indian prisoners, who were languishing in Pakistani jails. India reciprocated the gesture by announcing the release of 200 Pakistani prisoners from the Indian jails.

In February, 1978, Indian Foreign Minister, Mr. Vajpayee paid an official visit to Pakistan and tried to create a more congenial and hopeful environment in the Indian sub-continent. He declared that India fully respected the sovereignty and territorial integrity of Pakistan. He further observed at a press conference that, "though India is big and large country yet it has never and it would never try to play the role of a big brother in South Asia." Mr. Vajpayee was successful in establishing a good report with the Pakistani leadership. The restrained stand that Janata government took in respect of India's Nuclear Policy also has a salutary effect on Pakistan. In March, 1976, the Pakistani Foreign Secretary, Mr. Agha Shahi came on a return visit to India. The talks at New Delhi produced, on 12th April, 1978, an agreement over the Salal Dam Project. It ended the 30 years old dispute. By this agreement India secured the right to build Salal Dam and a power project on the Chenab river in J&K and in return agreed to respect some of the Pakistani views in respect of the design and nature of the project. The Delhi talks further gave strength to the acceptance of bilateral negotiations as the best means for promoting bilateral relations. It proved valuable strength to the concept of 'Beneficial Bilateralism' between the two countries.

Prime Minister Desai, in an interview with Pakistani Journalist on 14th April 1978, expressed India's readiness to solve all outstanding issues with Pakistan, including the issue of Kashmir in a reasonable manner. In September 1978, Desai-Zia meet at Nairobi further improved the environment of Indo-Pak relations. In October 1978 India and Pakistan agreed to open, on reciprocal basis, their consulates at Karachi and Bombay respectively. In November 1978, an Indian cricket team visited Pakistan and cultural and sports relations between the two countries started making a good headway.

All these can be described as happy developments in Indo-Pak relations, but much more remained to be done. The premature end of Janata era in January, 1980, and the development of Indo-Pak differences over the crisis in Afghanistan gave a new twist to the Indo-Pak relations in 1980s.

Simla Agreement: With a view to end the strained and tense environment that came to govern the relations between India and Pakistan after December 1971 war, both the countries agreed to meet at Simla in June 1972. The historic Summit meeting between Prime Minister Indira Gandhi and President Bhutto opened on 28th June 1972, at Simla and in a spirit of goodwill and compromise. In the inaugural speeches both the leaders laid stress upon the need for putting an end to the era of conflict and confrontation between two countries, and for a new turn in their relations. Mr. Bhutto declared that his country wanted to make a break with the past strife and that he would work for the securing of good relations with India. Mrs. Indira Gandhi also had declared in several of her speeches delivered after 1971 war that India did not have any desire to capitalise out of the grave situation which had come to develop in Pakistan after the war. She, while appreciating the views of Mr. Bhutto as expressed over Radio Pakistan, expressed her sincere desire for peace and for a new beginning in our relations.

The Simla Summit as such was held in a spirit of reconciliation, and it was because of this that initial differences over the issue of repatriation of Pakistani POWs: troops withdrawal particularly in the J&K sector and the issue of recognition of Bangladesh and Kashmir issue were handled successfully and were not allowed to hinder the signing Simla Agreement. Through negotiations between the official delegations of the two countries and through the final July 2 meeting between Mrs. Indira Gandhi and Mr. Bhutto the historic Simla Agreement was successfully drafted and signed on 3rd July 1972.

Simla Agreement can be legitimately described as an important landmark in the bilateral relations of India and Pakistan, because its provisions successfully provided a sound and practical basis for Indo-Pak normalisation in the post-1972 period. It, indeed was instrumental in giving a new beginning to the relations between the two countries. The text of the Simla Agreement is as under:

"The Govt. of India and the Government of Pakistan are resolved that the two countries put an end to the conflict and confrontation that have hitherto marred their relations and work for promotion of a friendly and harmonious relationship and the establishment of durable peace in the sub-continent, so that both countries may henceforth devote their resources and energies to the pressing task of advancing the welfare of their people."

In order to achieve this objective the Government of India and the Government of Pakistan have agreed as follows:

(*i*) That the Principles and Purposes of the Charter of the United Nations shall govern the relations between the two countries.

(*ii*) That the two countries are resolved to settle their difference by peaceful means through bilateral negotiations or by any peaceful means mutually agreed upon between them. Pending the final settlement any of the problems between the two countries neither side shall unilaterally alter the situation and both shall prevent the organization, assistance or encouragement of any acts detrimental to the maintenance of peaceful and harmonious relations.

(*iii*) That the pre-requisite for reconciliation, good neighbourliness and durable peace between them is commitment by both the countries to peaceful co-existence, respect for each other's territorial integrity, and sovereignty and non-interference in each other's internal affairs on the basis of equality and mutual benefit.

(*iv*) That the basic issues and causes of conflict which have bedevilled the relations between the two countries for the last 25 years shall be resolved by peaceful means.

(*v*) That they shall always respect each other's national unity, territorial integrity, political independence and sovereign equality.

(*vi*) That in accordance with the Charter of the United Nations, they will refrain from the threat or use of force against the territorial integrity or political independence of each other.

(*vii*) Both the Governments will take steps within their power to prevent hostile propaganda directed against each other. Both countries will encourage the dissemination of such information as would promote the development of friendly relations between them.

(*viii*) In order to progressively restore and normalise relations between the two countries step by step, it is agreed that:

(*a*) Steps shall be taken to resume communications, postal telegraphic, sea, land, including border posts, and air links including over flights.

(*b*) Appropriate steps shall be taken to promote travel facilities for the nationals of the country.

(*c*) Trade and co-operation in economic and other agreed fields will be resumed as far as possible.

(*d*) Exchange in the fields of science and culture will be promoted. In this connection delegations from the two countries will meet from time to time to work out the necessary details.

(*ix*) In order to initiate the process of establishment of durable peace, both the Governments agree that:

(*a*) Indian and Pakistani forces shall be withdrawn to their side of the international border.

(*b*) In Jammu and Kashmir, the line of control resulting from the cease-fire of December 17, 1971, shall be respected by both sides, without prejudice to the recognised position of either side. Neither side shall seek to alter it unilaterally, irrespective of mutual differences and legal interpretations. Both sides further undertake to refrain from the threat or the use of force in violation of this line.

(*c*) The withdrawals shall commence upon entry into force of this agreement and shall be completed within a period of thirty days thereof.

This agreement will be subject to ratification by both countries in accordance with their respective constitutional procedures and will come into force with effect from the date on which the instruments of ratification are exchanged.

"Both the Governments agree that their respective hands will meet again at a mutually convenient time in the future and that in the meanwhile, the representative of the two sides will meet to discuss further the modalities and arrangements for the establishment of durable peace and normalisation of relations including the questions of repatriation of prisoners of war and civilian internees, a final settlement of Jammu and Kashmir and the resumption of diplomatic relations."

With these provisions, and above all with the spirit of goodwill and reconciliation that marked its conclusion the Simla agreement can be described as a historic documents of the highest importance, it constituted a timely and healthy attempt to end the era of cold war and wars and to usher Into-Pak relations into a new era of bilateralism, goodwill, co-operation and friendship. It was a bold attempt to secure an end to the strained relations and to work for the development of friendly co-operation and relations. In this way it can be described as the charter of Indo-Pak detente.

It is laudable because it provided for peaceful settlement of all Indo-Pak issues and disputes through bilateral negotiations or by any other mutually agreed upon peaceful means. It successfully heralded the new era of constructive relationship aimed at the securing of durable peace in South Asia. The repudiation of the use of force for settlement of disputes and the resolve to end the era of conflict and confrontation amounted virtually to a

No-War Pact. The provision for re-stablishment of economic trade and cultural relations constituted a positive attempt to secure normalisation in the years to come. The provision for troops withdrawal and exchange of territories won in war was designed to secure military disengagement on the borders. Further India successfully maintained its right to keep those areas to POK which were won by it during the 1971 war. The agreement over the new line of actual control and cease-fire made the presence of U.N. observers in Kashmir superfluous. The clause for ratification of the Agreement by the two sides further gave it a solid legal base and in this way it involved a distinct improvement over the Tashkent Declaration. Its conclusion through direct bilateral negotiation further was a matter of great satisfaction and credit. Whereas the Tashkent Declaration was made without any outside help or pressure. This process involved a highly significant development in so far as it reflected the desire and determination of both the countries to come out of the era of dependence upon outside powers for securing a breakthrough in their relations. Indeed the Simla Agreement was the outcome of the free will of India and Pakistan and reflected the political maturity of both Mrs. Indira Gandhi and Mr. Bhutto.

It was because of its merits and the spirit in which it was concluded, that the Simla Agreement came, to be praised as a bold and healthy move for Indo-Pak detente. Both the super powers and many other countries of the world hailed it and a grand achievement which was both timely and highly useful.

In India, the press and public praised the Simla Agreement as a substantial step forward towards peace and friendly relations despite certain limitations. Almost all the political parties of India accepted that the Simla Agreement was a positive step towards peace and good neighbourly relations with Pakistan. However, the Janasangh President Mr. Atal Behari Vajpayee described it as a "sell out' by India because India failed to secure the package deal and to use the territorially advantageous position for securing a solution to certain other issues like vacation of Pakistani aggression in Kashmir, war damages, settlement of public debts, evacuee property and compensation for the burden of Bangladesh refugees. Another point of criticism raised by socialist leader, Mr. Samar Guha was that it envisaged no guarantee that Pakistan would reduce its military spending. The majority opinion, however, felt that it was too much to expect that all Indo-Pak issues and problems could have been solved at Simla in one stroke through a single agreement. India definitely showed a sense of accommodation and reconciliation with Pakistan and did not try to unduly capitalise out of her strong position.

The Indian Press Welcomed the Agreement: Most of the newspapers welcomed the spirit of bilateralism and the beginning that it sought to make towards the normalisation of relations with Pakistan. *The Hindustan Times* in its editorial of 4th July, 1972, expressed the view that "Simla Agreement postulated a momentous transformation of the relationships on the sub-continent from confrontation to co-operation... The cardinal principles agreed to related to the renunciation of the use of force and an acceptance by both countries to peaceful-co-existence, respect for each other's territorial integrity, sovereignty and pact of bringing peace and stability to a region that had been instability and war. The closing of ranks among the three principal nations of the sub-continent would add immeasurably to their individual and collective strength and stature".

In Pakistan also, the Public and Press welcomed the Simla Agreement as an epoch-making agreement. Against the unfavourable and hot reception accorded to the Tashkent Declaration, the Simla Agreement got from them a positive and mature reception. *The Pakistan Times* applauded it for breaking the ice and *The Dawn* praised it for the attempt to evolve a new pattern of relationship for the two countries. Similar sentiments were expressed by the Pakistani political parties. However, it was also criticised by some for its failure to provide for the repatriation of the Pakistani POWs.

The world press and Statesman also appreciated this bold attempt made by India and Pakistan for peacefully handling their bilateral affairs. The Soviet President described it as an important step towards normalising Indo-Pak relations. British leaders welcomed it as the first step towards friendly relations between India and Pakistan. American and Chinese leaders decided to praise Bhutto's efforts towards peaceful resolution of Indo-Pak issues and problems U.N. Secretary General, Kurt Waldheim described the agreement as the first step on the long and necessarily arduous road to peace in the sub-continent. The External Affairs Minister of Bangladesh Mr. Abdus Samad regarded it "as a success towards achieving more success." Similar words were used by the world Press for welcoming this agreement. The Simla Conference was described as a model of conciliatory diplomacy and the Simla Agreement as the first essential step towards peace in the South Asian sub-continent.

The issues that Simla Agreement failed to resolve were: (*i*) The repatriation of POWs; (*ii*) A final settlement of Kashmir; (*iii*) A direct No-War Pact; (*iv*) A joint machinery for handling the Indo-Pak relations, and (*v*) The differences over arms-race in South Asia. The Simla spirit made it possible for the two countries to successfully resolve the first issue through direct negotiations leading to the Delhi Agreement and the Tripartite Agreement of 1974. So far as the other issues are concerned both the sides are currently engaged in negotiations over the issue of a No-War-Pact/a Treaty of Peace, Friendship and Co-operation between India and Pakistan. The establishment of Indo-Pak Joint Commission for handling the trade and cultural relations between the two countries in 1983 further filled the gap left by Simla Agreement. The provisions of Simla Agreement and the Simla spirit is still the basis of all Indo-Pak talks which are currently being held from time to time for strengthening the normalisation of relations and for making the two countries live as good neighbours with strong bonds of friendship and developed economic trade, scientific and cultural relations.

VI. The Current Problems

The nature and history of Indo-Pak relations in the eighties can be analysed by reviewing the interactions between the two countries over the issue of No-War Pact/Treaty of Peace, Friendship and Co-operation. After having successfully normalised their relations on the basis of Simla Agreements and through a number of other trade and cultural agreements, both the countries, finding themselves face to face with certain far-reaching changes in Asia, particularly in the West Asia, and with the realisation that further development of relations between them required certain positive bold steps, are currently engaged in negotiations for effecting a comprehensive treaty of Peace, Friendship and Co-operation as proposed by India or a No-War Pact as proposed by Pakistan. Indian proposal for such a treaty has come as a better and positive alternative to the No-War Pact proposal of Pakistan. A bi-product, nevertheless a highly significant development, came in the form of the establishment of a Joint Indo-Pak Commission for promoting wide ranging economic, cultural and scientific co-operation between them. This Commission held its first meeting at Islamabad on 1st June 1983 and it produced certain fruitful decisions. This institutionalisation of Indo-Pak relations reflects a maturity that the Governments of two states have been able to develop as a result of the detente since the Simla Agreement of 1972, The issue of No-War Pact/The Treaty of Peace, Friendship and Co-operation and the handling of Indo-Pak economic trade and cultural relations through the Joint Commission as such are the two vital aspects of Indo-Pak relations in the eighties. It has been due to this fact that we are inclined to analyse Indo-Pak relations in the eighties through an in-depth analysis of the issue to No-War Pact/The Treaty of Peace, Friendship and Co-operation.

Every discussion on the issue of No-War Pact between India and Pakistan must be prefaced by answers to two questions: (*i*) How far there is a possibility of a new war between India and Pakistan which gives rise to the necessity of a No-War Pact? (*ii*) What was the fate of No-War Pact offers which India made prior to the current Pakistani offer?

For answering the first question we have to take into account certain factors, issues and disputes that continue to serve as irritants in the Indo-Pak relations. These factors suggest a possibility of another war between the two countries.

1. The Legacy: The unnatural partition and the three Indo-Pak wars, continue to remain as a background factor of Indo-Pak relations. Many persons in Pakistan still feel that India has not reconciled with the loss of Pakistan and that it is keen to prevent the emergence of a strong and united Pakistan. Many others in Pakistan still talk of war for redeeming the lost prestige of Pakistan. There are others, who still favour or accept possibility of a military solution of Kashmir. In India too; many people believe that history of Indo-Pak relation is bound to be infested with strains which can lead to a war. This belief is superstitiously based upon the past experience.

2. Existence of Military Dictatorship in Pakistan: Ever since its inception, Pakistan has been living under long periods of military dictatorship with short intervals in the form of civilian rules. No doubt, the nature of Government that runs Pakistan is an internal affairs of Pakistan, nevertheless, India can't remain totally unconcerned because militarism in Pakistan has been in the past a source of pressure and tension for India. The military rulers of Pakistan, invariably always, have indulged in strengthening their legitimacy by creating a fear of Indian aggression against Pakistan and by justifying the need to strengthen the military power of Pakistan. At the times of 1965 and 1971 wars, Field Marshal Ayub Khan and General Yahya Khan respectively were in power in Pakistan. The present military regime of General Zia in Pakistan is as such naturally regarded as not a healthy factor for the growth of Indo-Pak relations. The present drive to make Pakistan a highly advanced and disproportionately big military power is apprehensively viewed by many persons in India.

3. Difference over Kashmir: The continued differences over Kashmir also constitutes a negative factor which makes it possible for many persons to talk of another Indo-Pak war. The leaders of Pakistan at times still talk in terms of war with India for securing "the liberation of Kashmir."

4. Differences over the Supply of Highly Sophisticated American Arms to Pakistan: As a result of the Afghanistan crisis Pakistan believes that its security stands threatened and pressurised, and this development necessitates the strengthening of Pakistan's defence power in a big way. America accepts this view and considers Pakistan as a frontal state which must be militarily strengthened for checking the possible further advance of the Soviet Union towards the warm waters of the Persian Gulf. Consequently, America has been supplying to Pakistan highly sophisticated arms, war planes, missiles and radars, on concessional rates. This development has been the source of fear for India. The past experience tells us that Pakistan, has never hesitated, rather it has always tried, to secure arms for securing an edge over India's military power. The acquisition of superior and sophisticated weapons has always given Pakistan the encouragement to solve Indo-Pak issues and disputes through war. The present flow of highly sophisticated and technologically advanced U.S. weapons into Pakistan is naturally regarded as a very dangerous development by India that can upset the balance of power in South Asia and lead to a new war.

5. Fear about Each Other's Nuclear Policy: Ever since India conducted her first PNE in May 1974, Pakistan has been harping upon the threat to its security from Nuclear India. It has been consistently refusing to accept the view that Indian Nuclear Policy is a peaceful policy designed purely for helping India to secure the gains of nuclear technology for use in the industrial and economic development of India. On the contrary, Pakistan has been engaged since 1974, in the pursuit of developing, as Mr. Bhutto named it, an Islamic Bomb. It has secured in an clandestine manner the technology to enrich uranium—a technology which is considered essential for making nuclear weapons. Even some of the Americans have accepted that Pakistan is heading for the development of nuclear weapons. Mr. Coheon has expressed the apprehension that Pakistani rulers believe that it is only by securing nuclear weapon that they can attempt to militarily secure Kashmir from India. Pakistani Press keeps on talking about Indian design to destroy Pakistani nuclear installations. Now, Pakistan has herself admitted that it has tested a nuclear trigger. Both these developments indicate that Pakistan is heading towards the manufacture of nuclear bombs. India, though has the ability to do the same, remains committed to peaceful uses of nuclear technology. It views Pakistani attempts as harmful and dangerous developments which are designed to lead to an arms race in South Asia.

6. Beijing-Pindi-Washington Axis and Growing Indo-Soviet Co-operation and Friendship: Since 1962, Pakistan has been engaged in developing axis-type special relations with China. It has been instrumental in exploiting Sino-Indian differences for securing Chinese support, help and aid for itself. There exists an important military link between the two countries in the form of supply of Chinese arms to Pakistan. Pakistan, by accommodating China through a favourable boundary agreement and through the opening of Karakoram Highway and the Khunjerab pass, has been in a position to commit Chinese support for Pakistani view of Kashmir and of security in South Asia. Between China and America, Pakistan played the role of a broker in early seventies and since then it has been serving as a link between them. The Sino-US identity of views in regard to the dangers of growing Soviet power and presence in Asia, particularly after the Soviet intervention in Afghanistan, has given rise to the emergence of Peking-Pindi-Washington axis. Since there happens to be friendship, co-operation between the Soviet Union and India, the Peking-Pindi-Washington axis is always at pains to criticise both India and Soviet Union, Pakistan and China imagine that growing Indo-Soviet Friendship is an anti-Pindi and anti-Beijing development against which both of them must unite their powers. With the destabilisation of peace in West Asia as a result of the Iran-Iraq war and due to the Soviet presence in Afghanistan, Pakistan believes that the U.S. decisions to strengthen Diego Garcia base, to station the RDF in the Gulf region and to strengthen Pakistan in South Asia are justified steps in the interest of peace and stability in Asia. This Pakistan view is totally opposed to Indian view that US security policy in Asia is designed to increase the super power rivalry in Asia and particularly in the Indian Ocean. India strongly disfavours the growing Peking-Pindi-Washington axis in its neighbourhood. It believes that the US decision to arm Pakistan as a frontal defence state against the Soviet Union involves the risk of destabilisation of peace and power-balance in South Asia. Pakistan, however, feels the other way. It regards India's opposition to the acquisition of US arms by Pakistan as an unfriendly act. It has been mainly to assure India and in the process to justify the acquisition of F-16 plane, and other sophisticated arms, that Pakistan has now expressed its desire to sign a No-War Pact with India.

The very fact that Pakistan, after having rejected several times in the past, the No-War Pact offers made by India, now seeks to have a No-War Pact shows that Pakistan still accepts the possibility of a war with India. India too, on the basis of the past experience with the Pakistani policies in South Asia, fears that there exist chances of a new war with Pakistan. The Pakistani rush for arms, its nuclear programme the continued presence of a military dictatorship and the almost unchanged attitude towards Kashmir, are the factors which indicate a possibility of a new Indo-Pak war. Pakistan fears the growing power of India and believes that a powerful India is bound to create such troubles for Pakistan as can lead to a war in future. Thus, for a variety of reasons both the countries admit the possibility of a future war between them. To reduce the chances, rather to eliminate the chances of a future war, Pakistan now advocates a No-War Pact with India. India, however, regards that a comprehensive treaty of peace, friendship and co-operation between the two countries can be a better positive device for putting to an end to the chances of another Indo-Pak war and for giving a solid basis and healthy outlook to the growth of Indo-Pak friendship and co-operation in various spheres of relations.

The History of No-War Pact Offers: After having answered the first question we come to the answering of the second question *i.e.*, the history of No-War Pact offers—the past and the present ones. When we analyse the history of Indo-Pak relations, we find that prior to the present No-War Pact offer made by Pakistan in September 1981. India had made at least ten such offers to Pakistan which the latter rejected on one ground of the other. As early as on 22nd December 1949, Prime Minister Nehru proposed to Prime Minister Liaquat Ali Khan of Pakistan that the two governments should sign a joint no-war declaration. This offer was rejected by Mr. Khan, who wanted the settlement of Indo-Pak issues and disputes, particularly the Kashmir dispute as a pre-condition for signing the No-War Pact declaration. Prime Minister Nehru continued to repeat the Indian offer to Pakistan for signing a No-War Pact and on two distinct occasions in 1958 and 1963, he made definite proposals to negotiate and sign the pact with Pakistan. All these offers were rejected by Pakistan. In 1958, President Ayub proposed a Joint Defence agreement to India. This offer was designed to be 'Joker clause offer' since it was a known fact that India as a Non-aligned nation was least expected to accept the offer. Moreover, Nehru's query as to joint defence against whom, failed to get an answer from President Ayub and hence the offer got an immediate burial in Pakistan itself. In reply to the No-War Pact offer made by India in 1963, Mr. Bhutto declared "let India arrive at an equitable and honourable settlement with Pakistan over Kashmir, we can have not one but a thousand No-War Pacts....while the Kashmir dispute exists, it is inconceivable that we should accept India's offer of a No-War Pact." In July 1963, again he declared, "Pakistan would never accept India's offer after even a hundred years from now."

After the 1965 Indo-Pak war, Prime Minister Shastri renewed the offer of No-War Pact to Pakistan. In fact, at the Tashkent Conference India made it a basis for the negotiations with Pakistan. Even at this time President Ayub and Mr. Bhutto failed to respond positively to the offer. Pakistan expressed her inability to accept the offer once again on grounds of differences over Kashmir.

On 15th August 1968, the offer of a No-War Pact was repeated by Prime Minister Indira Gandhi. She even supplemented this offer by the proposal to have a joint Indo-Pak machinery for handling and resolving all the outstanding Indo-Pak issues and problems. Even this offer failed to get a favourable response from Pakistan. While criticising the Indian offer of a No-War Pact and for the arms control on reciprocal basis, Mr. Bhutto in his book, "The Myth of Independence" published in 1969 observed: "A reduction in armed forces of India and Pakistan would freeze the disputes forever and would benefit India. It would amount to a *de facto* recognition of India's supremacy in the sub-continent." Later on General Yahya Khan rejected these offers and observed: "It is our sincere conviction that amity and friendship will continue to elude India and Pakistan, if our two governments run after the shadow that the peripheral issues are and evade the reality that our two outstanding disputes regarding Kashmir and the Ganges Water represent....".

At the Simla Conference, the issue of No-War Pact was raised again but Mr. Bhutto, while accepting the possibility, expressed his inability to sign the No-War Pact on the ground that due to the weak position of Pakistan after 1971 war, it would appear to be a pact made under pressure and hence would lose its very purpose. In 1977, Prime Minister Morarji Desai expressed his government's readiness to sign a No-War Pact with Pakistan. This was offered as an attempt to further fortify the Simla Spirit and to allay the Pakistani apprehensions about India's Nuclear Policy. Pakistan failed, once again, to reciprocate the offer. India, through its Foreign Secretary Mr. Jagat Mehta renewed the offer to Pakistan in 1980, but General Zia-ul-Haq and his men failed to accept the offer. In fact, General Zia in an interview with an Indian Journalist clearly expressed his opposition to a No-War Pact when he observed: "No-War Pacts, non-aggression pacts were not worth the paper on which they were written. History tells us that a number of No-War Pacts, non-aggression pacts and peace treaties have been proved good for nothing."

Thus, from 1947 to 1980 Pakistani rulers always rejected on various grounds the Indian offers for a No-War Pact between the two countries. From the need to settle the Kashmir dispute as the first condition to the ideological opposition to no-war, non-aggression pacts and peace treaties, were used by the rulers of Pakistan to reject Indian offers. No wonder then, when on September 1981, India found Pakistani rulers taking a 180° turn and advocating No-War Pact, it decided to regard it as a non-serious loose talk on the part of Pakistani leaders.

The Pakistani Offer: It was on 15th September 1981, that Pakistan's readiness to enter into immediate consultations with India for the purpose of exchanging mutual guarantee of non-aggression and non-use of force in the spirit of Simla Agreement was published in a press report. Explaining the view Mr. Agha Shahi observed, "If they (Indians) still think it (Pakistan defence preparations) is a threat to their security, we are ready to enter into a non-aggression pact, a No-War Pact with them."

Reasons behind Pakistan's Offer of No-War Pact: The question that demands an answer is: As to why there appeared a total reversal of Pakistan's earlier opposition to No-War Pact a what where the factors and considerations which prompted Pakistan in 1981 to offer No-War Pact with India? The following factors can be explained as the reasons behind the change in Pakistani view:

1. Pressures on Pakistan's security as a result of the Soviet presence in Afghanistan and the fear of Soviet thrust into Pakistan for eliminating the Afghan guerrilla camps in Pakistan. Pakistan, in 1981, realised the need to make its eastern borders with India 'soft'.
2. The need to justify the flow of sophisticated and technologically advanced U.S. weapons into Pakistan. Washington and Islamabad felt that the smooth flow of U.S. arms to Pakistan could be better ensured by neutralising the strong Indian opposition to the induction of sophisticated weapon system and advanced war technology in the South Asia.
3. The attempts of the Zia regime to whittle down the Simla Agreement which was negotiated and signed by Mr. Bhutto.
4. The growing fear of India's nuclear policy.
5. The Chinese and American pressures on Pakistan to arrive at some rapprochement with India with a view to secure a reduced Indian dependence on Soviet Union.
6. The attempts of the Zia regime to increase its legitimacy in Pakistan.
7. The experience of Pakistan regarding the futility of the dreams of victory over India. The lessons of 1965 and 1971 wars made it essential for the Pakistani rulers to review their policy towards India. The realisation that no outside power would, in the event of war, really help Pakistan to offset India's superior power as a big and better developed country.
8. The hope to neutralise Indian support for the Soviet Union's role in Asia.
9. The Iran-Iraq war and the consequent realisation about the futility of war as a device for the settlement of a territorial dispute.

10. The need to concentrate upon the objective of securing economic development in Pakistan. The high-level of defence spending has been a big limitation upon Pakistan's economy.
11. Finally, the necessity to neutralise the internal opposition in Pakistan to General Zia's militarism cloaked with Islamic fundamentalism and the opposition to the growing armament race in South Asia.

All these factors prompted Pakistan to forget its past opposition to No-War Pact and to propagate the Pakistani desire and readiness to have a No-War Pact with India.

India's reaction to the Pakistani Offer: In the initial stages India did not deem it fit to give any real importance to the Pakistani offer. This was government by the view that Pakistan was not serious and was talking of a No-War Pact only as a means to show its good intentions towards India at a time when Pakistan was faced with both internal and external pressures and because it needed a propaganda base to justify the acquisition of American arms. India's decision to ignore the Pakistani offer was based upon the following grounds:

1. Pakistan's known opposition to No-War Pact, as was reflected by the previous rejections of Indian offers and the ideological grounds adopted by Pakistan to prove the futility of no-war non-aggression pact and peace treaties.
2. The flimsy manner in which Pakistan made the offer of a No-War Pact through a public speech and press without the use of diplomatic channels, made India doubtful about the Pakistani intentions. As the then External Affairs Minister of India, Mr. P.V. Narasimha Rao, observed, "Pak's offer was contained cryptically in a public statement released to media on an entirely different subject."
3. The continued and increased Pakistani attempts to secure more and more arms from America and China along with the attempts to prove its commitment to No-War Pact with India were viewed by the Indian leadership as 'double talks' and 'double standards'. On

6th October, 1981, Prime Minister Indira Gandhi observed, "The Pakistan statement about the Non-Aggression Pact has come after acquiring arms in a big way." She further commented on 7th October "You cannot prepare for war and yet talk of a No-War Pact". India as such regarded the Pakistani offer as a propaganda stunt raised by the Pakistani leadership for neutralising India's opposition to the flow of U.S, arms into Pakistan. It was regarded by India, as Dr. Satish Kumar observes, as a part of Pakistani design to secure favourable public and Congressional opinion in the U.S.A. for getting approved the U.S. decision to sell large quantities of arms to Pakistan for the professed purpose of meeting the threat to the Pakistani security that had developed in the wake of Soviet intervention and continued presence in Afghanistan.

4. In the presence of the Simla Agreement, which proved for the peaceful settlement of Indo-Pak issues through bilateral negotiations and other peaceful means, and which rejected the use of force for settling disputes or unilaterally effecting a decision, India felt that there was no need to sign a No-War Pact with Pakistan.
5. India felt that the Pakistani offer was just a device for gaining time which Pakistan needed for developing its nuclear bombs.
6. The existence of strong internal opposition to the regime and policies of General Zia in Pakistan further compelled caution on the part of India. The issue of No-War Pact involved a major new policy decision on the part of Pakistan and India felt that the weak legitimacy and narrow support base of General Zia's regime along-with strong internal political opposition to the policies of Zia Government made it essential to go slow towards the direction of a major agreement of the nature of a No-War Pact.

Because of all these reasons, India initially suspected the bona fides of the offer and decided to play cool to the Pakistani offer. But, later on, when it found that Pakistan was using the offer to 'show' its peace loving character and for maligning India as a country not interested in a durable peace through a No-War Pact, India decided to meet the Pakistani diplomacy first by opening negotiations with Pakistan and then by offering a comprehensive Treaty of Peace, Friendship and Co-operation to Pakistan as a better alternative for securing more friendly and co-operative bilateral relations leading to durable and stable peace in South Asia. India decided:

(*i*) To open negotiations with Pakistan on the issue of No-War Pact.

(*ii*) To offer a comprehensive and broad Treaty of Peace, Friendship and Co-operation designed to serve as a solid foundation for the development of strong economic cultural, trade, scientific and technological links with Pakistan; and

(*iii*) To secure further development of Indo-Pak trade, economic and cultural relations on the basis of the letter and spirit of the Simla Agreement.

It was on the basis of these objectives that Government of India, in late 1981, started opening out towards Pakistan. Official as well as non-official level contacts were encouraged and developed. These contacts revealed that there was a marked change in the attitude of the Pakistani people towards relations with India. A number of Indian scholars and journalists, who visited Pakistan in the years 1981 and 1982 came back with the impression that a wind of change was blowing in that country as far as the attitude towards India was concerned. No doubt, there still was popular rejection of India's stand on Kashmir, on the question of arms acquisition by Pakistan and there were differences in perceptions regarding the role of super powers, interpretation of Non-alignment and meaning of bilateralism as visualised in the Simla Agreement, yet along with this there realisation of the futility of previous wars with India and hence there was a general support for more meaningful detente and co-operation with India. In India too, the scholars and journalists started advocating the need to adopt a more positive, liberal approach towards relations with Pakistan. At the government level also the leaders and the External Affairs Minister increased their contacts with the Pakistani leaders and officials. There emerged a process of regular and frequent exchange of visits between them. Official level contacts and diplomatic links were used to exchange views Pakistan, in June, 1982, submitted a text of its war pact proposal to India for consideration and further negotiations. In August, 1982, the Indian Foreign Secretary Mr. M.K. Rasgotra visited Islamabad and held important talks with his counterpart, Mr. Niaz A. Naik as well as with General Zia. He also gave to the Pakistani Government the text of the proposed Treaty of Friendship, Peace and Co-operation that India was prepared to sign with Pakistan in preference to a No-War Pact. Prior to this Mrs. Indira Gandhi had, in her reply to President Zia's letter, clearly stated the Indian policy of building up highly friendly and co-operative relations with Pakistan. In January 1982, the foreign secretaries of the two countries met at Delhi and discussed the issue of No-War Pact and the progress of relations between them. Moreover, an Indian draft for the setting up of a joint Indo-Pak commission on a permanent basis for tackling issues concerning trade, travel, cultural exchanges and co-operation in science and technology, was also sent to Pakistan before the Secretary level talks.

In the August 1982 talks, the delegations of the two sides held free and frank discussion on the Pakistani proposal of a No-War Pact and the Indian proposal for a Treaty of Friendship, Peace and Co-operation. The details of the two drafts were kept secret but it became known that the Pakistani draft provided for: (*a*) A joint commitment to renounce war and non-aggression; (*b*) Settlement of Indo-Pak disputes exclusively through peaceful means, and (*c*) Joint commitment to promote good neighbourly relations between India and Pakistan. Indian side, however, found the Pakistani draft inadequate in many respects. It was considered to be an attempt to dilute the Simla Agreement and which in no major way provided for provisions aimed at strengthening Indo-Pak relations. The draft further did not contain anything for strengthening bilateralism between the two countries.

The Indian draft for the Treaty of Friendship, Peace and Co-operation on the other hand, involved a comprehensive plan for putting Indo-Pak relations on solid foundations of friendship, co-operation and commitment to peace and bilateralism. It advocated the need to accept bilateralism as the principle of Indo-Pak relations and the necessity to include the provision that no country shall give on its soil military bases to any foreign power. The Indian draft was an omnibus document meant to find the two countries to live in peace forever. It reaffirmed the principles of territorial integrity, inviolability of borders, peaceful coexistence, non-interference and sovereign equality of the two nations. It also implied acceptance of bilateralism as the principle for settlement of disputes. The Pakistani side advocated that the Indian draft stood for "too much too soon in one great leap forward". It felt that a step by step approach can alone be the best way. Further, it felt that the Indian draft sought to place a limitation on the sovereign right of Pakistan in so far as it provided for the renunciation of the right to give military bases and the right to secure settlement of dispute through means other than bilateral negotiations. Regarding the proposal for a joint Indo-Pak machinery, the Pakistani side proposed the establishment of a consultative commission for tackling such Indo-Pak issues as trade, travel, cultural exchange and co-operation in science and technology. The Indian side, however, felt that the establishment of a permanent joint panel for securing this purpose would be better and that an Indo-Pak treaty of Friendship, Peace and Co-operation and not a mere No-War Pact can really provide for durable peace and co-operation between the two countries. During these talks, there came to light certain differences between the approaches and views of the two countries. Nevertheless, the talks were characterised by cordiality and warmth. It was also agreed that the two sides shall again meet in New Delhi in the near future for carrying cut the talks. These talks as A.P.P. reported: "'Further contributed to dissipating apprehensions of tensions between India and Pakistan".

A really important and valuable development in Indo-Pak relations took place on November, 1, 1982, when Prime Minister Indira Gandhi and General Zia agreed, in their short summit level meeting, to establish a joint Indo-Pak penal or handling the development of non-political, non-military relations. They also agreed to resume in December, 1982, Secretary-level talks on No-War Pact/treaty of Peace and Friendship issue. The summit meeting produced a welcome thaw in Indo-Pak talks. The talks hinted that there were present good chances for the linking of the Pakistani proposal contained in the No-War Pact draft and the Indian proposals contained in the peace treaty draft. The public opinion and press in both the countries welcomed the decision to institutionalise the conduct of Indo-Pak economic, trade and cultural relations. Indo-Pak mini-summit was followed by the November, and December 1982 talks between the foreign secretaries of two countries for finalising the statute of the proposed Indo-Pak Joint Commission in November 1982, a 22-member business delegation of India visited Pakistan and found positive evidence of a strong desire in Pakistan to expand and diversity economic relations with this country. This further gave weightage to the decision for the establishment of the joint commission for conducting economic and trade relations in December 1982, the foreign secretaries of the two countries met at New Delhi and initialed the draft which provided for the organisation and functions of the Indo-Pak Joint Commission. They also exchanged views on the drafts of the No-War Pact and the peace treaty as submitted by Pakistan and India respectively. In January 1983, Mr. Natwar Singh visited Islamabad and tried to build bridges of understanding between the two countries. This visit was a part of the Indian efforts to narrow down the differences between the two countries on the interpretation of Non-alignment and on some other political and security matters. Pakistan entry into Non-aligned Movement rise to be possibility of Pak using the Non-aligned forum for raising Indo-Pak issues and problems. India wanted to prevent this and it was for its reason also that the Indian draft for treaty of peace and separation contained specific provisions for accepting bilateralism of the means for resolving all Indo-Pak issues. Moreover, India desired to Pak should undertake the responsibility of not allowing the establishment of foreign military bases in its territory. This was considered essential for giving real shape to the desire for peace between the two countries. But Pakistan expressed the view such an undertaking would amount to a renunciation of its sovereign right. India believed that acceptance of Non-alignment by Pakistan involved the duty to refrain from allowing foreign bases on Pakistani soil and as such Indian proposal for such an undertaking simply means a bilateral reaffirmation of the duty to prevent the establishment of foreign bases in the country. India as such wanted to discuss at length with Pakistan the implication of the acceptance of Non-alignment and to eliminate differences in perceptions about Non-alignment. India further hoped to impress upon Pakistan the necessity and desirability of remaining out of the superpower strategic consensus on Asia.

It was in March 1983, during General Zia's visit to New Delhi for attending the Seventh Summit of the Non-aligned, that the Foreign Secretaries of both India and Pakistan signed and exchanged the document which provided for the establishment of Indo-Pak Joint Commission. It was also agreed to hold the first meeting of the Joint Commission in June 1983 at Islamabad.

The fruitful culmination of the efforts to further strengthen the Indo-Pak normalisation and development of more co-operative economic and cultural relations came on June 1, 1983, when the first meeting of the Indo-Pak Joint Commission was held at Islamabad. In this meeting, Foreign Ministers of the two countries, not only exchanged the instruments of ratification pertaining to the establishment of the Joint Commission but also made significant progress in substantive matters, "Thereby, 'writers Dr. Satish Kumar,' extricating Indo-Pak relations from a state of fresh uncertainty and mutual suspicion in which they stood entangled in the past few months." The Commission set up 4 sub-commissions on (*i*) Economic matters dealing with industry, agriculture, communications, health, science and technology; (*ii*) Trade; (*iii*) Education, information, culture, sports and social science, and (*iv*) Travel, Tourism and Counsellor matters. As a result of the negotiations done through these sub-commissions, the Joint Commission agreed to cut postal rates by 1 to 20 per cent and to improve and argument the existing tele-communication facilities. It was agreed to encourage exchange of visits of businessmen and industrialists for identifying opportunities for collaboration between them and for establishing co-operative projects in the two countries and in their countries of the third world. It was also agreed to exchange visits to and information for the development of small scale and cottage industries and for securing co-operation in the field of Science and Technology. Measures for facilitating travel between the two countries were also agreed upon. The two sides agreed on measures for expediting the exchange of civilian prisoners. There were agreements for co-operation in the agriculture and shipping sectors and in the fields of information, education, social sciences, culture and sports.

The second meeting of the Joint Commission was held in July, 1985 and the process of developing Indo-Pak trade and cultural relations was further strengthened.

After the Simla Agreement, the agreement to establish Joint Commission for promoting Indo-Pak co-operation can be described as a major step towards the objective of securing highly friendly and co-operative relations between the two countries.

The success towards the institutionalisation of Indo-Pak economic trade and cultural relations constituted an important breakthrough in the relations between the two countries and it brightened the hopes that through mutual accommodation and goodwill the two countries shall be in a position to narrow down further the differences over the issue of No-War Pact or treaty of peace and friendship. An integrated agreement or a No-War Pact followed by steps for concluding a comprehensive treaty of friendship, peace and co-operation appeared to be a solution for ending the stalemate over these issues.

There are some clear indications that such a development can take place because:

(*i*) Both India and Pakistan now realise the importance and utility of mutually co-operative and friendly relations;

(*ii*) Both want to remain away from the super power strategic circles;

(*iii*) Both are Now-aligned countries;

(*iv*) Both now realise fully the futility of war and cold war type relations;

(*v*) Both have now come to realise fully the value and benefits of bilateralism;

(*vi*) Both have been successful in securing positive normalisation in their relations since 1972;

(*vii*) Both want to cut out their dependence on super powers and other big powers;

(*viii*) Pakistan now realises better that its security needs require friendly and co-operative relations with India;

(*ix*) Both are now more mature in respect of conducting mutual relations;

(*x*) Both the countries are now not prepared to let the differences over Kashmir come into the way of the development of bilateral relations;

(*xi*) Both are now tacitly accepting the *de facto* division of Kashmir along the line of actual control as determined on December 17, 1971 and,

(*xii*) Both realise the importance of regional and bilateral economic co-operation.

All these factors suggest a positive and hopeful view of the future of Indo-Pak relations. However, it must be stated that the path of negotiations and final agreement in this respect is bound to be difficult, uneven and problematic. The existence of certain irritants forces give us to this view:

(*i*) Differences over No-War Pact *vs*. The Treaty;

(*ii*) Pakistan's refusal to accept the provision for the acceptance of bilateralism as the only means for settlement of Indo-Pak issues and disputes and to accept the position that neither country would give military bases on its soil to a third country;

(*iii*) The continued Pakistani drive to acquire more and sophisticated and advanced war planes and arms;

(*iv*) American attempts to keep Pakistan as a country involved in strategic defence plan in the South and South-West Asia and the Soviet attempts to prevent the over-stepping of Indo-Soviet Treaty of 1971 by any Indo-Pak Agreement;

(*v*) The apprehensions about each other's nuclear policy;

(*vi*) The weak legitimacy of General Zia's regime and the known stand of the Pakistani political parties like PPP to oppose and reject every agreement that might be reached under General Zia's government;

(*vii*) The possibility of a sudden change which is always there in a dictatorship, in the internal politics of Pakistan;

(*viii*) China factor is bound to weigh heavily on both India and Pakistan. The existence of strong Sino-Indian differences over the border issue and the dependence of Pakistan on Chinese friendship and co-operation in Asia are bound to be irritants in Indo-Pak relations. China, though it would like to see India and Pakistan living in peace and a reduction in Indian dependence on relations with Russia, would not like to accept the development of Indo-Pak friendship and co-operation to the disadvantage and exclusion of China;

(*ix*) The Indian opposition to Sino-Pak links regarding the Karakoram Highway and the Khunjerab pass;

(*x*) The Pakistani practice of raising Kashmir issue at every international conference;

(*xi*) The Pakistani fear about a cultural invasion from India and the Indian charge that the Pakistani is providing help to the extremists in Punjab;

(*xii*) The Pakistan helps to anti-India forces;

(*xiii*) Pakistan's negative role during Punjab crisis;

(*xiv*) The militarisation drive in Pakistan;

(*xv*) The fear of Pakistan's nuclear policy, and

(*xvi*) Dispute over the ownership of Siachen Glacier.

All these are negative and hindering factors which are keeping limited the present drive towards more and more positive friendship and co-operation between India and Pakistan. The establishment of the Joint Commission and the good work done by it coupled with Indo-Pak attempts to establish and utilise

SAARC give rise to a hope that India and Pakistan can be successful in overcoming the existing differences over the issue of No-War Pact/treaty of peace, friendship and co-operation. Prime Minister, Rajiv Gandhi's initiative in strengthening India's friendship and relations with the neighbours, particularly with Pakistan and the good response from Pakistan further strengthen the optimism for peace, friendship treaty cum No-War Pact between the two countries. However, as already stated, ups in Indo-Pak relations are quite often followed by downs. This prevents us from making a deterministic positive prediction about the future course of Indo-Pak relations. The chances for a fuller and maturer agreement aimed at securing of durable peace and friendship, good neighbourliness and co-operation between the two countries at the moment appear to be quite good. It is hoped that long-term interest and wiser perception of South and world scene will influence both the countries to maintain and promote further the present thinking for securing mature friendly and co-operative relations. Both must try to avoid involvement in an arms/nuclear arms race.

Promotion of friendship, co-operation and goodwill with the other countries, especially with India's neighbours is among the principal planks of Mr. Rajiv Gandhi's foreign policy. During the past ten months of his regime, he has taken several bold and timely initiatives for cultivating and promoting friendship and co-operation between India and her neighbours in general and with Pakistan in particular. He has been very alert to the growing danger of an arms race — with a potential to become a nuclear arms race in South Asia. As a result of the increasing super power involvement in the affairs of south Asia, particularly due to the big U.S. involvement in South-West Asia and the Gulf, and the Soviet Union's continued presence in Afghanistan, there has come to be developed a danger of destabilisation of peace in this region of Asia the big flow of huge quantities of highly advanced and sophisticated U.S. weapons and equipments into Pakistan coupled with Pakistan's own attempts to go nuclear are viewed by India as very dangerous drifts and developments which need an immediate attention and a necessary halt. For this, the vital need is a maturer friendship and co-operation among the countries of South Asia in general, and India and Pakistan in particular. The history of Indo-Pak relationship — with three wars, limited relations and suspicious environment, make it essential for both India and Pakistan to work out a fruitful course of friendly, peaceful and co-operative bilateral relations. It was with this end, in view that Rajiv Gandhi decided to give an immediate restart to the process of Indo-Pak talks for securing better and more mature bilateral understanding, friendship and co-operation, which since 1983, had been bogged down under the weight of Indo-Pak suspicions and differences arising particularly due to Pakistan's support to the extremists in Punjab and India's strong exception to the disproportionately large acquisition of U.S. Military hardware and weapons by Pakistan. The decision to send the Foreign Secretary, Mr. Romesh Bhandari to the neighbouring capitals was a part of India's decision to do her to boost "constructive peace" in the region so that the people of India and its neighbour could grow in strength economically. To step up existing co-operation and to identify and remove the irritants were the specific objectives of this visit. This step, and President Zia's decision (25th January 1985) to put the hijackers of the two Indian Airlines aircrafts on trial, paved the way for the reopening of Indo-Pak dialogue on improvement of their relations, particularly through a peace-friendship co-operation treaty/No-War Pact. It was described as a "good first step" and a positive step for reviving Indo-Pak dialogue which had been in suspension since mid-July 1984.

India's Foreign Secretary visited Islamabad from April 3 to 5, 1985 and held talks with his Pakistani counterpart and with General Zia. The talks resulted in a general accord to review and step up efforts for increased understanding and co-operation but no concrete agreement on the pending bilateral problems was reached. The decision "to change the past atmosphere of tension and hostility step by step" was the result of the visit. The people of Pakistan, according to Mr. ' Bhandari, appeared to recognise that friendship with India was an absolute necessity for that country. "The effort would, therefore, be to establish people to people contacts and promote exchanges at different levels."

Rajiv Gandhi's View of Indo-Pak Relations: In an interview to "The Muslim"—a Pakistan daily, Prime Minister Rajiv Gandhi gave a categorical assurance to Pakistan that India had no designs against any of its neighbours, especially Pakistan. "We will not like to see a dismembered weak country bordering us". He, however, called upon Pakistan to stop acquiring highly sophisticated offensive weapons and respond positively to India's fresh initiatives to establish confidence and trust between the two countries. The quantum jumps in the level of arms technology in the regions, resulting from Pakistan's present policy of importing U.S. weapon, can only work to the detriment of our people". Hoping that a more positive response would be forth-coming from Pakistan, the Prime Minister advocated the need for "bringing about a sort of de-escalation" through step-by-step approach for normalisation. This, he said, was necessary for making successful the forthcoming ministerial level Indo-Pak Joint Commission talks on the issue of No-War Pact/treaty of peace, friendship and co-operation. He cautioned against a nuclear arms race in the Indian sub-continent, saying "it would only subject both the people to worst fate on earth".

Indo-Pak Talks: The three-day second meeting of the Indo-Pak Joint Commission was held in New Delhi on 2nd, 3rd and 4th July, 1985. The Indian side was led by Minister of State for External Affairs, Mr. Khursheed Alam Khan and the Pakistani side by the Foreign Minister of Pakistan, Sahibzada Yaqub Khan. The meeting was held in an atmosphere of friendship, constructive co-operation and mutual accommodation and discussed a number of proposals and decided to continue an exchange of views in areas where there could be no agreement. After the end of the meeting the leaders of the two sides described the talks as "productive and satisfactory and a stop towards the establishment of a relationship of cordiality, co-operation, mutual trust and understanding between our two people".

The meeting agreed on through rail bookings of seven pairs of designated railway stations on either side as well as additional telephone facilities from August between Bombay-Islamabad, Calcutta-Lahore, and Jalandhar-Lahore. This was to be later on extended further to Lucknow-Kashmir, Calcutta-Karachi and Bombay-Karachi. A bilateral agreement for co-operation in agricultural research and development was also signed. It envisaged Indo-Pak co-operation and collaboration through their executing agencies — the Indian Council of Agro-Cultural Research and the Pakistan Agricultural Research Council It was agreed to encourage people to people contacts to check smuggling, particularly drug smuggling and to promote cultural contacts between the two countries.

A review of the progress at the talks reveals that no substantial or concrete progress in the field of trade was secured. The talks had all the diplomatic eloquence but built little tangible results. No major trade or cultural agreement was signed. Pakistan's decisions not to buy wheat from India and to keep on the drive towards acquisition of U.S. weapons continued to provide the background in which there could be no material advancement in the deliberations of the Joint Commission. The armed clashes in the Siachen Glacier and the Pakistani claim to this territory made the environment of Indo-Pak talks further unhealthy and hence no concrete result could emerge from this exercise. At best, it was a dialogue for understanding each other's view points and not for reaching concrete and durable agreements.

Foreign Secretary Level Talks: In the last week of July, the Foreign Secretaries of India and Pakistan conducted a round of talks over relations between the two countries. But here again the process of talks was friendly and cordial but without results. While reviewing the talks, Mr. Rajinder Sareen in his article: Peace Treaty with Pakistan (*The Tribune*, August 4 1985) observed: "The note of cordiality that marked the conclusion of the current round of talks between these Foreign Secretaries of India and Pakistan at Delhi last week cannot obfuscate the fact that they failed to make any headway in their quest for evolving a framework of peace and harmony between the two countries." To the credit side, the two Foreign Secretaries expressed their resolve to "continue efforts aimed at the conclusion of a comprehensive treaty between the two countries". That there existed divergence of views between the two countries over this issue was clear from the joint press statement in which it was stated that "both sides sought further clarifications." "So what it boils down to is", observers Mr. Rajinder Sareen, "that the

Foreign Secretaries could not attain any worthwhile measure of approximation in their perceptions, but at the same time they accepted the political compulsion to continue the effort."

Thus, Indo-Pak relations in their present phase continue to be governed by the desire "to build bridges of understanding" and to promote friendship and co-operation between the people of the two countries and their governments. However, the legacy of past relations and mutual fears and suspicions continue to act as barriers.

Pakistan's Perceptions: Pakistan continues to fear that India has hegemonious intentions in South Asia, particularly in relations with Pakistan (*The Tribune*, August 5, 1985). It views the fast growing power of India as a dangerous development for the security and integrity of Pakistan. India's secularism and its advocacy of people to people relations is viewed as attempts at the cultural invasion of Pakistan. Further, Pakistan, particularly due to the Soviet intervention and continued presence in Afghanistan, views growing Indo-Soviet friendship and co-operation as a danger signal for its security. As a way out, Pakistan regards the acquisition of U.S. weapons, development of highly close ties with China and U.S.A., and the strengthening of Pakistan by developing its own nuclear technology including the ability to manufacture weapons, as the *sine quo non* of Pakistan's security and developmental needs. The continued desire to secure Kashmir further makes Pakistan adopt a very cautious approach towards relations with India. It, therefore, wants a sort of No-War Pact with India which will reduce the security threat, to Pakistan from its eastern borders but which will not, in way check its drive to strengthen its military might and to acquire full nuclear technology. "The upshot is that Pakistan wishes to have a perceptibly reduced level of hostility with India but would like to be left alone to pursue its options of defence and economic linkages away from it. While Pakistan is keen on concluding a simple agreement to exchange guarantees on non-use of force, it wants to leave aside the basic question of how the two countries stand in relation to each other in the context of the world and the security environment of the sub-continent".

Indian Perceptions: India fully realised the importance of normalisation of relations with Pakistan for keeping South Asia free from power-rivalry, arms race and super power interferences. India further fully realised that normalisation with Pakistan can, beside helping her to concentrate fully on internal socio-economic development, strengthen her *vis-a-vis* China. The ability of China and to some extent of the U.S.A. fully to exploit Indo-Pak conflict/confrontation for keeping Pakistan dependent for securing its defence needs, ultimately limits India's ability to concentrate on her internal development. By pumping huge quantities of sophisticated and advanced technology weapons into Pakistan, the U.S.A. is indirectly forcing India to spend large sums on military purchases from the Soviet Union, and other countries like France and England. India, wants a normalisation in relations with Pakistan as a means for checking the impending arms race. India is greatly concerned about the possibility of third party linkages (China and the U.S.A.) in form of foreign military bases in Pakistan and the possible fall out on India's strategic interests. India is, therefore, keen to pursue Indo-Pak talks over No-War Pact/treaty of peace, friendship and co-operation.

India prefers a comprehensive a peace-friendship co-operation and treaty with Pakistan for providing a solid foundations to the future course of their relations. India wants treaty aimed at promoting beneficial bilateralism in all aspects of Indo-Pak relations. A mere No-War Pact can be no remedy to the irritants that characterise Indo-Pak relations. India believes that a comprehensive Indo-Pak treaty alone can solve the real problems of their relations and usher the two countries into an era of peace, friendship, harmony, and co-operation. India views treaty with Pakistan as a culmination of the process of normalisation, where as Pakistan views the No-War Pact as the first step which will pave the way for future full normalisation in due course of time as such, there exists a gap between the perceptions of two countries.

The Irritants: India believes that some of the current Pakistani policies and moves constitute major hindrances in the way of full normalisation between the two countries through a pact or a treaty. These are:

1. Pakistan's import of disproportionately large quantities of highly sophisticated and technologically advanced offensive weapons.
2. Pakistan's nuclear programme, which from all indications ability to enrich uranium, possession of the nuclear trigger, open talk of Islamic bombs and assertion of Pakistan's right to manufacture nuclear weapons, all indicate that the Pakistan is following a weapon-oriented nuclear programme.
3. Continued Pakistani support to anti-India elements, particularly to the Punjab extremists, who continue to get help and training in Pakistan.
4. Pakistan's unwillingness to open trade relations with India, and reflected in its decision to import American instead of Indian wheat.
5. Pakistan's attempts to forcibly occupy Siachen Glacier.
6. The continuance of anti-India propaganda by several Pakistani leaders and sections of press.
7. Sino-Pak relations with their known anti-India character.
8. Pakistan's apprehension that Indian emphasis on bilateralism is aimed at imposing its hegemony on Pakistan.
9. Differences over the provisions of the Indian draft of a peace-friendship co-operation treaty and the Pakistani draft of a No-War Pact.
10. Pakistan's encouragement to anti-India activities in Kashmir and its continued desire to activate the Kashmir issue in all international forums.

All these irritants, believes India, are keeping the Indo-Pak dialogue over No-War Pact/peace treaty limited and unproductive. Pakistan on her part regards India's unhelpful role in the Afghanistan crisis, growing strength of India's power, India's refusal to sign NPT, India's nuclear capability potential, India's relations with the Soviet Union, India's structural interferences in Pakistan etc., as the major hindrances in the way of full normalisation of their relations. The existence of mutual suspicions, fears and disagreements continue to keep the process of Indo-Pak normalisation slow and limited even during the era of their mutual relations in which the leaders of both the countries fully realise the need for full normalisation. Only by adopting a more positive approach, by exposing their mutual anxieties and concerns and by adjusting their national perceptions and correlating them to the political and strategic imperatives of South Asia, and the world at large, the two countries can overcome the existing era of continued suspicions and fears. What Mr. T.N. Kaul observed in his article, India in South Asia (World Focus, Fourth Annual Number, November-December, 1983), while analysing the scope of Indo-Pak normalisation as a part of drive for peace and stability in South Asia, holds true even today. To quote him, "Unless therefore, Pakistani rulers are willingly ready and sincere to enter into a long-term agreement with Indian leaders to stop their subversive activities and encourage more peaceful and fruitful ventures, there is little likelihood of any lasting peace and friendship between the two countries. At the same time, it is necessary that any suspicions in the minds of the Pakistani people about India's intentions and motives regarding Pakistan be removed." It is for this purpose there is every need to maintain and develop further the present system of increased contacts between the two countries both at the formal governmental as well as non-governmental informal people to people levels.

1. Zia's Six-hour Halt at New Delhi: India and Pakistan agreed not to attack each other's nuclear installation when Prime Minister Rajiv Gandhi and Pakistan's President Zia met at New Delhi during Zia's six-hour stopover in the Capital while on his way to Islamabad from Maldives. Both the leaders held free and frank discussions and got engaged in a confidence-building exercise. Both the leaders also agreed to merge the draft of the No-War Pact proposed by Pakistan and that of treaty of peace and friendship offered by India. This was to be done at a meeting of the foreign secretaries of the two countries in Islamabad in January 1986. Both the leaders also discussed the issues of terrorist problem and dispute over Siachen Glacier.

2. Trade Accord, January 1986: Prospects of developed economic relations between India and Pakistan received a big boost when in January, 1986, the Finance Ministers of the two countries signed a Memorandum of Understanding for increasing bilateral private trade. The agreement allowed the private sector in Pakistan to import 42 items from India. In the public sector the two sides agreed to double the quantum of trading during 1986-87. This trade agreement appeared to be a significant step forward in the two countries' search for a framework of mutually beneficial bilateralism. However, in actual practice the progress in this sphere remained very limited even after the signing of this agreement.

During 1986, Indo-Pak relations continued to develop very slowly. SAARC provided opportunity to both the countries for keeping up the process of bilateral relations in order. India continued to work for step by step normalisation of relations with Pakistan. In December 1986, Indian Home Minister led a delegation to Pakistan and held useful talks. Both the sides reaffirmed their commitment to the Simla Agreement and to seek solution of problems discussed: illegal border crossings, terrorist problem, smuggling of arms and narcotics across the borders etc. Both the sides agreed to strengthen their border security forces and to take up specific measures such as joint surveillances of the border and a joint mechanism with solemn and binding obligations. On a reciprocal basis, against allowing the use of their respective territories for any acts or activities directed against internal peace, stability and territorial integrity of the other state. However, the Foreign Secretaries of the two countries in their December 1986 talks failed to resolve the differences over the issue of No-War Pact/Treaty of peace and friendship. India wanted that Pakistan must commit itself against the grant of foreign basis whereas the latter believed that there was no need to do it because of its membership of NAM and because it was signatory to the 1971 U.N. resolution on keeping the Indian Ocean a Zone of Peace, free of super power rivalry. Thus, the impasse continued. Along with it the U.S. decision to upgrade air bases in Pakistan further dampened the issues.

3. The New Tensions-chances of a New War and the Troops Pull Out Accord in February 1987: The inability to harmonise their bilateral relations combined with the continued anti-India stance of Pakistan's policies in South Asia, created an environment which let to a real crisis in relations. The militarism in Pakistan got strengthened as a result of the big flow of sophisticated advanced technology weapons and arms into Pakistan. Pakistan, on the pretext of meeting the "menace posed by Indian forces" started amassing its troops on the borders. Actually, India was conducting its triennial battle exercise in the bigger way for testing its capability to defend itself and it had duly notified the same to Pakistan. Pakistan's forces were placed in big strength on all strategic points and these constituted a big threat to Indian security as these increased the chance of an accidental Indo-Pak War. India took up the counter-action and ordered its troops to the borders. The situation became grim. India took up a timely stop to de-escalate tension. Foreign Secretary level talk were proposed, which took place in New Delhi in early February 1987. After five days (31st January to 4th February 1987) of hectic negotiations, Mr. A.S. Gonsalves, Secretary in the Indian Ministry of External Affairs and Pakistan's Foreign Secretary, Mr. Abdul Sattar signed the minutes of consultations which contained a blue print for defusing tension along Indo-Pakistan borders. It was agreed:

1. Both sides agree not to attack each other.
2. Both sides agree to exercise the maximum restraint and to avoid all provocative action along the border.
3. Both sides agree to adopt a sector-by-sector approach for the pull out of troops. The first such sector was to be the Ravi and Chenab corridor.

Similar other agreements were reached for effecting a complete deescalating of tensions. India, however, maintained her right to conduct its "Operation Brass Tacks exercise as planned. This agreement came as a source of big relief to both the countries.

It, however, highlighted, the very delicate and instable nature of Indo-Pak relations and once again gave strength to the ideas in favour of increased Indo-Pak normalisation through bilateralism, SAARC and comprehensive peace/no war agreement.

On March 2, 1987 another Indo-Pak agreement was signed for completing the pull out of deployed troops on Indo-Pak borders, further de-escalation also came through "cricket diplomacy" when the President of Pakistan, General Mohammad Zia-ul-Haq came to India for watching the second day's play of the third cricket Test between India and Pakistan. His stop over at New Delhi was used as an opportunity for conducting high-level talks between Prime Minister Rajiv Gandhi and President Zia. Both the sides agreed that lack of communication was responsible for the border crisis of January 1987, and decided to keep up speedy and regular communications for minimising the chances of accidental tensions.

4. Indo-Pak Clashes in Siachen Area: The tensions which are always present in Indo-Pak relations once again surfaced in new heights, when on September. 24 and 25, 1987, Pakistan attacked the Indian position in the Siachen Glacier. India was in a position to successfully meet the division-level Pakistani attack and Indian troops inflicted heavy casualties in the battle. The Pakistani attempt to gain Sia La Indira Col. Bilafond and Saltoro passes was foiled by the Indian troops. Siachen continues to be a bone of contention between the two countries. During President Zia's December 1985 visit, it was agreed to sort out the issue through negotiations. Two meetings were also held but these could produce no solution. Pakistan, as such, decided to impose its will by force but had to receive a beating at the hands of Indian troops. Pakistan's adventurism however, repeated its performance in January 1988 and this time Bana Post of the Bilafond area was the target. India continues to hold a strong post for over the Siachen Glacier. Lt. General B.C. Nanda GOC-IN-C Northern command in a press conference, as reported by *the Tribune*, dated January 14th 1988, observed that India was in complete occupation of the 76-km. long Siachen Glacier.

Indo-Pak relations, as such even today continue to be what these have been since 1947 — relations characterised by tensions, strains, possibilities of war. 'Kashmir' continues to guide Pakistani policies. Siachen issue has further made the Pakistani attitude rigid. The big and almost free flow of the US arms, the ability to keep its nuclear (weapons) programme intact, and the ability to exploit fully the US interests in Asia have together helped its policy-makers to keep up a tough line in respect of its relations with India. It is stepping up its military modernisation programme with the import of new Chinese aircrafts, French missile system, US AWACS and the like. It continues to regard India as its chief opponent. SAARC spirit has failed to really reduce Indo-Pak tensions the issue of No-War Pact *vs.* the treaty of peace friendship and co-operation appears to have gone into background. Process of normalisation of trade and cultural relations continues to be slow. The peoples of the two countries find themselves culturally and emotionally very close, but the foreign policies of the two countries continue to work along different lines. India continues to feel apprehensive about the big militarisation of Pakistan as well as about Pakistan's nuclear programme, which from all available date appears to be fast heading towards a weapons programme. The existence of an entente type of Washington-Islamabad-Beijing relationship continues to develop in Asia. India finds herself not in a position to change the Pakistani attitude. Membership of NAM has not deterred Pakistan from developing an alliance type of relations with USA and China. It has become a frontline state in American strategic plan. India, too, has found it essential to develop further for "time-tested friendship" with the Soviets. And this continues to be viewed with suspicion by Pakistan. As such the signs for the development of Indo-Pakistan relation either through "mutually beneficial bilateralism" or through SAARC appear to be dim.

4

Bangladesh

As the champion of Panchsheel, India has maintained cordial relations with neighbouring countries. So also it has maintained a cordial relationship with Bangladesh right from its emergence in 1971.

I. India's Role in the Emergence of Bangladesh

It has been a consistent and vitally important principle of Indian Foreign Policy to refrain from any interference in the internal affairs of other countries and more particularly, in the internal affairs of its neighbours. But the dirty struggle for power that emerged in Pakistan after the first ever General Elections held in March 1970, created a highly taxing and dangerous situation in East Pakistan, which forced India to support, on humanitarian grounds, the rights of the Bengalese living in East Pakistan. Ever since the creation of Pakistan in 1947, the people of its eastern half-the East Bengal of East Pakistan, as it has subsequently named, were struggling against the domination of their culture and economy by the people of West Pakistan. For instance when in 1949, Pakistan adopted Urdu as its only national language, the people of East Bengal came out with strong resistance against the move. It led to the organisation of Awami League—the party committed to secure the rights of the people of East Bengal. In 1956, they opposed the move to deny them their due share in the political and economic life of Pakistan. In 1957, the East Bengal Assembly adopted a motion demanding full autonomy for East Bengal. It was designed to oppose strongly their economic exploitation by the Western half of Pakistan. After 1947, the people of West Pakistan established and then maintained with vengeance, their superior position in all spheres *vis-a-vis* with the people of East Bengal. The Government of Pakistan, being dominated by the people of West Punjab, did nothing to meet the legitimate demands and aspirations of the people of East Bengal. The result was a gradual but definite consolidation of anti-West Pakistan feelings in East Bengal. The East Bengalese started feeling that their part of Pakistan was nothing but a Colony of West Pakistan which was deliberately being kept economically backward and underdeveloped, and whose foreign exchange earnings resulting from the export of jute and tea were being used for developing the economy and life of West Pakistan. It has been in this context that many scholars opine, and rightly so, that the rise of Bangladesh as a sovereign state in 1971, was an outcome of a long-drawn movement spread over two decades or so and not merely a producer of the post-March 1970 developments and the subsequent war of December 1971.

The people of East Bengal, till 1970, did not voice their support for liberation from the clutches of West Pakistan. It were the attempts of General Yahya and Bhutto's PPP to prevent the transfer of power in Pakistan to the East Bengal based on Sheikh Mujib's Awami League that created a sharp and violent protest and reaction in East Bengal and which forced the people of East Bengal to launch a Civil disobedience movement for securing their legitimate rights, and for ending the era of exploitation. The failure of General Yahya to transfer power to the Awami League, which had secured clear majority in the March 1970 Elections, the arrest of Sheikh Mujib in March 1970, and the military crackdown inflicted on the people of East Bengal gave rise to a revolution against West Pakistan and to the declaration of Bangladesh as a sovereign republic.

Initially, India decided to maintain strictly its policy of keeping away from internal affairs of Pakistan. It viewed with alarm the happenings in East Bengal but decided to maintain complete neutrality. However, later on, the atrocities committed by the army of General Tikka Khan on the men, women and children of East Bengal compelled India to voice support for the protection of their human rights. Further, when the big influx of refugees from East Bengal into India took place in the post-

March 1970 period, India found herself burdened with the responsibility of looking after the primary needs of these refugees. This involved a big strain on Indian economy and consequently, it forced the Government of India to demand the normalisation of conditions in East Bengal and the return of refugees to their homes. The Government of Pakistan, on the other hand, decided to put the blame on India. It began charging India of interfering with the internal affairs of Pakistan. It issued a white paper in which it tried to link the crisis of East Pakistan with the Agartala Conspiracy Case, and observed that India was behind the trouble in East Pakistan. The Government of Pakistan, it appeared, was as such been to transform the East Bengal crisis into an Indo-Pak problem and issue.

This charge was strongly refuted by India and it refused to accept the view that crisis in East Bengal was a part of Indo-Pak problem. India therefore decided to secure world public opinion in favour of the human rights of the people of East Bengal. The Indian Prime Minister, Mrs. Indira Gandhi and the External Affairs Minister, Mr. Swaran Singh under-took world tours for securing support or a political settlement of East Bengal crisis which can secure the safe return of refugees to their homes. India also raised the issue at the UN and in other International forums. However, these moves and efforts failed to produce any meaningful result. In 1971, India became aware of the fact that it would have to intervene in the crisis for effecting a settlement of the crisis. On 15th June 1971, Mrs. Indira Gandhi declared in the Rajya Sabha that: "We will have to go through hell to meet the challenge posted by the developments in Bangladesh." From then onward India started providing help to the refugees and their Muktibahini for securing their rights, which involved the liberation of Bangladesh. The crisis soon developed into the December 1971 Indo-Pak War. The Indian Army formed a joint command with Muktibahini and both jointly fought against the West Pakistani army in East Bengal. After a highly efficient and successful military operation of nearly two weeks, the joint command, led by Lt. General Jagjit Singh Arora, was in a position to secure the liberation of Bangladesh on 16th December 1971. Meanwhile, on 6th December 1971, India had granted recognition to Bangladesh.

After the defeat of West Pakistani army in Bangladesh, the administration of the country was entrusted to the leaders of Bangladesh. Soon afterwards, Bangladesh was granted recognition by other States and this completed the process of liberation of Bangladesh.

India played a leading role in the liberation of Bangladesh. Its people made bold sacrifices for securing to the people of Bangladesh their freedom and their rights. These historic and unparalleled sacrifices made by the people of India and the material and moral support that they gave to the people of Bangladesh combined together to provide a solid foundation for the development of warm and highly friendly and co-operative relations between India and Bangladesh.

II. Relations between India and Bangladesh during Mujib Era

It was on 6th December, 1971, the Prime Minister Mrs. Indira Gandhi, amidst thunderous applause informed the Lok Sabha the decision of the Government of India to grant recognition to the People's Republic of Bangladesh. Since this fateful day, the two countries have been engaged in the process of developing friendly and co-operative relations between them. The immediate goal of securing the liberation of Bangladesh from the clutches of Pakistan was accomplished on December 16, 1971, by the Joint Army command of the two states and this was followed by certain bold steps to usher the history of Indo-Bangladesh relations into an era of friendship and co-operation based upon the spirit of mutual respect for each other's territorial integrity and sovereignty, and commitment to the principles of Panchsheel, Non-alignment, beneficial bilateralism and peaceful means for the settlement of all issues and problems.

The similarities in the foreign policy perceptions of the two countries, the understanding regarding the common needs, goals and objectives, the recognition of the sacrifices made by India for securing the liberation of Bangladesh, the dependence of Bangladesh on India for meeting the immediate security and economic needs, and the mutual understanding among the leaders of the two countries gave good support to the cause of developing highly co-operative and friendly Indo-Bangladesh relations. The tone was set right on 6th December 1971, when Mrs. Indira Gandhi, while announcing the decision to grant recognition to Bangladesh observed: "In future the Governments and people of India and Bangladesh, who share common ideals and sacrifices, would forge a relationship based on principles of mutual respect for each other's sovereignty, territorial integrity, non-interference in internal affairs, equality and mutual benefit."

The first Chancery of Bangladesh was formally opened on 9th December 1971, and it was formally announced that the two countries had entered into a number of mutual agreements. By these agreements India pledged its military support, help and involvement in the struggle (war) for the liberation of Bangladesh. India further undertook the pledge to withdraw its armed forces from liberated Bangladesh, agreed that liberated areas would be immediately handed over to the Government of Bangladesh, and that India would defend Bangladesh against any external threat. The agreements affirmed allegiance to Panchsheel and non-alignment. However, no restriction was sought to be placed on the rights of the people of Bangladesh to have their own independent foreign policy. By another agreement, India decided to give ₹100 crores immediately to Bangladesh for helping the initiation of the process of socio-economic reconstruction in that country. Both the Governments also entered into a detailed trade agreement envisaging an annual trade of ₹100 crores between the two countries. On 16th December 1971, Bangladesh was liberated and the Government of Bangladesh took over the administration of the country. It was on 8th January 1972 that Pakistan announced its decision to release Sheikh Mujib, who was under detention in Pakistan since 25th March 1971. During his brief stopover at New Delhi, on 10th January 1972, Sheikh Mujib paid glowing tributes to India for her historic role in the liberation of Bangladesh. He observed that the people of his country would never forget the sacrifices made by their Indian brothers for making it possible for them to achieve liberation. He declared that bonds of friendship and co-operation between the two countries are bound to become more and more mature and developed in times to come.

From 5th to 9th January 1972, the Foreign Minister of Bangladesh, Mr. Abdus Samad Azad paid an official visit to New Delhi for strengthening the relations with India. The visit resulted into an agreement under which India agreed to help Bangladesh; (*i*) By giving to Bangladesh goods and services to the tune of ₹25 crores in the shape of aid and grants, (*ii*) By meeting the foreign exchange requirements of Bangladesh through a loan ₹25 million which was to be repaid by Bangladesh after an initial lapse of 5 years and in 15 equal yearly installments. On January 22, 1972, India's special emissary Shri D.P. Dhar visited Bangladesh and discussed with its Foreign Minister Mr. Samad, the issues regarding the withdrawal of Indian troops from Bangladesh, trial of Pakistani POWs and the issue of food supplied to Bangladesh. On 2nd February 1972, Bangladesh's Finance Minister, Mr. Tajuddin Ahmed visited India and held talks for increasing Indo-Bangladesh economic co-operation. India agreed to give 5 million tonnes of food-grains to Bangladesh and to increase the quantum of aid to ₹125 crores.

Mujib's 1972 Visit to India: From 6th to 8th February, 1972, Sheikh Mujibur Rahman, the Prime Minister of Bangladesh, visited India and held important discussions with Indian Prime Minister and other leaders. In the joint statement issued on 8th February in New Delhi, Mrs. Indira Gandhi and Sheikh Mujib agreed that India would withdraw all its troops from Bangladesh by 25th March 1972, and that every means would be adopted for ensuring the return of the refugees from India. Both the leaders further expressed "their determination to promote in every possible way the co-operation between governments and people of the two countries inspired by a vision of lasting peace, amity and good neighbourliness." Similar views were expressed later on by Bangladesh President Mr. Abu Sayeed Chowdhary while accepting the credentials presented by the Indian High Commissioner, Mr. Subimal Dutt. India came out fully for helping the Government of Bangladesh in its drive for reconstructing the shattered country. It gave on loan two aeroplanes of Indian Airlines to Bangladesh Viman for getting initiated the new country's internal airline. India took efficient and early steps for troop's withdrawal from

Bangladesh and the task was completed on March 13, 1972, *i.e.*, 12 days in advance of the stipulated date. While taking salute at a ceremonial parade at Dacca on 13th March, Prime Minister Sheikh Mujib declared that friendship between India and Bangladesh would remain intact for ever and no power on earth would be able to destroy it. The immediate withdrawal of troops from Bangladesh amply proved the Indian desire of not occupying even an inch of Bangla territory and also of the desire to pave the way for recognition of Bangladesh by other members of the International Community.

Mrs. Gandhi's Visit to Dacca: Mrs. Indira Gandhi paid a return visit to Dacca in March 1972, and her visit further cemented the growing Indo-Bangladesh friendship and co-operation. Her visit produced a number of agreements, and also a 25 years Treaty of Peace, Friendship and Co-operation between the two countries. It was during this visit that both the countries decided to further strengthen bilateral co-operation by agreeing to hold bi-annual consultations among the officials of ministries of Foreign Affairs, Defence, Planning Commission and of departments dealing with economic, cultural, commercial and technical affairs of the two governments. It was also agreed to establish a Joint Rivers Commission (JRC) for surveying and studying the shared river systems and for formulating and implementing joint projects for flood control and irrigation facilities. Both the Prime Ministers approved the proposal for the revival of Trade and Transit Agreement for the border areas of the two countries. Further understanding was reached for the exchange of information regarding peaceful uses of nuclear energy, technological and scientific research for industrial development and utilisation of future space research for communication purposes. Along with this, the process of the delivery of Indian food supplied and economic assistance to Bangladesh was reviewed. The two Prime Ministers also agreed to take appropriate and concrete steps for strengthening cultural relations between the two countries. A very fruitful development however, came in the form of the Indo-Bangladesh Treaty.

Indo-Bangladesh Treaty of Co-operation, Friendship and Peace: On March 19, 1972, India and Bangladesh signed a 25 years Treaty of Friendship, Co-operation and Peace. It was a bold-attempt to cement the Indo-Bangla friendship. The Treaty, with 12 Articles and a Preamble, was designed to maintain fraternal and good neighbourly relations, to transform the borders into a border of external peace and friendship, to uphold Non-alignment, peaceful co-existence, to safeguard peace stability and security, to promote and strengthen the existing relations of friendship and co-operation, and to reaffirm the determination to follow peaceful means for the settlement of disputes as well as to uphold the aims and principles of the U.N. Charter.

The 12 Articles of the Treaty provided for the steps agreed by both the countries as the means for securing the ideals and objectives listed in the preamble. Both the countries declared that there shall be lasting peace and friendship between the two countries and their people and that each side shall respect the independence, sovereignty and territorial integrity of the other and refrain from interfering in the internal affairs of the other side. The two shall further develop and strengthen the relations of friendship, good neighbourliness and all-round co-operation existing between them. Under Article 2, both sides condemned colonialism and racialism in all forms and affirmed their determination to strive for their final and complete elimination. Both agreed to co-operate with other states in achieving these aims. Under Articles 3 and 4, both the sides reaffirmed their faith in Non-alignment and peaceful co-existence and to resolve to maintain regular mutual conflicts on major international problems affecting the interests of both the states. In the next Article *i.e.*, Article 5, both the countries agreed to continue to strengthen and widen their mutually advantageous and all-round co-operation in economic, scientific, technical, trade, transport and communications fields. Under Articles 6 and 7 both the countries agreed to make joint studies and take action in the field of flood control, river basin development and the development of hydro-electric power and irrigation, and further to promote relations in the fields of art, literature, education, culture, sports and health. Each side solemnly declared under Article 8, that it shall not enter into or participate in any military alliance directed against the other party and that both the countries shall refrain from any aggression against the other and shall not allow the use of its territory for committing any act that may cause military damage to or constitute a threat to the security of the other. Article 10 of the Treaty declared that: "Each of the high contracting parties shall refrain from giving any assistance to any third party taking part in an armed conflict against the other party. In a case either party is attacked or threatened with attack the high contracting parties shall immediately enter into mutual consultations in order to take appropriate effective measures to eliminate the threat and thus ensure peace and security of their countries. Each of the high contracting parties solemnly declared that it shall not undertake any commitment, secret or open, towards one or more states which may be incompatible with the present treaty." In the last two articles it was stated that the Treaty was for 25 years and was renewable by mutual agreement, and that any differences in interpreting the Treaty that may arise shall be settled bilaterally through peaceful means in a spirit of mutual respect and understanding.

Evaluation: With these provisions the Treaty constituted a bold attempt towards the securing of peace stability in South Asia. This Treaty affirmed India's respect for the sovereign equality and territorial integrity of Bangladesh and set at rest the Western a Pakistani propaganda that India had an eye over Bangladesh. The Treaty, observed the Patriot, was the first formal and certainly unique step taken up by two important Asian countries for the stabilisation of peace in this sub-continent. It cemented the growing Indo-Bangla friendship and laid solid foundations for the extension of bilateral co-operation between the two countries. It was neither a defence pact nor a security pact designed against any other country. Like the Indo-Soviet Treaty of Peace, Friendship and Co-operation, the Indo-Bangladesh Treaty was a bilateral treaty for positive bilateral co-operation. It was a solemn treaty solemnly signed for strengthening both world peace and bilateral relations. Indeed, this treaty was a welcome and fruitful way of ushering Indo-Bangla relations into an era of enduring peace, friendship and co-operation.

Indo-Bangla Co-operation in Trade, Economic tie, Cultural Fields in the Post-Treaty era: After the signing of the Treaty, both the countries conducted further negotiations for enlarging trade between them. On March 28, 1972, the two countries entered into a trade agreement providing for a trade of nearly ₹100 crores. Firstly, this agreement provided for border trade for people living within 15-km. belt of the borders and its aim was to help the people of border areas to meet their day-to-day requirements. But, the trade was restricted to specific commodities. Secondly, it provided for a ₹50 crore two-way trade goods of special interest to both the countries on a balanced basis. Thirdly, this agreement laid down that if India exported goods worth more than its share-25 crores, then the payment of the overflow shall be in the form of temporary loan to Bangladesh and shall not carry any interest. This agreement was indeed a symbol of liberal and friendly attitude of India towards its new neighbour. On July 5, 1973, Indian and Bangladesh signed a new three years Trade Agreement and it was agreed that the two countries would now export goods worth ₹30.5 crores each way. The trade relations were given a new big boost on May 16, 1974, through a number of agreements on wide ranging bilateral economic and trade co-operation. India agreed to give three credits of the value of ₹41 crores to Bangladesh. Though these agreements, closer collaboration was envisaged in respect of jute export and for the setting up of industrial projects for common benefits. It was also agreed to set up a ministerial-level commission for closer co-operation in the production, trade, technical development, manufacture and promotion of jute. By the trade protocol of December 1974, both the countries agreed to switch over to trade in freely convertible currency *w.e.f.* January 1st, 1975. In 1975, Bangladesh agreed to export fish worth ₹3.5 crores to India. Further, a protocol for exchange programme in the fields of culture, education, information and sports was signed by India and Bangladesh on September 27, 1974. India offered to give 100 scholarships and fellowships to Bangladesh nationals for pursuing higher studies and research in India.

Indo-Bangladesh Co-operation in the Spheres of Science, Technology and Trade: For promoting co-operation in the fields of science and technology, India and Bangladesh agreed, on June 10, 1972, for co-operating in the peaceful uses of atomic energy and space research. On August 27, 1973, a treaty was signed for exchanging information on atomic research and literature between the two countries. Scientists of both the countries were to be given opportunities for research and training in atomic research laboratories in either country. In May 1974, when India conducted her first underground and fully controlled peaceful nuclear explosion (PNE), Bangladesh welcomed the development as an important step towards the development of developing countries. *The Bangla Times*, an influential daily of Bangladesh, described India's PNE as a matter of pride for developing countries. It wrote that this explosion will have deep impact on the politics of Asia and the sub-continent. It called upon the neighbours not to feel unduly apprehensive from India because India's nuclear policy was a peaceful policy.

Major Indo-Bangladesh Agreements: Thus, close co-operation in the fields of trade, commerce, education, cultural activities and sports was registered in the post-Treaty period of Mujib era. Particularly, after the understanding reached during May and September 1974, meetings between the leaders and delegations of the two countries, some very important and major agreements were reached for effecting closer co-operation between the two countries. The May 1974 Summit conference between India and Bangladesh produced very healthy and fruitful results. The following Four Joint Ventures were cleared: (*i*) A cement plant at Chatak in Bangladesh based on Limestone supplied from Meghalaya in India; (*ii*) A Clinker plant in Meghalaya for supplying Clinker to Bangladesh; (*iii*) A Fertilizer Plant in Bangladesh for the supply of urea to India, and (*iv*) A Sponge Iron plant in Bangladesh with the supply of iron ore from India. The decision to constitute a Joint Commission on Jute was another landmark achieved at the summit. All these steps for bilateral economic collaboration were commendable. For promoting co-operation in the fields of science and technology, India and Bangladesh agreed on 10th June 1972, for co-operating in the peaceful uses of atomic energy and space research. On 27th August 1973, a treaty was signed for exchanging information on atomic research and literature between the two countries. Scientists of both the countries were to be given opportunities for doing research and training in atomic research laboratories in either country.

Border Agreement: Realising the necessity of settling the border problem, both India and Bangladesh conducted negotiations which led to the signing of Border Agreement on May 19, 1974. Under this agreement, India retained the Berubari enclave and in exchange Bangladesh received Dahagram and Angarpota enclaves and a perpetually leased corridor for connecting Dahagram with Panbari Mouza of Bangladesh. "The border demarcation was to be so framed as to cause the least disturbance to the population, to be as far as possible on both sides and to make it easy to recognise the borders between the two countries." It also provided for exchange "expeditiously of all enclaves." Another feature of the agreement was regarding the fixation of midstream boundaries along Muhuri and Fenny rivers. This ensured that two sides would get water from the rivers all the lime. The Border Agreement was as *The Tribune* of May 21, 1974, observed, "an example in good neighbourliness and a major friction remover."

Exchange of Visits and Close Political Relations: Increased contacts and exchange of visits became regular features of Indo-Bangladesh relations in the post-Treaty years of Mujib era. In November 1972, President of Bangladesh, Mr. Abu Sayeed Chowdhry paid a 10 days state visit to India and in June 1974, President of India, Mr. V.V. Giri returned the state visit to Bangladesh. Both the visits strengthened the bonds of friendship between the two countries. The visits revealed that there was close identity of views between the two countries. Similar contacts at the ministerial level were also maintained. In April, 1973, the Foreign Minister of Bangladesh visited India and in return Mr. Swarn Singh, Indian Minister of External Affairs, paid an official visit to Bangladesh in February 1974. During these visits, the progress of Indo-Bangladesh relations and co-operation was reviewed. After the discussions the determination to give practical shape to the deeply felt and just aspirations of the people of two countries for socio-economic well-being, was expressed.

The Summit Conference 1974: With a view to further strengthen the very friendly relations existing between the two countries a Summit Conference between Mrs. Indira Gandhi and Sheikh Mujib was held on May 2, 1974. It was during this conference that important discussions were held over matters of mutual interests and International problems. The exchange of views was held in an atmosphere of friendship, cordiality and in the background of traditional friendship and understanding between the two countries. Discussions on matters like trade and commerce, sharing of Ganga waters, functioning of Joint Rivers Commission, boundary disputes, expansion of co-operation in field on Jute export, issue of joint ventures etc., were objectively discussed and certain agreements were reached. Similarly international problems, like energy crisis were discussed. On May 19, 1974, India and Bangladesh signed the Border Agreement and announced that an understanding had been reached regarding the resolution of Farakka Barrage issue.

Indo-Bangladesh Joint Statement: In the joint statement issued after the end of the Summit, it was stated that the Prime Ministers reviewed the whole gamut of Indo-Bangladesh relations and reached a clear understanding regarding the nature of future economic and trade relations between the two countries. Besides the Border Agreement and the understanding on Farakka issue, agreements for establishing 4 joint ventures were reached. After reviewing the international situation both the Prime Ministers reaffirmed that, "the policy of Non-alignment to which both countries were deeply committed, constituted a positive force in strengthening the national sovereignty, independence and the attainment of peace, stability and just international economic order, in accordance with the aspirations of people the world over." This Summit and the agreements it produced gave further strength to the development of Indo-Bangladesh friendship and co-operation. It constituted, as The Bangla Observer described "a milestone on the road to the sub-continental peace realised on the basis of sovereign interests."

Similarly, India and Bangladesh exhibited complete understanding and co-operation at the time of Simla Summit between India and Pakistan. Bangladesh welcomed wholeheartedly the Simla Agreement and the Delhi Agreement between India and Pakistan, as two positive steps towards peace and stability in South Asia—India kept Bangladesh fully informed about the nature, scope and progress of the discussions with Pakistan. In April 1973, India and Bangladesh jointly prepared a three points programme on the basis of which was to conduct negotiations with Pakistan. The Indo-Pak agreement of 1973, reflected the fact that India fully upheld the commitments that had been made with Bangladesh in respect of the repatriation of POWs and refugees.

Further, India left no stone unturned for helping Bangladesh to get recognition from other countries and its due place in the United Nations. India gave full support to the August 9, 1972 application made by Bangladesh for getting the membership of the United Nations. However, the Chinese veto against Bangladesh prevented success in this direction. In February 1974, Pakistan gave recognition to Bangladesh and it was followed by the accord of recognition by China. This development cleared the way of Bangladesh's entry into United Nations. In the context of Indo-Pak-Bangladesh relations, the April 1974 tripartite talks between India, Pakistan and Bangladesh produced an important agreement leading to the repatriation of 195 Pakistani POWs, who were still being detained in India because of Bangladesh's earlier decision to try them on charges of genocide and war crimes.

Interim Agreement on Farakka: Even the complex issue of Farakka was temporarily resolved through an interim agreement of April 18, 1975. Under an interim and short-term agreement reached at Dacca, it was agreed that India was to draw a specified quantity of water for its feeder canal for the benefits of Calcutta Port. The Following schedule was fixed:

Period	Daily withdrawal of water by India
21st to 30th April	11,000 cusecs
1st May to 10th May	12,000 cusecs
11th May to 20th May	15,000 cusecs
21st May to 31st May	16,000 cusecs

The remaining water was to flow to Bangladesh.

It was further agreed that a joint team of experts would supervise and observe the effect of withdrawals on Bangladesh and the Hooghly river. A joint team was to be stationed at Farakka was keeping a record of the water fed into the feeder canals.

The agreement was an important breakthrough in the Farakka dispute between India and Bangladesh. It was hoped that this short-term agreement would pave the way for an amicable long-term accord on Farakka. It was an agreement reached through bilateral negotiations and this gave it added importance.

The above account of Indo-Bangladesh relations during the Mujib era (1973-75), clearly reveals that the conduct of relations between the two countries got a positive and good start. During a short period of just four years both the countries were in a position to solve the Border disputes and reach an interim agreement on Farakka. Both were in a position to establish highly friendly and co-operative relations in spheres of trade, economic, cultural, educational relations and scientific and technological co-operation. The 25 Years Treaty of Co-operation, Friendship and Peace gave a solid foundation to Indo-Bangladesh friendship and co-operation. India, after having helped the emergence of Bangladesh as a sovereign independent republic, came forward wholeheartedly to help the new country in overcoming the problems of socio-economic reconstruction. Through loans and aids, material and model support and a series of trade and economic agreements, India gave valuable help to Bangladesh during the initial years of its independence. The Government of Bangladesh, particularly Prime Minister of Bangladesh Sheikh Mujibur Rahman, recognised fully the sacrifices made and the help given by India to Bangladesh and, therefore, felt indebted to India. All the agreements reached during this period were backed by complete understanding and mutual respect for each other's needs, desires and interests.

Irritants in Indo-Bangladesh Relations: However, along with this positive development, the march of time produced certain irritants in Indo-Bangladesh relations. Particularly, the carrying out of anti-India propaganda by certain sections of Bangla press and vested interests, at times, made the environment of Indo-Bangladesh relations quite heavy. This negative development became a source of concern particularly towards the close of Mujib-era. Some scholars even go to the extent of saying that Mujib's friendship with India was a factor in the August 1975 coup against Mujib's regime. The following factors were responsible for the emergence of anti-India propaganda in Bangladesh during the closing years of Mujib era:

1. Existence of pro-Pakistan factors in Bangladesh.
2. Internal opposition to Sheikh Mujib's policies particularly to the centralisation and concentration of authority into his own hands.
3. The Pakistani and Chinese propaganda that India was having imperialistic designs over Bangladesh.
4. The difference over Farakka Barrage issue.
5. Rise of communalism in Bangladesh.
6. The strong dissatisfaction in Bangladesh over the increased corruption, shortage of essential commodities, particularly food-stuff, and uncontrolled smuggling on Indo-Bangladesh borders.
7. The strong criticism by the Indian Press (West Bengal based) of the role of opposition in Bangladesh, produced a strong reaction and gave rise to considerable opposition to the role of India in the sub-continent. In particular, this made Maulana Bhashani and his party a strong critic of India.
8. The failure of the Government of Bangladesh to effectively run the administration and check the spread of ani-India propaganda.

III. Post Mujib Era

Indo-Bangladesh relations during the post-Mujib era have been governed by the domestic compulsions of Bangladesh. The August, 1975 coup against Sheikh Mujib opened an era of political instability in Bangladesh which seriously impaired the process of Indo-Bangladesh relations. The emergence of strong anti-India propaganda after the murder of Sheikh Mujib, the inability of the new regime of Bangladesh to control growing lawlessness the rapid and violent political changes in Bangladesh, gave a big blow to the cause of Indo-Bangladesh relations. India felt greatly disturbed by the events in the new republic, but it strictly adhered to the policy of keeping away from the internal affairs of the friendly neighbour. However, due to its close borders on all sides of Bangladesh, India felt concerned with the turmoil in Bangladesh and as such felt no hesitation in condemning political murders and violence and in calling upon the people of that country to work for the unity, integrity and development of *Sonar Bangla*.

After the murder of Sheikh Mujib on August 15, 1975, political uncertainty came to engulf Bangladesh. The regime headed by Khondaker Mostaq Ahmad, which came into existence after the 15th August coup, could remain in power for only 11 weeks and on November 3, 1976 it was overthrown by the Army. The lawlessness that erupted in Bangladesh led to the murder of a number of important and popular national leaders, who had played a key role in the liberation of Bangladesh. On November 6, Justice A.S.M. Sayem took over as the President of Bangladesh. He immediately announced the dissolution of parliament and promised to hold fresh elections before February 1977. However, his regime failed to acquire credence and Bangladesh continued to live under political instability. On April 21, 1977, the political power in Bangladesh once again passed into the hands of army when President Sayem resigned from his office on grounds of failing and handed over the reins of office to Gen. Zia-ur-Rehman, Chief of Army staff and Chief Martial Law Administrator. General Zia-ur-Rehman continued in the office till 30th May, 1981, when he was assassinated by army rebels. Acting President Abdul Sattar proclaimed a state of emergency and suspended most of the civil rights of the people. Soon afterwards, Mr. Abdul Sattar had to quit under pressure from the army and this brought into operation the military dictatorship of Lt. Gen. H.M. Ershad, who still continues to rule Bangladesh. Such frequent and violent changes in Bangladesh have been problematic for the course of Indo-Bangladesh relations. In India too, a vital political change took place with the coming into power in March 1977, of the first non-Congress Government—the Janata government. But this change did not materially affect India's relations with Bangladesh because new government, in the main kept on following the foreign policy principles and objectives when had been previously followed by Mrs. Indira Gandhi's government. The Janata Government's policy of giving more importance to the development of India's relations with the neighbouring countries gave a welcome change to Indo-Bangladesh relations and an interim agreement on a complex issue like Farakka was reached through mutual negotiations and in the spirit of give and take. The return of Mrs. Indira Gandhi to power in India in January 1980 and certain bold moves initiated by the two countries further made the relations better through not as harmonious and co-operative as these were prior to August 1975. Lt Gen H.M. Ershad has been very soon to sort out and solve the outstanding issues and problems with India. After the summit meeting in October 1982, between Mrs. Indira Gandhi and General Ershad and the March 1983 meeting at the time of the 7th Summit Conference of the Non-aligned nations, there re-emerged a process of re-building bridges of understanding between India and Bangladesh. But the existence of certain irritants like the Farakka and New Moore Island and issues of checking illegal crossing of borders by Bangla nationals into India, the recurring anti-India propaganda in Bangladesh continued to affect adversely the course of Indo-Bangladesh relations.

Mr. Rajiv Gandhi has now taken several bold steps towards the securing of more developed friendship and co-operation with Bangladesh. His visit to Dacca for expressing India's concern for and sympathy with the people of Bangladesh has produced a healthy impact. The chances for growth of Indo-Bangladesh relations and the solution of Farakka dispute now appear to be quite good.

The history of Indo-Bangladesh relations since 1975 can be analysed through an analysis of the following problems:

1. Border problem,
2. Problem of illegal crossing of borders,
3. Economic relations,
4. Controversy over New Moore Island,
5. Farakka dispute,
6. Anti-India propaganda in Bangladesh.

1. Border Problem: It was in 1974, that the Delhi Agreement was reached between India and Bangladesh and the problem of enclaves was solved. However, in the post-Mujib era, the Government of Bangladesh once again tried to activate the border problem with India. It was along' the Tripura, Meghalaya and Assam borders that Bangladesh Rifles resorted to firing first in April 1976, and then in November 1976. In April 1976, the borders out-post at Dumnikura, in the Garo Hills district of Meghalaya was fired upon by the Bangladesh Rifles. In November, 1976, the Bangladesh authorities claimed an Indian area measuring about 8 hectares in the Muhuri Char area in the Belonia sub-division of Tripura. It became the object of dispute between India and Bangladesh, and the crisis became deeper when the Bangladesh Rifles repeatedly opened fire upon the Indian farmers. The demarcation of border along Tripura, Assam, Meghalaya had been pending issue because of certain changes in the course of Muhuri river. To sort out the matter, the first of talks between Bangladesh Rifles and Indian Border Security Force representatives was held at Comilla on 11th November 1976, but there could be reached no agreement. Each side then blamed the other for taking rigid and unreasonable stand. Bangladesh accused India of having unilaterally constructed nine spurs for deflecting the course of Muhuri river. The allegation was refuted by India. A second round of talks was held in Dacca on November 19, and both the sides agreed to prevent the recurrence of border incidents. After a meeting of the Joint Rivers Commission in Dacca, it was declared on November 20, that both sides have tried to understand each other's view point regarding the border near Muhuri Char land and that both sides have agreed to take steps for removing the irritants. A committee for river site and for determining the issue of spurs was instituted. This was a welcome move but the net result negligible because on November 22, Bangladesh Rifles again resumed firing in this sector. The civil defence exercised and the hectic activity on the Bangladesh side of the border further made the issue more complicated. To defuse the situation, a six-member Bangladesh delegations came to India on December 12, and held discussions with the counterpart over the issue of differences over border demarcation as stipulated in the 1974 Boundary Agreement. The talks again failed to produce any tangible result. The Bangladesh delegation refused to accept the steps listed by India for normalising the situation on Tripura-Bangladesh border. It demanded that the whole of Muhuri Char area should be made a "no man's land' with the provision for joint patrolling on the Indian side by Indian and Bangladesh border forces. This was an indirect way of inducing a change in the 1974 Agreement and hence it was rejected by India. The talks produced only one small agreement whereby both sides agreed to maintain normalcy in the Muhuri Char area.

In February 1980, Secretary level meetings between India and Bangladesh were held in Dacca for resolving the issue. The talks, however, ended after just striking a note of optimism for future course of Indo-Bangladesh relations. After the August, 1980 visit of Foreign Minister P.V. Narsimha Rao, it was declared that India and Bangladesh would hold high-level talks in October 1980 for working out details regarding the implementation of 1974 Border Agreement. Consequently, the 3-day official level talks were held in New Delhi in October and it was agreed that within two years the two countries shall complete the demarcation of boundary on the basis of 1974 Agreement. The talks helped the countries to remove certain apprehensions and to accept status quo in Muhuri Char area till the completion of some more surveys in this area. It was in July 1983 that the agreement over the perpetual lease to 'Tin Bigha' Corridor to Bangladesh was reached.

2. Problems of Illegal Crossing of Borders: Even after 12 years of the independence of Bangladesh, the process of illegal crossing of borders by the Bangla nationals, with a view to secure a settlement on the Indian side of border, has been in operation. The affected Indian States have been Assam, Meghalaya, Tripura and West Bengal. The 4000-km. Bangladesh border with these states of Indian Union passes through difficult terrain which makes it difficult for India to check the illegal crossings. Bangladesh because of administrative weaknesses and because of its cold attitude has not been able to prevent the influx of refugees' into India. By 1979 the situation became highly grim and Prime Minister Desai, during his visit to Bangladesh, discussed this issue with President Zia-ur-Rehman. Both the leaders then agreed to take effective steps for preventing the illegal crossing of borders. It was also agreed that Bangladesh would hold the drive against Mizo rebels operating from sanctuaries in Bangladesh.

But in spite of such an agreement, the influx of illegal Bangla immigrants into India continued almost unabated. The problem became very dangerous when there developed a strong reaction against Bangla refugees in Assam and other Indian States along the Indo-Bangladesh border. In May 1980, India sent an *aide memorie* to Bangladesh in which it listed the steps taken by India to check this dangerous development and called upon Bangladesh to help the stopping of illegal infiltration of Bangla nationals into India. India further intensified border patrolling for checking the illegal practice. The problem continues to be there even today. Now, as a strong and effective deterrent, the Assam Chief Minister Mr. Hiteswar Saikia has proposed the construction of a 270-km. boundary wall for preventing illegal immigration from Bangladesh. Bangladesh has reacted against this proposal. As reported in *The Tribune* of 13th July 1983, Bangladesh has recalled its High Commissioner in Delhi for urgent consultations .... an authoritative Bangladesh source has said "we will certainly object to such plans because they militate against our border agreements." The 1975 Border Agreement prohibits construction of any kind within 150 yards of the borders. The Centre has not given permission to Assam to go ahead with the construction of border wall, but the proposal to have a barbed wire fence is under consideration. Mr. Khursheed Ahmed Khan, Minister of State for Foreign Affairs, has recently stated India's decision to raise a barbed wire fence along the Eastern Border with Bangladesh. The work is stated to be in progress. The issue of illegal immigration as such still needs an effective and expert handling. There continues to be an urgent need for checking the illegal crossing of borders. If Bangladesh is not prepared to accept the construction of a border wall, it must take effective steps for preventing its nationals from crossing over to India and it must fully co-operate with India for detecting and repatriating the Bangladesh refugees who have illegally entered India after 1971.

3. Economic Relations: The economic and trade agreements which had been signed during 1972-75 period did not succeed in reaping a rich harvest in the form of increased and diversified trade between India and Bangladesh. The complementary nature of their economies, geographical contiguity and the trade agreements as well as Indo-Bangladesh Treaty could not lead to the expected vital and close economic and trade links between the two countries because of the existence of certain problems and irritants. Even the switch over from barter to free convertible currency dealing failed to produce the desired results. The political instability in Bangladesh after August 1975 coup and the consequent emergence of strong anti-India propaganda in Bangladesh, created a situation in which both the countries found it difficult to capitalise through mutual trade and economic links. Nevertheless, the two sides kept on trying to maintain and improve mutual trade and economic co-operation.

In January 1976, both the countries reached an agreement for checking the decline in bilateral trade and for securing increased two-way trade between them. It was also agreed that ₹4.9 crores due to India for providing technical credit to Bangladesh, should be converted into a loan payable in installments. Agreement in respect of commercial exchange of fish, coal, jute and newsprint was also reached. This trade agreement was a bold attempt to rerail Indo-Bangladesh trade relations. It was indeed an important breakthrough in trade relations designed to repair the decline registered after August 1975. In December 1976, India, Bangladesh and Nepal agreed to form a Jute International for co-ordinating the Jute export policy of the three countries.

By another trade agreement of February 1978, New Delhi agreed to purchase 10,000, 20,000, 60,000 and 15,000 tonnes respectively of newsprint, naphtha, furnace oil and chloroquin phosphate from Bangladesh during the year 1978. In return Bangladesh agreed to purchase 3,00,000 tonnes of steam coal from India and also to consider the purchase of 75,000 tonnes of Assam coal. In October 1979, the Janata government entered into another trade agreement with Bangladesh for developing and diversifying the trade between the two countries. It was agreed to strengthen tele-communication facilities and also to remove transport bottlenecks between the two countries. On 4th October 1980, both the countries entered into another trade agreement which envisaged measures for expanding and promoting mutually advantageous trade between the two countries. A decision to promote trade and economic links through exchange of visits and through the organisation of trade exhibitions and fairs was also reached.

In October 1982, the Summit between Mrs. Indira Gandhi and General Ershad produced a decision to revive the plan to set up sponge iron, cement, textile and sugar units in Bangladesh. The decision to establish these units was reached in 1972-73, but the internal compulsions of Bangladesh had made these non-starter.

In November 1982, the first meeting of the Indo-Bangla Joint Commission was held and it gave a fresh impetus and new direction to the economic co-operation between the two countries. The meeting identified measures to be taken on a priority basis for expanding trade and reducing the trade imbalances. It was decided that an Indian team of experts will visit Bangladesh for formulating a medium-term plan of co-operation in the field of small and cottage industries. The Commission decided to constitute committee headed by the Secretary of Indian External Affairs Ministry and the Secretary of the Bangladesh External Resources Division of the Finance Ministry, for ensuring the effective functioning of the existing and new bodies and to follow-up the Commissions work.

It was also agreed that to promote the establishment of industrial and infrastructure projects in Bangladesh, and that India would provide a Government to Government credit of ₹20 crores which would be used for import of Indian capital goods and equipment. India would also provide credit of ₹40 crores from the Export-Import Bank to finance the import of Indian capital goods and equipment for projects in both the public and private sectors.

India agreed to procure 50,000 tonnes of urea and 20,000 tonnes of newsprint annually from Bangladesh for the next three years, India also decided to purchase 20,000 tonnes of bitumen in 1983. In addition to it, India agreed to explore the possibility of importing sarees, viscose yarn and timber from Bangladesh.

India expressed its willingness to continue exports of 1,00,000 tonnes of high steam coal annually and offered to supply 3,00,000 to 5,00,000 tonnes of special low volatile coal to Bangladesh.

Both sides agreed to set up joint ventures and range of industrial projects discussed included sponge iron and steel, cement, concrete sleepers, modernisation of railway workshops, manufacture of coaches and wagons as well as modernisation of four sugar mills of Bangladesh. This agreement revived the hopes that in the years to come. Indo-Bangladesh trade and economic relations are bound to grow. Yet any complacency is bound to be counter-productive. There exists ample opportunities for expanding Indo-Bangladesh co-operation in economic, trade, industrial, technological and scientific development spheres and every effort must be made to utilise these opportunities in actual practice. Both the countries can harvest rich gains through mutual economic and trade co-operation. Now, under the aegis of SAARC Indo-Bangladesh economic, trade and cultural co-operation is bound to grow further.

4. Controversy over the New Moore Island: Towards the middle of 1981, Indo-Bangladesh relations developed serious strains over the issue of occupation and ownership of the New Moore Island or the South Talpatti as Bangladesh calls it. Born in 1970, with barely 1.5 sq. in area, the New Moore Island became a major matter of dispute between India and Bangladesh. So much so that in May 1981, there appeared a danger of armed naval clash between the two countries. Before 1970, this land-mass was nothing more than a low tide elevation which became visible only when the sea subsided during a low tide. It surfaced in an effective way only in 1970.

The Island has great economic implications and its ownership involves various maritime and other territorial rights over about 4,000 sq. nautical miles of the sea. The possibility of using the land-mass and sea around the New Moore Island for securing sea food, mineral resources and natural gas makes the Island very important in the eyes of India and Bangladesh.

Indian case regarding the ownership and sovereignty over the Island is clear and supported by facts. It has been in possession of New Moore ever since 1970. The Island lies at a distance of barely 5.2 km, from the nearest Indian land-mass as against 7.6 km from the nearest land-mass of Bangladesh. As such it is relatively close to India than Bangladesh.

The Indian Navy made an early survey of the Island and erected identification pillars on it in 1974 in accordance with international practice. India further notified the British Admirality and the U.S. Navy about the existence of Island and its Indian ownership. Shri Inderjit, writing in *The Tribune* of 29th September 1981 (Thaw in Delhi-Dacca Ties), observed "Latest British and American naval maps show New Moore as an Indian Island. Both London and Washington are said to have taken Dacca into confidence in the matter before doing so."

During the Indo-Bangladesh talks in 1974 on the issue of delimitation of maritime boundary, India brought to the notice of Dacca neither at this stage nor at the time of subsequent talks over maritime boundary in 1975, questioned India's ownership of the Island. Even in 1978, when talks between the two countries in maritime boundary were resumed during the regime of President Zia-ur-Rehman, Bangladesh did not question the Indian claim. A little after this, the West Bengal police sent one of its patrol boats to the island and the Indian Tricolour was hoisted on the island which was now renamed as Purbasha. The occasion was enthusiastically celebrated by the people of India, especially in Calcutta. The Bangladesh press published the historic occasion in a big way with photographs.

This time Dacca reacted suddenly and sharply to the press reports taking Delhi completely by surprise. It questioned the Indian claim for the first time in 1978 and even mounted a popular agitation on this issue. It started disputing India's claim over the island. In December 1978, Dacca presented to India a US satellite map showing India, Bangladesh and the river Hariabhanga. On the basis of this map, Bangladesh staked its claim to the island as a territory on the Bangladesh side of the mutually accepted river boundary. Afterwards, in April 1979, during the visit of Prime Minister Desai to Bangladesh, the authorities in Dacca laid serious claim to the island and proposed a joint survey for determining the ownership issue. Mr. Desai, observed Inderjit, was anxious to build bridges with neighbours and hence promptly agreed to the proposal. Prime Minister Desai refused to accept his advisers' view that it was an unfair concession to Bangladesh since there existed no doubt about India's ownership of the New Moore Island and its physical occupation by India for the last 10 years. Bangladesh decided to follow-up the matter actively and in June 1979, its Deputy Prime Minister, Mr. Mandood Ahmed, during his visit to Delhi for a meeting of Joint River Commission on Farakka, pressed Delhi for a joint survey of the Island area. However, a proposal could not materialise because of the fall of Desai's Government in July 1979 and Prime Minister Charan Singh's refusal to accept Mr. Desai's line in respect of the New Moore island.

In January 1980, Mrs. Indira Gandhi returned to power in India and endorsed the stand that had earlier been taken by Mr. Charan Singh. In August 1980, the matter was rediscussed during the visit of Mr. Narasimha Rao to Dacca. A broad understanding was reached on the issue and the joint statement issued at the end of this visit noted that the two ministers had discussed the 'issue' of the island and agreed to exchange data and hold talks for resolving it.

This was regarded by India as a welcome development because Dacca was made to drop the demand for joint survey. But Dacca had its own view. It was pleased that India had conceded that the New Moore Island constituted an issue between the two countries. It was pleased because Delhi agreed to exchange data on the island. Subsequently, Bangladesh presented an up-to-date version of the satellite map and claimed its right of possession over the island.

On 14th April 1981, India sent its survey ship *Sandhayak* to New Moore for collecting fresh data. Dacca reacted a month later when it summoned Indian High Commissioner Mr. Mukh Chand Dubey to the Foreign Office and demanded withdrawal of the ship. New Delhi maintained its ownership and sovereignty over the island and advocated that the *Sandhayak* was merely performing a routine practice which was ten years old. Dacca escalated the situation on May 15 by sending two of its gunboats to the Island. Delhi reacted sharply and rushed one of its frigates-INS Andamans. Dacca reacted through holding the anti-India demonstrations on May 19. India then decided to station 30 to 40 of its armed personnel at New Moore. One move followed the other and eventually Bangladesh sent 5 of its naval ships including a frigate to the island. India responded by sending six naval ships. All this made the situation very alarming and there appeared chances of a clash between India and Bangladesh naval forces.

Fortunately, such an adverse development was averted through discussions along diplomatic channels. On September 6, 1981, in a statement issued simultaneously in Dacca and Delhi, it was announced that the two countries have succeeded in materially defusing the tension over the New Moore Island. The announcement said that the two sides also agreed to undertake all further necessary steps to remove the remaining causes of tension and resolve the issue. As agreed upon by the External Affairs Minister of India and Foreign Minister of Bangladesh in August 1980, both governments stand for a peaceful settlement of this problem. '"With a view to continue our joint efforts for a peaceful resolution of this and all other outstanding problems between Bangladesh and India and also with a desire to reinforce mutual trust, understanding and friendship between the two neighbouring countries, the External Affairs Minister of India has invited the Bangladesh Foreign Minister to visit New Delhi. The Bangladesh Foreign Minister has accepted the invitation and will be visiting Delhi within this week."

Commenting upon this announcement, *The Times of India*, in its Editorial on 8th September 1979, described the announcement as 'A Happy Turning' and observed "One reason for the welcome change in the situation may well be New Delhi's policy of combining firmness over New Moore with patience over the sustained anti-Indian campaign in Bangladesh which died down only some days ago."

On 11th September 1981, Foreign Minister of Bangladesh, Mr. Shamsul Haq arrived at New Delhi and for two days held discussions with his counterpart Mr. Narasimha Rao. He also had a meeting with Mrs. Indira Gandhi. The two Foreign Ministers agreed that this and other issues should be resolved on the basis of mutual trust and benefit. Mrs. Indira Gandhi assured

Mr. Haq that "India was committed to fostering co-operation and friendship with Bangladesh and that her approach towards solving the outstanding issues would be constructive, practical and rational." Mr. Haq also emphasised that his visit was to foster friendship and trust between the two countries. This visit further helped the two countries to defuse tension over the New Moore Island. Even before this visit, both sides had withdrawn their naval ships from the region. But Indian personnel continued to remain on the island and this situation tacitly continues even today.

The New Moore Island continues to be an issue in Indo-Bangladesh relations. Bangladesh continues to base its claim for ownership over the island on the basis of the satellite map. India is equally clear and forthright in asserting its claim which is based upon three main foundations: (*i*) That New Moore Island is closer to Indian land-mass; (*ii*) That the main channel of the Hariabhanga and the estuary flows along the eastern side of the island and not the western side as claimed by Dacca, and (*iii*) That India owns the island since its birth in 1970.

5. **Farakka Dispute:** Another major irritant in the Indo-Bangladesh relations of post-1975 era continues to be the dispute over Farakka. The Interim Agreement of April 1975 was replaced in November 1977 by another agreement on Farakka. The new Farakka Agreement had a short-term and a long-term agreement. The short-term agreement laid down the quantum of water that India was to withdraw below Farakka during the lean session in which the flow of Ganga comes down to around 55,000 cusecs. In fixing such a proportion a highly considerate and sympathetic view of Bangladesh's needs and desires was taken into consideration. The Janata government, which signed the Agreement, did not press for securing a larger quantum of Ganga water that was necessary for the health and safety of Calcutta Port. Instead, it tried to win over the friendship and co-operation of Bangladesh by giving to it certain vital concessions. The long-term agreement was for studying the alternative ways for increasing the water flow of the Ganga during the lean session. The Agreement was severely criticised by Indian Press and people because it failed to safeguard the interests of India. The Janata

Government justified the Agreement on various grounds and the short-term agreement was operationalised. For reaching a long-term agreement negotiations were opened with Bangladesh. Mrs. Indira Gandhi's Congress I returned to power in January 1980. The new Government felt that 1977 agreement was harmful to Indian interests but accepted it as a legacy of Janata rule. At the same time, it initiated speedy moves for securing a long-term final settlement over Farakka.

The Indo-Bangladesh task over the question of ways to augment the flow of Ganga, however, got deadlocked because of a big difference in the approach and ideas of the two countries. Whereas Bangladesh wanted to augment the flow of Ganga during lean session by using water stored in reservoirs which were to be constructed in Nepal, Himalayas. India advocated the construction of Brahmaputra-Ganga link Canal for achieving the desired goal. Further, whereas Bangladesh wanted to involve Nepal in negotiations over Farakka. India wanted to settle the issue bilaterally. Such a difference in approach made the Farakka talks dead-locked in 1981-82. The 1977 Agreement was for a period of five years and was to expire on 4th November, 1982. To overcome the deadlock, Prime Minister Indira Gandhi and Bangladesh President H.M. Ershad, in their summit meeting of October, 1982, reached an understanding over the nature of agreement for sharing the Ganga waters after the expiry of the 1977 Agreement. They also agreed to effect a final long-term settlement of Farakka issue through mutual negotiations. For this purpose, the Indo-Bangladesh JRC was given the responsibility to study the feasibility of all possible alternatives which can lead to the augmentation of the Ganga flow during the lean session. The JRC was also directed to complete the assignment within 18 months.

The JRC has been meeting at regular intervals for evaluating facts and data regarding the possible ways in which augmentation of Ganga waters can be secured. Its 25th meeting was held at Dacca on 18th July 1983. At this meeting both the sides were successful in reaching an *ad hoc* agreement on the sharing of Teesta waters. This agreement is to remain in force till 1985 by which date the JRC is to complete its studies. This agreement, (as revealed by the leader of Indian team Mr. R.N. Mirdha, the Union Minister of State for Irrigation in his press conference at New Delhi Airport on 20th July, 1983) divides Teesta waters in the ratio of 39: 36 per cent between India and Bangladesh and leaves 25 per cent water as unaccounted water flow. Similarly, an agreement has been reached to study the economic, technical and implementability aspects of all the proposals for augmenting the flow of Ganga below Farakka. Both sides are conducting negotiations for a peaceful, amicable and mutually beneficial solution to the problem. Prime Minister Rajiv Gandhi has initiated several moves to strengthen bilateral relations between the two countries and a welcome change in the psychological environment has appeared. Thus, it hoped that such change shall be very helpful in finding a solution to Farakka dispute.

Anti-India Propaganda in Bangladesh: In the post-Mujib era, certain sections of Bangladesh press and people have been carrying out anti-India propaganda with the vicious objective of preventing the development of harmonious, friendly, co-operative relations between the two countries. These sections are backed either by pro-Pakistan or by the pro-left lobby and by the desire to establish a support base in international politics by posing 'the danger from India'. Unfortunately, at times, the Bangladesh rulers have also been giving encouragement to such a propaganda by tolerating the anti-India tirade for securing their regimes. The legacy of the Pakistani practice of securing internal consolidation by giving air to supposed dangers from India,' continues to be followed by Bangladesh. This has, on many occasions, given a big setback to the course of Indo-Bangladesh relations, particularly during the period under review.

In fact, since the August 1975 coup anti-India propaganda has come to be regular ritual with certain sections of Bangladesh press and political parties. After the coup, it was alleged by these sections that India was behind the miscreants who were indulging in anti-social activities in Bangladesh. The Indian diplomats in Dacca were dubbed as agents and spies of India. On 26th November 1975, the Indian High Commissioner Mr. Samer Sen was shot at in Dacca by six young men. The Government of India and the Indian press strongly reacted against the dastardly attack. The Government of India sent a strong protest note to Dacca in which it warned of "serious consequences that might follow if campaign-insidious and mischievous propaganda against India; was allowed to be continued. Bangladesh then realised its responsibility and sent a delegation headed by the Justice Abdul Sattar the Special Assistant to President A.S.M. Saye, to New Delhi for high-level talks with India. The meeting between his delegation and the team of representatives of Indian External Affairs Ministry helped the sorting out of differences and misunderstandings and reaching of understanding about the situation. In a joint statement, both sides reaffirmed the view that promotion of Indo-Bangladesh friendship and co-operation on the basis of sovereign equality and mutual benefit was a common objective of both the countries and the achievement of this objective was the supreme condition necessary for peace and stability of the region as well as for the progress and well-being of their people. This high-level meeting definitely removed certain apprehensions but only temporarily. Towards the end of January 1976, once again there appeared renewed outbursts of anti-India propaganda in the Bangladesh press. The Government of India decided to take a lenient view because it felt that behind such a development were the domestic compulsions of Bangladesh. In February 1976, anti-India propaganda was stepped up in Bangladesh over the issue of Farakka Barrage. Maulana Bhashani's Awami League played a frontal role in the organising the anti-India tirade in Bangladesh. In 1981, the issue of ownership of the New Moore Island further gave rise to strong anti-India propaganda in Bangladesh. The gun-boat diplomacy under-taken by the Government of Bangladesh further made Indo-Bangladesh relations very tense. Recently, there has been strong tiff between the two countries over the issue of harassment of the Indian High Commissioner at Dacca. At the October, 1982 summit between Prime Minister Indira Gandhi and Chief Martial Law Administrator of Bangladesh, Lt. General H.M. Ershad, both the countries decided that each side must take effective steps against all such sections of the press and people as were found engaged in making false propaganda against the other country. "The summit talks between Mrs. Indira Gandhi and General

Ershad covered a wide area of understanding and mutual accommodation," observed *The Tribune*, Editorial of 9th October 1982, "which augurs well for future relations between India and Bangladesh."

However, such an understanding and goodwill between the countries still continues to be marred by the outbursts of anti-India propaganda in Bangladesh. On 1st June, 1983, a public demonstration of resentment against India was held. The rulers of Bangladesh did nothing to control it. On the contrary they seemed to have encouraged it. In this demonstration an effigy of Mrs. Indira Gandhi was burnt at Dhaka (Dacca) and a campaign against the purchase of Indian goods was launched. This anti-India campaign was launched by a committee set-up to resist the present arrangement of Farakka. This committee, in its meeting on this day, also demanded the cancellation of the 23 years Indo-Bangladesh Treaty of Peace, Friendship and Co-operation. Speeches made at meeting left little room for doubt that the anti-India campaign was well-organised and not a spontaneous outburst of anger. Earlier in May 1983, even Lt. General Ershad in his speech before a seminar had accused India of holding back Bangladesh's share of Ganga waters. This was definitely much against the letter and spirit of the Memorandum of Understanding which Lt. General Ershad had himself signed after the October, 1982 summit talks with Mrs. Indira Gandhi. Such a development, like other developments, involving anti-India propaganda, constitutes a big irritant in way of the development of Indo-Bangladesh relations. Bangladesh rulers must realise the dangers inherent in carrying out anti-India campaign in their country. Steps must be taken to prevent the outburst of false propaganda against India. India has, in the previous years, tolerated this negative feature as a compromise with the domestic turmoil's in which Bangladesh has been living since 1975, but the continuance of hate-India or criticise India campaigns in Bangladesh is bound to evoke in future strong reaction from Indian people and press. Such a development would certainly harm the cause of Indo-Bangladesh relations and hence must be prevented. The present rulers of Bangladesh must take effective steps against such a possibility. They should themselves stop using anti-India propaganda as a device for maintaining and strengthening their legitimacy. With the new determination of Rajiv Gandhi's government in respect of peaceful settlement of all outstanding issues and disputes with her neighbours and with the new positive relations in Dacca about the need for developing friendship and co-operation with India, it should be possible for both India and Bangladesh to resolve these issues amicably and in the stipulated time.

IV. Farakka Issue

With a view to flush out the silt, which entered the Calcutta Port as a result of the slow follow of the Ganga waters, and for securing an optimum utilisation of these waters, the Government of India, in 1951, decided to construct a barrage at Farakka across the Ganga and a 26-mile long feeder canal to take off from the barrage for supplementing the waters of Bhagirathi at a lower point. The Project was designed to reduce the frequency and intensity of tidal waves which move up the Hooghly and affect the shipping services at Calcutta, and to augment the supply of fresh water to Calcutta.

The Problem: This decision of Government of India was not liked by the Government of Pakistan because it felt that the construction of Farakka Barrage would adversely affect and jeopardise the economy and irrigation system of East Pakistan (Now Bangladesh) because these were dependent upon Ganga waters which entered East Pakistan just 9 miles below Farakka. The Government of Pakistan took up the matter with the Government of India and suggested that India should consult Pakistan before starting the construction of Farakka Barrage. India over ruled the objection raised by Pakistan on the grounds that the Pakistani view lacked substance, but at the same time it assured Pakistan that Farakka Barrage would in no way harm the interest of East Pakistan. India fully justified its right to utilise Ganga waters on the basis of the construction of Farakka Barrage and the Feeder Canal. Pakistan then started mounting pressure on India for sharing Ganga waters with Pakistan. During 1968-70 period, a series of talks were held between India and Pakistan for resolving the issue but no agreement could be reached.

In 1971 when Bangladesh came into existence as a sovereign independent state with the territory which previously constituted East Pakistan, the dispute over Faraka came to be an Indo-Bangladesh dispute. Being good friends, committed to maintain good neighbourliness, the two countries agreed to resolve the Farakka issue amicably through mutual negotiations. In 1972, both the countries established a Joint Rivers Commission (IRC) which was given the responsibility to formulate schemes aimed at securing equitable utilisation of common river waters between Indian and Bangladesh. In May 1975, India gave a commitment to Bangladesh that Farakka Project, which was nearing completion, will not be commissioned before an agreement on the sharing of Ganga waters was reached.

The 1975 Interim Agreement: In April 1975, India and Bangladesh entered into an Interim Agreement regarding the sharing of Ganga waters below Farakka. By this agreement India got the right to run the Feeder Canal and withdraw between 11,000 to 16,000 cusecs water during the lean session—April 21 to May 31. After this Farakka Barrage was commissioned by India but at the same time negotiations were initiated with Bangladesh securing a final settlement over Farakka. It was hoped that the existence of strong bonds of friendship and high-level of co-operation between Bangladesh under Sheikh Mujib and India under Mrs. Indira Gandhi would make it possible for the two countries to amicably settle the Farakka issue through mutual negotiations and in the spirit of mutual accommodation. However, the future was not destined to be so smooth. The murder of Sheikh Mujib on 15th August 1975 and the coup of Bangladesh gave a big setback to the course of Indo-Bangladesh relations in general and to the negotiations over Farakka in particular.

From that day till today, the dispute over Farakka continues to be an irritant in the Indo-Bangladesh relations. The Interim Agreement of 1975 failed to be a basis for future settlement of dispute. In fact, it was a patch-work which could neither satisfy the objective of securing the health of Calcutta Port nor could meet the irrigation needs of the two countries. The agreement was signed with the limited objective of enabling the running of

Feeder Canal till the determination of allocation of the minimum flow of Ganga during the lean months.

Farakka Dispute in Post-Mujib Era: In the Post-Mujib era, the atmosphere for further talks in Farakka became vitiated because of the anti-India tirade carried out of the Bangladesh Press which included the demand for a prior approval by Bangladesh of any water that India wanted to withdraw from Farakka. In February 1976, when India sent an official proposal to Dacca for discussions of the lean month discharges from Farakka, Dacca came out with the view that all such talks are bound to be meaningless so long as India continues to unilaterally withdraw Ganga Waters at Farakka. Along with such a stand, Bangladesh started highlighting the alleged ill-effects of such withdrawals on the irrigation, economic and industrial needs of the country. It even tired to internationalise the issue. Later on, Dacca realised the importance of bilateral talks on Farakka and the two rounds of talks between the officials of the two countries took place in April and May 1976. It was agreed that the two teams would jointly observe the effect of Farakka Barrage and its Feeder Canal at Haldia and Farakka. However, the opposition parties of Bangladesh in general and Maulana Abdul Hamid Khan Bhashani's Awami Party in particular, started a vicious tirade against India on the Farakka issue. At one time Maulana Bhashani threatened to cross the borders, gherao Farakka and stop its functioning. This threat could not materialise because of a strong Indian stand and Mrs. Indira Gandhi's firm declaration that "India was willing to discuss and settle the Farakka issue peacefully and any attempt to solve it through threats and agitations shall be harmful and counter-productive." The March to Farakka, as organised by Maulana Bhashani, was abandoned at Sibganj, about 5-km. from Indian border of Malda. In May, 1976, General Zia-ur-Rehman, while participating in the Islamic Ministers Conference at Islamabad, called upon the Muslim countries to support Bangladesh on the Farakka issue. In August 1976, again an attempt was made to raise this issue at the Colombo Summit of the Non-aligned nations.

Indo-Bangladesh Talks on Farakka: In the first week of September, 1976, India sent an invitation to Bangladesh for holding bilateral negotiations on Farakka. Along with it, India declared that there were to be no preconditions and negotiations were to be conducted with an open mind. The invitation was accepted by Bangladesh and Indo-Bangla talks on Farakka opened on September 8, 1976. In the talks, both the short-term and long-term aspects of Farakka issue were discussed but there could be reached no agreement because Bangladesh, by that time, had decided to internationalise the issue by moving to the U.N. for securing an agreement with India. India refused to accept the demand that pending the long-term solution, the flow of Ganga during the lean session should be restored to Bangladesh on the ground that it would amount to the closure of view that a joint study of all possibilities, including the construction of a link canal between Brahmaputra and Ganga for augmenting the flow of Ganga should be made by experts of India and Bangladesh. Later on, Bangladesh proposed that for breaking the deadlock three steps should be undertaken:

(*a*) To restore normal flow of Ganga below the Farakka Barrage.

(*b*) To work out a new interim agreement.

(*c*) To include Nepal in the Farakka negotiations.

These proposals were obviously designed to further complicate the issue and hence were rejected by India.

Dacca's View of the Farakka Dispute: In September 1976, Bangladesh issued a white paper on Farakka and highlighted its view of the adverse consequences of Farakka Barrage on the economy and agriculture of Bangladesh. In this very month, Bangladesh raised the Farakka issue at the United Nations. It requested the United Nations' Security General to include Farakka issue in the agenda of the General Assembly. On 24th September, the General Assembly of the U.N. decided to include the item in its agenda and to allocate it to the Special Political Committee for consideration. India opposed the move and felt that such a move would complicate the issue and prevent its final solution that can be reached through bilateral negotiations. In November 1976, the Special Political Committee considered the question. In it, Bangladesh advocated the view that Ganga was an international river and Indian decision to construct and utilise Farakka Barrage for its own interest was bound to affect adversely, rather it has already adversely affected, the economic interests of nearly 35 per cent of the people of Bangladesh, who inhibit the Ganga basin.

Indian View of Farakka Issue: India is strongly opposed to the Dacca's view of the Farakka issue and of the issue of rights over Ganga waters. It argued, on the basis of geographic, economic, cultural grounds the Ganga is an Indian river, which towards its final stages towards the sea entered Bangladesh. As such, India had the first and foremost right to use Ganga waters. The construction of Farakka Barrage was essential for preventing the silting of Calcutta Port and that it was in no way designed to harm the interest of Bangladesh. Bangladesh was a country with plenty of natural rainfall and hence not depended upon Ganga waters. India further criticised Bangladesh for unnecessarily involving the General Assembly into a bilateral problem between the two neighbours. It strongly repudiated the claim made by Dacca that India had no right to withdraw water at Farakka without the prior consent of Bangladesh. India, therefore, asked the U.N., to support bilateral efforts for reaching a solution to this problem.

1976 U.N. General Assembly Statement on Farakka: In November 1976, India and Bangladesh reached a consensus through mutual talks. Bangladesh thereupon withdrew its draft resolution and the Special Political Committee approved a consensus statement which was adopted by the General Assembly on November 26, 1976. The consensus statement declared: "The parties affirmed their adherence to the Declaration on the Principles of International Law concerning friendly relations and co-operation among states in accordance with the Charter of the U.N., and stressed in that regard their unalterable commitment to strengthen their bilateral relations by applying those principles in settlement of disputes. Further, the parties agreed that the situation called for an urgent solution' and decided to meet urgently at Dacca for negotiations with a view to arrive at a fair and expeditious settlement of the Farakka issue."

Though India had taken a very serious view of the attempt made by Bangladesh to internationalise the Farakka issue by raising it at U.N., yet when the consensus was reached and Bangladesh withdrew its draft resolution, it came out even more openly to solve the issue through bilateral negotiations. The final fate of the Bangladesh's move to the U.N. also vindicated the consistent and reasonable approach of India towards Farakka Issue.

Resumption of Indo-Bangladesh Talks on Farakka: After the consensus at the U.N., India and Bangladesh resumed bilateral talks on Farakka issue at Dacca on December 6, 1976. After exchange of views the talks were adjourned with the understanding that as soon as possible the two sides would meet again.

In March 1977, when the Janata Party came to power in India it was decided to speed up the process of building more friendly and co-operative relations with neighbouring countries. In the context of relations with Bangladesh, it demanded speedier efforts for resolving the Farakka issue. Consequently, in April 1977, talks between India and Bangladesh were held at Dacca and an understanding was reached on the issue of sharing of Ganga waters. The officials of the two countries were then directed to work out the details for operationalising the understanding that was reached. India was understood to have made major concessions to Bangladesh.

After two rounds of talks held in May and July 1977, both Indian and Bangladesh officials were successful in evolving a broad consensus and in further narrowing down the differences between them. By September 1977, both sides got finalised a short-term and long-term agreement over Farakka, and it was on November 5, 1977 that Indian Agriculture and Irrigation Minister, Surjit Singh Barnala and Advisor to the Bangladesh President on Flood Control and Irrigation, Rear Admiral Musharraf Husain Khan signed the Farakka Agreement between the two countries.

The Farakka Agreement, 1977: The Agreement contained a Preamble and 15 Articles. In the Preamble both sides reaffirmed their determination to promote and strengthen their relations of friendship and good neighbourliness... that both recognised the need for an interim agreement for sharing the

Ganga waters at Farakka for a solution of the long-term problem of augmenting the flow of the Ganga and hence were entering into this agreement.

The agreement provided for a short-term and a long-term solution to the problem of sharing the Ganga waters at Farakka. The short-term agreement specified the quantum of water that the two countries were to withdraw during the five months period from January to May every year. The long-term agreement committed the Governments to work out an economic and feasible scheme for augmenting the water flow of the Ganga during the lean session.

It was estimated that during the first 5 months of each year the flow of Ganga ranged between 55,000 to 98,500 cusecs with the lowest lean period between 21st to 30th April and the highest flow period between 1st to 10th January. While fixing the share of each country only 75 per cent of the estimated flow as taken as the basis. The plan of distribution was fixed as under:

	Month and period	Estimated flow at Ganga (Cusecs)	India's share (Cusecs)	Bangladesh's share (Cusecs)
Jan.	1-10	95,500	40,000	58,500
	11-20	89,750	38,500	51,250
	21-31	82,500	35,000	47,500
Feb.	1-10	79,250	33,000	46,250
	11-20	74,000	31,500	42,500
	21-28/29	70,000	30,750	39,250
March	1-10	65,250	26,750	38,500
	11-20	63,500	25,500	38,000
	21-31	61,000	25,000	36,000
April	1-10	59,000	24,000	35,000
	11-20	55,500	20,750	34,750
	21-30	55,000	20,500	34,500
May	1-10	56,500	21,500	35,000
	11-20	59,950	24,700	35,250
	21-31	65,500	26,750	38,750

It was agreed that water released to Bangladesh shall not be reduced by India below Farakka except for reasonable uses of waters and not exceeding 200 cusecs between Farakka and the point on the Ganga where both its banks are in Bangladesh (Art. 111). For observing and recording the daily flow below Farakka, and in the Feeder Canal as well as the Hardinge Bridge, a Joint Committee (JC) of the representatives of two governments was to be set up. The Joint Committee was asked to work out of the procedural details. Differences between the representatives of the two countries were to be referred to panel of experts constituted in equal partnership by the two governments.

Regarding a long-term arrangement, it was agreed that both sides shall co-operate for finding a solution to the problem of augmenting the flows of Ganga during the dry session. The Indo-Bangladesh Joint Rivers Commission (JRC estbd. 1972) was given the responsibility to undertake surveys and studies for formulating and suggesting schemes for achieving the above purpose. The two governments were to consider the recommendations made by the JRC and formulate schemes "that may be mutually agreed upon by the sides." Any difference or dispute arising out of this part of the agreement was to be resolved through mutual discussions at appropriate governmental levels.

The agreement was valid for 5 years but was to be reviewed by the two governments at the expiry of 3 years of the stipulated term and again six months before the expiry of the agreement. It could be extended for a specified period by mutual agreement and in the light of such reviews (Article XIII).

The Reactions in India and Bangladesh: At the time of signing of the agreement, Surjit Singh Barnala observed that it reflected clearly the spirit of accommodation and the desire for co-operation. He referred to the considerable sacrifice made by India for accommodating the wishes of Bangladesh and hoped that necessary steps would be undertaken speedily for activating the JRC and for finding a long-term solution for augmenting the flows of Ganga during the dry session. Admiral Khan, who signed the agreement on behalf of Bangladesh, described it was an historic agreement and a meaningful step of far-reaching importance in the way of finding a lasting solution to the problem.

However, the agreement produced a mixed reaction in India while it was praised as an agreement between two friendly neighbours for resolving a long drawn and complex problem. It was also criticised for ignoring the vital interests of India, particularly the Indian interest to save the Calcutta Port from rapid and heavy silting.

This objective required, as the experts reported, a minimum flow of 40,000 cusecs of water into Calcutta Port for flushing out the silt. The agreement was in no way near to the grant of such a quantum of Ganga water to India during the first 5 months of each year. Some observers, like Margaret Alva described it as 'sell out'. "It would affect Uttar Pradesh and Bihar in the long run and also the Calcutta Port and certain smaller towns along the banks of the river." The agreement made India concede much without adequate return. The Congress I and its leader Mrs. Indira Gandhi, who was now in opposition, strongly criticised the Agreement and charged the Janata government of having sacrificed India's vital interests and even sovereign rights. "By accepting a minority share in Ganga waters the Janata government was guilty of changing the consistent stand that India has been taking prior to 1977. Further, that the agreement was designed more to reverse the stand taken by the previous Congress I government and less to satisfy the needs and interests of India. It was executed without any regard for the opinion of the experts."

However, Prime Minister Desai while speaking in the Lok Sabha strongly defended the agreement on following grounds:

1. It is a historic agreement of extraordinary significance since it has removed a major dispute between two neighbours and has thereby helped the two countries to cement their friendship and co-operations.
2. The agreement has been reached through bilateral negotiations on the basis of mutual goodwill and on the basis of accommodation. It was checked the possibility of the inter nationalisation of the Farakka issue by Bangladesh.

3. It was an agreement based upon recognised practices of International Law and the Helsinki Rules of 1966.
4. The short-term agreement was an improvement over the interim arrangement of 1975 under which India could withdraw water between 11,000 to 16,000 cusecs.
5. The long-term agreement for taking steps for augmenting the flow of Ganga during the lean/dry session was designed to settle the problem on a permanent basis. In fact, it alone constituted the effective feasible and useful method for settling the Indo-Bangladesh differences over the rights to withdraw Ganga water below the Farakka Barrage.
6. The Government was fully alive to the need of saving the Calcutta Port from silting by providing for the flushing out of the silt with an increased flow of Ganga into the Hooghly. He observed that for this purpose 40,000 cusecs of water was not needed. Around 20,000 cusecs of water along with such other measures as dredging, river training, prevention of soil erosion etc. were needed for saving the Calcutta Port.
7. The agreement makes the responsibility of the two Governments to study all possible ways for augmenting the flow of the Ganga during the lean session.
8. The real importance of the agreement was reflected in the approach and the spirit which had made it possible. "Such an approach and spirit, if applied to the larger spectrum of our relations with Bangladesh, can lead to an ever-widening co-operation between the two countries, both bilaterally and in multi-lateral forum and it should constitute to the furtherance of our objective of promoting peace and development in the sub-continent and of working together towards a better world order.

Similarly, External Affairs Minister, Mr. Atal Behari Vajpayee defended the agreement on the ground that it honoured the commitments made by the previous Government. He commented that in the leanest season the flow of Ganga came down to 55,000 cusecs and under the circumstances it could not be expected that Bangladesh would agree to the Indian demand for 40,000 cusecs.

The opposition parties in the Lok Sabha launched a severe criticism against the Agreement. In particular, the MPs from West Bengal came out with solid objections against the Agreement. Mr. Samar Guha strongly criticised the Agreement and charged the Government of making the whole Farakka Barrage virtually useless. He felt that there was no necessity for getting the permission of Bangladesh, the lower riparian country whose share of water was less than 10 per cent, for withdrawal of water below Farakka. The Janata government, he charged, was guilty of not consulting Hydrological experts before taking a decision on Farakka. Mr. Chitta Basu moved a resolution which called upon the house to disapprove the Agreement as being inadequate for supplying water to Bhagirathi so as to save the Calcutta Port. The Janata government was, however, successful in getting the Agreement approved by the Lok Sabha.

The Follow-up: After the Agreement, India and Bangladesh kept up the efforts both for implementing it and for devising schemes for a long-term settlement. The Farakka Agreement was discussed between President Zia-ur-Rahman and Prime Minister Desai during the state visit of the former to India in December, 1977. The Joint Communiqué issued after the visit said: "They attached importance to a speedy solution of long-term problem of augmenting the flow of Ganga which was essential for adequately meeting the requirement of the two countries. They believed that the Agreement paved the way for optimum utilisation of the water resources of the region as a whole." The two leaders also discussed the Brahmaputra, Ganga Link Project as a possible means for augmenting the flow of Ganga but felt that JRC should be activated and asked to examine in detail all possible alternative proposals.

The 14th meeting of the JRC was held at Dacca in January, 1978 and various proposals were examined by it. A decision to continue the efforts was made. At the 15th meeting, the JRC decided to set up a joint committee for working out an agreement on the sharing of the Teesta water. Regarding the issue of augmenting the flow of Ganga, views were exchanged, methods of study were discussed and a decision to discuss these further was undertaken. In April Prime Minister Desai visited Dacca and discussed the issue of sharing water of Ganga and other rivers. In the joint communiqué issued after the talks, both the leaders reaffirmed that there was an immediate need for taking effective action for settling the issue of the Ganga water on the basis of the proposals that were to come from the JRC.

In January 1980, Mrs. Indira Gandhi and her Congress-I Party returned to power in India. In respect of Farakka Agreement this change gave rise to renewed criticism and opposition to the Farakka Agreement. Union Minister for Energy and Irrigation, A.B.A. Ghani Khan Choudhry in an interview on 16th January 1980, stated that the Government was examining the papers related to the Agreement for analysing whether there was anything in the Agreement of 1977 which could be regarded as a prejudicial to the interests of Calcutta Port.

Mrs. Indira Gandhi and President Zia-ur-Rahman discussed the issue of Farakka during latter's visit to India in January, 1980. Both the leaders affirmed the faith that all problems between the two countries can be resolved through bilateral talks.

The Deadlock in the Talks: The 18th meeting of JRC was held at New Delhi from 27th to 29th February 1980. The meeting brought to light many differences between the approaches of the two teams. Both sides advocated the need to review the 1977 Agreement but differed deeply in respect of the desired ends and methods. The Indian side opined that the real issue was the formulation and implementation of a project for augmenting the flow of Ganga and for this it favoured the construction of a Brahmaputra-Ganga link canal. The Bangladesh team, however, suggested the construction of water reservoirs in the Himalayas and for this advocated that India and Bangladesh should jointly approach the Government of Nepal for co-operation and participation in this direction. It rejected the Indian proposal for a link canal in the Bangladesh territory on the ground that it would seriously disturb the ecology of the region. As a result of the existence of such wide differences in approach in respect of alternatives, the JRC failed to draft an agreed report. The talk became deadlocked and the meeting of the JRC was adjourned.

Even the resumed meeting in April 1980 failed to break the deadlock. The Government of India voiced its dissatisfaction over the attempts of Bangladesh to distort the Farakka accord and to involve Nepal into the negotiations over Farakka. In April 1980, Mrs. Indira Gandhi observed that the 1977 Agreement was not in India's interest and it has to be looked into afresh. The Government of Bangladesh, though agreed with the need to review the Agreement. Outrightly disapproved the Indian scheme for augmenting the flow of Ganga through Brahmaputra Ganga link canal. Instead, it repeated the proposal for the building of reservoirs in Nepal. Because of the continuance of such big differences, the next meeting of the JRC, which was held in July 1978, also failed to reach any agreement. The leaders of the two teams—Indian Irrigation Minister Kedar Pandey and Water Resources and Flood Control Minister of Bangladesh Kazi Anwar-ul-Haq, agreed that discussions at higher level were required for breaking the deadlock. In November, 1980, two rounds of talks, first at Dacca and second at Delhi were held but both the countries failed to complete a review of the Farakka Agreement. The talks revealed that there were strong differences between the two countries over the implications of Farakka Agreement, and also regarding the possible long-term solutions. India rejected the Bangladesh view because it unnecessarily wanted to involve Nepal, and Bangladesh rejected Indian view on the ground that construction of link canal was not in the interest of Bangladesh.

On 4th April 1981, the JRC agreed to refer the issue to the respective Governments for a solution at the highest and political level. The Government of Bangladesh thereupon demanded that India should not operate Farakka Barrage without a new treaty, but the Government of India rejected this demand. The Farakka issue as such once again became a dispute between India and Bangladesh. It became a political dispute which got further complicated and hot when in mid-1981, India and Bangladesh appeared to be heading for a clash over the issue of ownership of the New Moore Island. This crisis was successfully defused in September/October 1981 through mutual diplomatic talks but this again left Farakka as the most complicated single dispute between

India and Bangladesh. The 21st meeting of Indo-Bangladesh JRC was held in February 1982 at Dacca. The issue of sharing the waters of Teesta river was discussed between the two sides. The discussion gave rise to possibility of an Indo-Bangladesh Agreement over this issue. Mr. Kedar Pandey told newsmen, "We are near a solution." However, this meeting failed to reach any consensus regarding the settlement of Farakka issue. Soon afterwards it became known that Government of India, after taking into account the experience of first five years, has come to the conclusion that it would not be possible to extend the present terms and conditions of the Farakka agreement because this agreement had proved to be harmful for Calcutta Port. Such a stand of the Government of India, and the regularity with which some newspapers of Bangladesh were carrying out anti-India propaganda further reduced the chances of an extension of Farakka Agreement. The intimidation and harassment of the Indian High Commissioner, Mr. Muchkund Dubey by the security authorities in Dacca on 25th February 1982, further damaged the course of Indo-Bangladesh relations and consequently, made the settlement of Farakka issue more difficult. In March 1982, Bangladesh proposed the reactivation of the standing committee for discussing the sharing of water between India and Bangladesh. This proposal gave rise to a fresh hope that Bangladesh was now prepared to resolve the issue through bilateral talks in May 1982. External Affairs Minister, Narasimha Rao visited Dacca and held important discussions with his counterpart on the issues of sharing of Ganga water, control over 'Tin Bigha', demarcation of boundary and the ownership of New Moore Island. The visit helped the removal of certain misgivings and both the sides reaffirmed their faith in the settlement of disputes through mutual consent. However, the meeting failed to bridge the gap fully. Bangladesh continued to maintain its earlier stand. Its representative at the U.N. Environment Programme meeting in Nairobi observed: "The use of Ganga water by India had serious effects on the economy, ecology and the overall environment in our country."

In August 1982, four-day talks between the two countries were held and a decision to continue efforts to find a mutually acceptable solution to the Ganga water's issue, was announced. The joint statement issued at the end of the talks said, "The two sides achieved greater understanding on the elements to be taken into account to find an equitable solution to the issue." The two sides decided to meet, as often as necessary at appropriate levels to find its solution. Commenting upon the outcome of this decision. *The Indian Express* in its editorial on September 2, 1982 wrote: Towards a Sane Decision: The Indo-Bangla talks on the Eastern rivers, just concluded in Dacca, have widened the area of understanding and prepared the ground for a Summit level meeting between General Ershad and Mrs. Indira Gandhi in Delhi later this year when discussions will centre on a formula for sharing the lean season flow of the Ganga below Farakka following the expiry of the 1977, accord on November 4. The Dacca round was noteworthy for having achieved some movement on the sharing of waters of some of the other smaller common rivers flowing into Bangladesh from Tripura and Cachar and, more particularly, the Teesta. Both sides have undertaken or proposed projects on several of these rivers Phase I of the Indian Teesta Project and barrages in the Khowai and Gomati should be ready for commissioning within the next 12 to 18 months. Further discussion and exchange of data has been remitted back to the Joint Rivers Commission which is expected to meet and report on these matters before the end of the year. This is an important gain, for if a climate of mutual trust and co-operation can be engendered, it will most certainly facilitate mutual accommodation on proposals for augmenting Ganga flows and an interim accord on sharing available summer supplies in the meantime.

"India seems inclined to link any interim arrangement with an accord on a framework for augmentation of Ganga flow. Expedition on this would be to mutual advantage and the most fruitful way to proceed would be for both sides jointly to examine the augmentation proposals already tabled by either party along with any other newer ideas on the subject. There is no reason to view the two sets of proposals previously exchanged as mutually exclusive they are complementary and necessary in any case and need to be phased in an integrated development programme.

The package could extend to a variety of water-related and other trade offers which would be mutually beneficial and forge numerous ties of co-operation and friendship."

"A solution of the eastern waters question is not primarily an engineering but a political question. What is involved is a determination of Indo-Bangla relationship in a number of areas over time."

The Summit Meeting of 1982 and the Memorandum of Understanding on Farakka: It was in October, 1982, during the Summit meeting between Lt Gen. H.M. Ershad and Prime Minister Indira Gandhi that an understanding on the sharing of water below Farakka after the expiry of 1977 agreement was reached. A Memorandum of Understanding on Farakka was signed and it provided; "While the 1977 Agreement will expire on November, 4 this year, the monitoring and inspection provisions, as also the elaborate system evolved for sharing of waters on Farakka during the lean session starting January, 1 till May 31, 1983 may be retained for a period of 18 months within which time experts from the two countries were to prepare feasibility studies on the long-term proposals". This time-bound decision was expected to lead to an agreement regarding the proposal for augmenting the flow of Ganga during the lean months. In fact, the long-term settlement for sharing of Ganga water below Farakka can be finally made only by accepting the importance of Ganga waters for both the countries and by dividing this water in such proportion as may enable the two countries to secure their respective interests in the Ganga basin area. The requirement of equitable share can be met only by augmenting the flow of Ganga during the lean session either by building Brahmaputra-Ganga link canal as proposed by India or by the construction of storage reservoir as proposed by Bangladesh. The joint feasibility studies agreed upon, for the first time, offered the hope for a mutually agreed long-term settlement.

"The return to bilateral efforts," wrote *The Tribune* in its Editorial on October 9, 1982 "will also enable India to convince Bangladesh about the mutually beneficial project to build a 200-mile canal linking Brahmaputra to Ganga in Indian and Bangladesh territories which will give the latter all the water it needs." In fact, the area of understanding and mutual accommodation covered during the Summit meeting, which included an agreement regarding the perpetual lease of 'Tin Bigha' to Bangladesh and an *ad hoc* agreement on Farakka, besides the welcome return to bilateralism, have rise to the hope that India and Bangladesh would be in a position to solve the Farakka issue bilaterally and amicably. This meeting definitely ushered Indo-Bangladesh relations into an era in which more fruitful co-operation between the two countries could be envisaged.

The Attempts to Resolve the Farakka Dispute: In December, 1982, a meeting of the Indo-Bangladesh JRC was held and it yielded an agreement for the establishment of a Committee to look into all the proposals for the augmentation of the lean session flow of the Ganga. The Committee was asked to prepare a time-bound schedule of work within the next few weeks. Commenting upon this development, *The Indian Express* in its Editorial on 25th December 1982 wrote: "Earlier rigidities appear to have eased Bangladesh is now prepared to look at the Brahmaputra-Ganga link canal proposed by this country while India seems ready to consider the Bangladesh proposal for Himalayan storages in Nepal which will necessarily entail a joint approach to that country at some stage, initially for data and later on, for substantive co-operation India believes that a transition from bilatcral to tripartite discussions might only complicate things further. This is, however, an exaggerated fear and it is possible Nepal's participation in joint talks might help break the Indo-Nepalese logjam on water resources development in the Kamali, Kosi and other river basins. The JRC has also made further progress in its deliberations on the joint sharing of the Teesta and other common rivers, notably the Gumti (in Tripura), and it is possible that a firm agreement may be reached at its next meeting. This would be highly significant as an agreement on the co-operative development of these smaller rivers could play a very important part in confidence-building and demonstrate the benefits of working together."

The Commission held deliberations in an atmosphere characterised by goodwill and understanding. The leader of the Bangladesh team, Agriculture Minister, Obaidullah Khan observed,

"This time we have agreed to seriously and objectively study each other's proposals." Mr. Kedar Pandey, the Indian Irrigation Minister said, "There is now a definite and specific dateline for us." Mr. Z.R. Ansari, Minister of State for Irrigation said, "Past, we have entered a new era in our relations with the signing of the Memorandum of Understanding. We are now working in a spirit of goodwill to solve a long outstanding problem."

In March 1983, another meeting of the Indo-Bangladesh JRC was held but it failed to conclude an agreement on the modalities for further examination of the proposals put forward by either side for augmenting the lean session flow of the Ganga above Farakka. Nevertheless, both the sides were able to discuss freely the whole issue and the differences between them were narrowed down.

Commenting upon the outcome of the meeting. *The Times of India* wrote in its issue of March 10, 1983, "The differences have narrowed down and there is an undercurrent of hope that the matter will be clinched at the meeting. It has already been agreed that each side will examine the scheme proposed by the other. India has suggested north storages on the Brahmaputra and Barak and an inter-basin transfer from the Brahmaputra to Ganga through a link canal. Bangladesh has proposed a dozen or so Ganga storages, in the Nepal-Himalaya, India has baulked at a joint Indo-Bangladesh approach to Nepal as suggested by Dacca, on the ground that the issue is the best settled bilaterally, with Delhi talking to Kathmandu directly with regard to the harnessing of any rivers in Nepal. The Nepalese for their part do not want to enter into the Indo-Bangladesh controversy but have indicated that they will consider a joint approach at the last meeting of the JRC there was some reference to a possible via media, namely, that India and Bangladesh, each may approach Nepal separately with a request that it be permitted to make a site inspection for purposes of a feasibility study and that the requests be so timed as to facilitate and actually result in a joint inspection."

"If this formula is acceptable to all concerned, the matter may be amicably settled...."

"Fortunately, the JRC meeting has registered somewhat greater progress on sharing Teesta water and satisfactory progress in reportedly being made in joint studies relating to the harnessing of the common rivers between Bangladesh and the Cachar-Tripura Mizoram region of India. Co-operation on the smaller rivers could help promote mutual confidence and illustrate the advantages of working together in order to ensure optimal benefits."

This editorial rightly summed up the whole issue as it stands today India and Bangladesh are now committed to solve the Farakka problem peacefully through negotiations in the spirit of goodwill and good neighbourliness. Through mutual accommodation both the countries should come forward to settle the issue. A great deal of time has already been lost. An expeditious settlement is of the essence. The 25th meeting of the JRC was held at Dacca on July 18, 1983. The Indian team was led by Mr. R.N. Mirdha, Union Minister of State for Irrigation and the Bangladesh side by Mr. Obaidullah Khan, the Agriculture Minister of Bangladesh. This meeting was successful and both the sides signed an *ad hoc* agreement on the issue of sharing of the Teesta water during the dry session. This agreement allocated 39 per cent water to India, 36 per cent to Bangladesh and left 25 per cent as unallocated water. This agreement is to be valid up to October, 1985. The JRC has been trying to sort out the river water issue in its regular meetings. Regarding the Farakka issue both sides agreed to study, "The economic, technical and implementability aspects of the proposals of the two countries for augmenting the flow of Ganga below Farakka."

Indo-Bangladesh Ganga Waters Accord: After a year of stalemate India and Bangladesh were successful in reaching an agreement on sharing of Ganga waters for the next three years. The breakthrough came after Prime Minister Rajiv Gandhi's meeting with Bangladesh President H.M. Ershad on October 18, 1985 at Nassau (Bhamas). The two leaders also agreed to undertake a joint study of the augmentation of Ganga waters soon after the finalisation of the terms of reference of the agreement. Both sides came forward to relent on their earlier stands. On the basis of this understanding a Memorandum of Understanding was signed by the two sides in New Delhi on

November 22, 1985. It was agreed that the joint study would identify alternatives for the sharing of the water resources common to both countries to the mutual benefit. This would include a long-term scheme or a scheme for augmentation of the flow of Ganga at Farakka, and on the sharing of the Ganga waters available at Farakka for the next three dry seasons.

Border Demarcation and Indo-Bangladesh Relations: On April 20, 1986, the two countries resolved to expedite the demarcation of the 60.8 acres Muhuri Char land below the South Tripura border town of Belonia. The sides, however differed on the outstanding issues of the dispute. Bangladesh kept up protesting against the construction of the revetment work and the 1.2-km, embankment of the India side on the ground that "it would prejudice the demarcation of boundary" of the disputed Muhuri Char. India overruled the protest and instead asked Bangladesh to stop the "unprovoked firing" by its forces upon Indian workers and justified the construction work, which was of temporary nature and which was fully covered by the provisions of the Indira-Mujib Pact of 1974. India further advocated the view that the revetment work was essential as a part of "anti-erosion measures which were necessary to meet the erosion threat posed by revetment work done by Bangladesh. The bilateral-relations, as such, got strained over the issue.

Ershad's Visit to India in July 1986: In July 1986, the Bangladesh President Lt. General H.M. Ershad visited India and conducted wide ranging talks with the Indian leaders. The two countries agreed to co-operate in checking cross-border insurgency and resolved to find an amicable solution to the river water issue. Bangladesh further agreed to take back all measures for enabling the Chakma tribals, who have illegally entered Tripura. Prime Minister Rajiv Gandhi and President Ershad agreed the negotiations on the maritime boundary between the two countries in the Bay of Bengal region be resumed. They also considered steps necessary for giving an impetus to the economic relations as well as accepted the need for an early convening of the Joint Economic Commission, India, further assured Bangladesh of its commitment to transfer the 'Tin Bigha' enclave. "The talks were held in an atmosphere of cordiality" which led to "a greater degree of understanding between the two countries and a willingness to co-operate in solving bilateral problems." The two countries agreed to hold further talks on demarcation of maritime boundary between them and to co-operate in putting down border insurgency. Bangladesh agreed to take back the Chakma refugees (around 18,000 in number) in India.

Farakka issue, however, continues to be the major problem of Indo-Bangladesh relations. It is hoped that the two countries would be successful in resolving the issue through mutual efforts. The commitment to keep up and strengthen further the friendly co-operation between the two countries provides a good basis for this prophecy. Currently, Bangladesh is passing through a tough time because of internal troubles. The opposition parties are making it increasingly difficult for President Ershad to keep limited the democratic aspirations of the people of Bangladesh. This factor can be a source of strains for Indo-Bangladesh relations, as internal problem can force Ershad either to adopt a rigid attitude or to keep pending the issue of foreign relations.

5
Sri Lanka

I. Background

The resplendent Island of Ceylon was often a victim of foreign invasions all through her history. The Sinhalese Kings were compelled to submit to the domination of the Pallavas, Cholas, the Chinese. Malayans and Burmans at different intervals before the advent of the European elements. The merchants from Egypt and the Western countries were attracted by the fabulous wealth in gems and the spices that were abundantly available in the Island. The Portuguese were in the first Europeans to create the settlement in Ceylon.

When the Portuguese landed on the shores of the Island in 1505, Kotte was the capital of the lowland Sinhalese. Kandy was the capital of the highland Sinhalese. Therefore, the highland Sinhalese are called the Kandyans. The Portuguese navigator Dom Lourenco de Almeida arrived at Colombo on 15th November 1505. It appears that the king of Kotte, Vira Parakrma Bahu VIII, was so weak that he was unable to protect his subjects against the incursions of the foreign races like the Moors in Colombo, the Tamils in Jaffna, and also the Sinhalese chiefs who were engaged in mutual wars in the highlands. Therefore, he asked the Portuguese, who had brought with them the large ship leads of Western arms, to protect the lowland Sinhalese. In return for the Portuguese protection the Sinhalese were to pay an annual tribute in the form of cinnamon which had great demand in the European markets. The Portuguese readily accepted this offer to promote their own interests. Very soon Portuguese fortifications appeared everywhere commencing from the city of Colombo, which was the centre of various foreign settlements.

The Portuguese settlements in Ceylon were to be administered by a resident Captain-General, who was subordinate to the Portuguese Government at Goa. The Portuguese enjoyed the monopoly of the Ceylonese Coasts forever 150 years.

During the 150 years stay of the Portuguese in Ceylon they had to confront several difficulties in exercising their control. The proud highlanders or the Kandyans did not tolerate the alliance between the King of Kotte and the Portuguese. The king of Sitawaka, Rajasinha I of the highlands became furious on hearing the brutalities of the Portuguese against those who opposed their authority. Rajasinha attacked Kotte and drove its king to Colombo. After having defeated the Portuguese, Rajasinha besieged the city of Colombo. He inflicted a severe defeat on the Portuguese. He also attacked and defeated the Kandyan king and drove him away from his capital. He was able to organise an excellent army and a navy. He established his authority all over Ceylon except the kingdoms of Colombo and Jaffna. However, he was defeated by a Sinhalese king.

After 1560 the Portuguese ascendancy in Ceylon began to spread unrestrained. It is believed that they captured the Sacred Tooth relic of Lord Buddha from Jaffna and it was taken to Goa. Regarding its return to Ceylon divergent views are held by the scholars. One version is that the Sacred Tooth relic was burned by the Archbishop of Goa and that one reported to have been returned to Ceylon and now preserved at the Temple in Kandy is a fake one. The other version is that the Tooth relic was miraculously saved from the Portuguese and that the one captured by them at Jaffna was not the original one. Whatever might be the truth about this episode the Portuguese had relentlessly suppressed the Buddhists, who enjoyed supreme control over the Sinhalese in every matter. The Portuguese made every effort to spread Roman Catholicism in the island. The natives were converted to Catholicism by them. The fabulous wealth of the island in gems, cinnamon, areca nuts, pepper, and the elephants, was greedily exploited.

The Portuguese monopoly was challenged by the Dutch not only in Ceylon but in the entire eastern waters. The Dutch won over the rulers of Kandy to their side in an attempt to drive the Portuguese out of the Island. The Portuguese were forced to surrender to the Dutch in 1656 when Colombo succumbed to the siege of the Dutch. Prom 1656 to 1796 the Dutch were able to enjoy the trade monopoly in the Island. They controlled most of the coastal cities and built fortifications on the Island. The Dutch East India Company of Amsterdam exercised control over the Dutch possessions in Ceylon through military governors. However, the Governor of Ceylon was subordinate to the Dutch Governor-General of Java. The Dutch introduced certain administrative changes by dividing Ceylon into provinces. They administered the territories under their control through a civil service. But they did not interfere with the local institutions under the Sinhalese chiefs.

The Sinhalese did not submit to Dutch without offering any resistance. The king of Kandy Rajasinha II harassed them by inflicting a brutal treatment. The Dutch ports and fortifications were attacked frequently. Therefore, the Dutch carefully concentrated their activities in the sea ports of Matara and Jaffna. The French Revolution influenced the European politics profoundly and the Dutch had to renounce their political interests in Ceylon and elsewhere in the east. The Dutch introduced a code of Roman Dutch law in Ceylon. They also set up missionary schools and churches. However, regarding the general welfare of the Sinhalese the Dutch evinced no interest to improve their conditions. Further, the Dutch influence in Ceylon was affected by the growth of the British East India Company. In 1796 the Dutch Governor in Ceylon surrendered to the British.

The British interests in Ceylon were not to acquire the monopoly of spice trade but to establish a naval base to protect their enlarged eastern possessions. For obtaining the naval port of Trincomalee the British had approached the king of Kandy as early as 1763. The French were also contemplating on the same. But it was captured by the British after a naval attack in 1782. Though it was returned to the Dutch very soon the British were offered an excellent opportunity when the king of Kandy Rajadhirajasinha sought an alliance with them against the Dutch.

Taking advantage of this situation the British captured Trincomalee, Jaffna, Negombo and even Colombo by February 1796. This confirmed the British supremacy in Ceylon. The newly-acquired possessions were governed by the British military Governors, who were subordinate to the Governor resident of the East India Company at Madras. Gradually, the British introduced administrative changes and employed the Indian Civil Servants in the Ceylonese administration.

Unlike the Portuguese and the Dutch, the British interfered with the Local Government of the Ceylonese. This attitude provoked the Ceylonese all over the Island. They organised serious insurrections against the corrupt British rule and their disregard for the traditions. On account of these developments the Ceylonese administration was taken over by the crown in 1798. Frederick North was appointed first Civil Governor of Ceylon. However, his regime was not peaceful. The political intrigues of the pretenders to the local throne often disturbed peace which resulted in chaos and disorder. Lawlessness was the order of the day. Sri Wickrama Rajasinha who ruled Kandy from 1798 to 1815 made a final bid to put an end to the British supremacy in Ceylon. He fought bloody wars with the British. But he was defeated and captured by the British on 14th February 1815. He was the last king of his dynasty which came to an end when he was deported to Madras. With the fall of Sri Wickrama Rajasinha the British were left unquestioned masters of Ceylon. They introduced administrative reforms and laid the roads to connect the important places. As a crown colony Ceylon came to enjoy an advantageous position than what she could under the Portuguese and the Dutch traders. It formed an integral part of the British Empire.

The Colebrooke and Cameroon reforms of 1833 removed all the vestiges of feudalism in Ceylon. They established uniformity in the administration of the three provinces of Ceylon. (The Sinhalese Maritime Provinces, the Tamil Maritime Provinces, and the Kandyan provinces). In the judicial field also uniformity was introduced and the courts were separated from the executive. The Governor was assisted by his executive and legislative councils in administering the territory. English education was introduced and it became the official language. Very soon some of the Ceylonese learned English and began to take interest in the administration. No doubt the legislative council introduced by the Colebrooke and Cameroon reforms formed the preliminary step towards a parliamentary system in Ceylon. But the legislative council was not vested with the necessary powers. It was only an advisory body. There was dissatisfaction among the Ceylonese, who demanded liberal reforms in every sphere. At the same time, there were also several European planters and merchants who had been interested in obtaining reforms. In fact petitions and appeals were presented by them to the Governor. In these the Government was urged to reconstitute the legislative council in order to include more non-official members so that it may obtain a representative character. The legislative council was to be given greater powers. Further, they also demanded the reduction in the large sums set apart for military expenditure from the Ceylonese revenues. The British import duty on Ceylon coffee was to be reduced so as to enable the planters in Ceylon to get more profits. Thus, in the 19th century the British administration in Ceylon was not free from local resistance and attacks. Serious demonstrations and uprisings were organised compelling the Government to bring liberal reforms. Instead the administration suppressed the risings mercilessly. The situation was discussed in the British House of Commons and the British policy was criticised by the eminent parliamentarians like Disraeli and Gladstone.

There was no communication between the rulers and the ruled. The people were not consulted in the administration of their land. The bureaucracy had been negligent to contact the people in the remote areas. They were extremely corrupt. Added to these the arrival of the European settlers and the acquisitions of vast areas of land to raise plantations affected the interests of the local population. Some of the officials themselves possessed vast areas of plantations. Naturally, they were totally indifferent towards their official duties. All these were mainly responsible to produce feelings of resentment among the Ceylonese. Therefore, several reforms were introduced by the British in the 19th century to appease the local interests. In the latter part of the 19th century Dr. Elliot the Editor of the newspaper 'Colombo Observer' led a movement demanding popular control of the Legislative Council of Ceylon. But it may be pointed out that Ceylon was a land divided. It composed of the varied population like the Sinhalese, Tamils, Moors, European Burghers and other factions. They did not identify themselves as a nation. Such a divergent population could not present an effective resistance to the British. Knowing this fully well the British ignored all such demands that came from the divided people in the 19th century.

II. Nature of Indo-Sri Lanka Relations

In respect of Sri Lanka, Indian Foreign Policy has always has governed by the desire and assure Sri Lanka that India fully respects the sovereignty and integrity of Sri Lanka. Moreover, India is keen to cement the traditional, cultural and trade ties by taking concrete steps towards the development of a more meaningful friendship and fruitful co-operation between the two countries.

Prime Ministers Nehru, Mrs. Indira Gandhi and Mr. Rajiv Gandhi took keen interest to maintain peace and friendship with Sri Lanka. So also the DMK and AIADMK governments in Tamil Nadu took sympathetic attitude towards Sri Lanka. In short, the Indian leaders have always been at pains to assure Sri Lanka that India fully accepts and respects the sovereign equality of Sri Lanka and its state as an important and equal member of the community of Nations.

Both the Sinhalese and Tamilians, who constitute respectively the 70 per cent and 12 per cent of Sri Lanka's total population, accept their traditional links with India. The Sinhalese accept themselves as the descendents of the Aryans of North India and the Tamilians accept themselves as the descendants of the Dravidians of South India. The Sinhalese language bears the influence of Hindi. Similarly the Tamilians speak Tamil—the language of a large number of Indians living in the South. Buddhism was introduced in Sri Lanka by India and even till today it continues to be the religion of the majority of the people of Sri Lanka. The National Day celebrations of Sri Lanka commence with a religious ceremony at Sri Mahabodhi, the sacred tree that was grown from a sapling from the Bodhi tree brought in the third century from Bodh Gaya in North India. Such cultural links between the people of the two countries have been a source of strength and have helped them to better understand and adjust with each other.

The similarities in the foreign policy of the two countries again constitute a helping and positive factor in Indo-Sri Lanka relations.

Both have, over the past 38 years, forged important economic, trade, industrial, communication and cultural links.

Both have successfully resolved the issue of demarcation of the Maritime Boundary and ownership of Kachhativu island in a spirit of mutual reconciliation and adjustment.

Both the countries have a similar perception about the desired status of Indian Ocean as a zone of peace.

The peaceful way in which both the countries reached agreements for repatriation of the people of Indian origin in Sri Lanka, also has been a source of satisfaction. Both have willingly shared their respective responsibilities towards the decision regarding the status of the stateless persons in Sri-Lanka.

Both are committed to Non-alignment; both have firm faith in Panchsheel: both are opposed to colonialism and radicalism.

The following factors and disputes have been the source of fear, suspicion and tension in Indo-Sri Lankan relations during the past 45 years:

1. Sri Lanka's fear of India and the complex that being a small country its interests and security is bound to be dependent upon the interests and policy objectives of India, has been a hindering factor in Indo-Sri Lankan relations.
2. The slow progress towards the implementation of agreement regarding the repatriation and settlement of people of Indian origin and the recent differences over the fate of the previous agreement over this issue, has been another hindering factor in Indo-Sri Lanka relations.
3. India believes that it has the right and the need to develop nuclear technology for peaceful purposes and as such is opposed to the Non-Proliferation Treaty (NPT).

India conducted its first PNE in May 1974 and holds that if necessary it shall conduct more such explosions for implementing the peaceful nuclear energy utilisation programme which is essential for promoting the prosperity and welfare of its people. Sri Lanka, on the other hand, feels otherwise and wants that India should sign the NPT. It did not look with favour the 1974 peaceful nuclear explosion conducted by India. Much to the dislike of India, Sri Lanka currently even supports the Pakistani demand for making South Asia nuclear free zone.

4. The existence of subversive elements in Sri Lanka, which become active at times, to demand autonomy/statehood for certain areas which are inhabited by minorities (mostly Tamil speaking people), has been a source of irritation in Indo-Sri Lankan relations because a section of the people of Sri-Lanka, consisting of mostly Sinhalese and the members of ruling elite, feels that the insurgents and terrorists operating in their country have their roots and bases in India.
5. Sri Lanka was on the first few countries who supported the demand for making the Indian Ocean a Zone of Peace. At the moment Sri Lanka, however, appears to be a little hesitant in making determined efforts for securing this objective. Behind this lack of efforts on its part is the fear that countries like India, and even China, would try to fill the power vacuum after the elimination of super power naval presences in the Indian Ocean. Sri Lanka, therefore, wants that the declaration of Indian Ocean as a Zone of Peace must also involve a commitment from the littoral states that none of them would increase its naval presence and strength in the area of Indian Ocean.
6. The desire of Sri Lanka to play safe and keep at a safe distance from both India and China, has also been a hindering factor in Indo-Sri Lanka relations. In the sixties, Sri Lanka even tried to secure friendship with China as a counterpoise to India.

These negative factors have been responsible for the slow progress of Indo-Sri Lankan co-operation in various spheres. At time, there had been responsible for generating tensions and strains for Indo-Sri Lankan relations.

III. History of Indo-Sri Lanka Relations Till 1985

While commenting upon the history of Indo-Sri Lanka relations, Dr, S.C. Gangal in his article: Indo-Lanka Ties Ambivalent (*The Tribune*, 3rd July 1982) writes: "Indeed during the last 30 years Indo-Sri Lanka relationship has been marked by a sort of ambivalence—an alternation between warmth, goodwill and co-operation on the one hand, and fear, suspicion and political and territorial disputes on the other." Such a conclusion is fully supported by the facts of Indo-Sri Lanka relations since 1948.

A study of the history of relations between these two South Asian states, which have strong cultural links between them, reveal that on the one hand, they have been successful in reaching agreements and resolving disputes through peaceful negotiations and in the spirit of mutual accommodation but on the other hand, there has been continuously present a sense of fear, suspicion and political problems and disputes between them. Even after 38 years of peaceful, friendly and co-operative living as India's South Asian neighbour, Sri Lanka continues to regard India as a critical factor in the South Asian regional power system and as a potential power which can inflict at will any harm to the security and other interest of Sri Lanka.

The recent tensions over the Tamil problem in Sri Lanka have once again made Indo-Sri Lanka relations somewhat strained and tense. The Colombo outburst against Indian nationals and property during the July, 1983, riots, once again brought chilling winds for the bilateral relations of the two countries. Since her independence, Sri Lanka has been in search of a counterpoise which can match or neutralise the growing power of India as a major power in South Asia. It continues to fear India as a state which can harm or limit the freedom of action and choice of Sri

Lanka. It is on record that Mr. Jaywardene, the President of Sri Lanka once remarked: "if some tyrant should get hold of India and wants to invade Ceylon, nothing on the earth is going to stop the invasion," Undoubtedly, it is a conditional statement, yet it clearly reveals that Sri Lanka accepts the possibility of an invasion by India. This factor, along with many other differences over the fate of stateless persons of Indian origin, the issue of alleged Indian support for Tamilian separatists in Sri Lanka, the nature of Indian Ocean as a peace zone and the issue of trade imbalances between the two countries, continue to be the sources of suspicion, tensions and strains in Indo-Sri Lanka relations. However, the existence of traditional links, similarities in policies and the realisation for the need of each other's help and support have been a source of strength which has helped the two countries to resolve the conflict over a number of issues—peacefully and through bilateral agreements. The steps initiated by Prime Minister, Mr. Rajiv Gandhi for allaying Sri Lankan fears and for stepping up Indo-Sri Lanka co-operation are bound to usher their relations into an era of new understanding, friendship and co-operation. During the past 38 years, the two countries have been successful in securing some important and major agreements which have been a source of big satisfaction for the two countries.

India became independent in 1947 and this paved the way for Sri Lanka's independence in 1948. The decision of England to leave Sri Lanka was prompted by the need to end the waste of efforts and resources in maintaining control over a small state after its withdrawal from India.

Both India and Sri Lanka got their independence from the British rule at about the same time, yet the objective was achieved in different ways and conditions. India attained independence from the yoke of British imperialism through a determined and strong national movement. As against this, Sri Lanka did not have to work that hard for securing its independence. It got independence because of the British decision to withdraw from South Asia.

After their liberations, both India and Sri Lanka decided to join the Commonwealth but on different grounds. India decided to remain in the Commonwealth for maintaining economic, trade and cultural links with Britain and members of the Commonwealth. As against this, Sri Lanka's decision to join the Commonwealth was designed to be a means for safeguarding its security interests against the 'possible invasion' from India and for not accepting a power vacuum in Indian Ocean area which involved the possibility of a march of communism in this area. The fear of communism also influenced Sri Lanka's decision to join the Commonwealth. In fact, during the initial years of independence the leaders of Sri Lanka's ruling United National Party shared the American view of containing communism and as such never hesitated to take a pro-West stand on almost all the cold war issues.

Between 1948-56, Sri Lankan Foreign Policy had a distinct bias in favour of the West. This was there despite the declarations made by the Prime Ministers of Ceylon that they would pursue the policy of middle path or Non-alignment. This pro-west bias of Sri Lanka became most evident during the Korean crisis. In the Korean war, on the one hand, Ceylon argued that it was a conflict between the Soviet Union and the U.N., and as Ceylon was not a member of the U.N., it was for U.N. to settle it, on the other hand, it granted permission to American warships to touch Colombo on their way to Korea on the plea that "They were engaged in opposing aggression by International Communism". Similar was the case during the Vietnam War. It permitted airport facilities to American globe masters carrying troops to Vietnam on the ground that they were going to "check the danger of Communist advance and expansionism."

Despite the resentment expressed by the opposition parties, Prime Minister John Kotelawala insisted on equating 'Soviet Colonialism' with Western Imperialism at the Bandung Conference. The signing of a defence pact with Britain and acceptance of the U.S. blessed Peace Treaty with Japan in 1951, were definitely at variance with the doctrine of Panchsheel and policy of Non-alignment as propounded by Nehru. Such aspects of Sri Lanka's foreign policy perceptions and actual behaviour at international level were totally different from the balanced approach of India. India at that time favoured equidistance from both the super-powers and their blocs. Nehru regarded Sri Lanka's foreign policy as not a policy of real Non-alignment. This difference in foreign policies of the two countries and certain other negative factors checked the development of Indo-Sri Lankan friendship and co-operation during 1948-56.

The Initial Irritants: Sri Lanka's fear of 'Indian expansionism', the complex regarding the small population and size of Sri Lanka as compared with India, the existence of the minority problem in Sri Lanka, Sri Lanka's fear regarding the emergence of Communist movement in South India, the suspicions regarding the demand for a separate state by the DMK of India, and the differences over the issue of citizenship of the people of Indian origin in Sri Lanka, further prevented the growth of Indo-Sri Lanka relationship during this period. The expression of sympathies for the rights of Tamils of Sri Lanka by the leaders of DMK and some other persons, like C. Rajagopalachari, further made things difficult for the course of Indo-Sri Lankan relations. In addition to all these, the Sri Lankan Prime Ministers, particularly D.S. Senanayake and John. Kotelawala, suffered from personal complexes against Nehru and were not keen to open out with the Government of India led by Nehru. These factors kept the Indo-Sri Lankan relations cool and checked. The growth of the friendship and co-operation remained very slow and limited during this period.

But all this should not be taken to mean that there was a total lack of friendship and co-operation between India and Sri Lanka. In 1949, both the countries sought to develop the traditional trade, and concluded an agreement for the exchange of essential commodities. This agreement was subsequently extended from time-to-time. In 1952, the schedule attached to the agreement included new items which were to be exported from one country to the other. In 1953, certain trade concessions in respect of trade in tobacco and 'bidis' were affected. In 1953 and 1954, cultural troupes were exchanged between the two countries when India's Indrani Rahman visited Sri Lanka and a 19-member Ceylonese Ballet troupe paid a visit to India.

The Indo-Ceylon Agreement (1954): In 1954, the Nehru-Kotelawala Pact — The Indo Ceylon Agreement, was signed by which India accepted the proposal that those persons of Indian origin as were to be registered as citizens of Sri Lanka, according to citizenship Act of that country, could apply for Indian citizenship and that they were to be registered as citizens of India if they satisfied the conditions laid down in Act 8 of Indian Citizenship Act. In 1954, the two countries further agreed that all such persons, who were in employment in Sri Lanka were not to be disturbed until they attained the age of 55. Besides these agreements, both India and Sri Lanka agreed to co-operate in the Colombo Plan. Further, both played important roles in popularising the concept of Afro-Asian solidarity and he took active part in the Bandung Conference. India fully appreciated the Sri Lankan decision to refuse the American offer for membership of SEATO because the decision gave strength to Non-alignment.

The rise of S.W.R.D. Bandaranaike and the ascendancy of his Sri Lanka Freedom Party to power in 1956 brought with it a welcome change in Indo-Sri Lankan relations. Prime Minister S.W.R.D. Bhandaranaike was a close personal friend of Nehru and was committed to follow the Indian version of Non-alignment. He was of firm conviction that Sri Lanka had nothing to fear from India. His participation in the two Asian Relations Conferences in 1947 and 1949 at New Delhi, had given him the opportunity to understand India better and to accept the need for securing Afro-Asian solidarity through consolidation of friendship and links with the new states of these two continents. This further gave strength to his desire to build-up friendship and co-operation with India. The stands taken by Sri Lanka on the Suez and Hungarian crisis of 1956 and the Tibetan issue in 1959, reflected such a change in Sri Lanka's foreign policy under the new Prime Minister. India and Sri Lanka worked together to secure the resolution of the twin crises of 1956 and the problem of Tibet. Sri Lanka accepted the stand taken by India.

But, unfortunately, this healthy development in Indo-Sri Lanka relationship could not make a very real headway because under the premiership of Sirimavo Bhandaranaike (1960-65), Sri Lanka, particularly after 1962, started moving closer to China. It did not brand China as the aggressor in the Sino-India Border War of 1962. In the Colombo Conference over the Sino-Indian Border war, Sri Lanka showed its eagerness to balance India and China by declaring its desire to maintain impartiality. Moreover, the emergence of the Indo-Ceylon dispute, the differences over the Maritime Boundary, and the Tamil Minority problem in Sri Lanka, further made the path of Indo-Sri Lanka relations uneasy. The encouragement that Sri Lanka gave to the Chinese and Pakistani attempts for winning its friendship against India further dampened the progress of Indo-Sri Lanka relations. But, in spite of these irritants, the leaders of the two countries kept up their contacts with each other and in certain directions they were successful in resolving bilateral issues and in co-operating at international level for strengthening the process of securing their shared objectives.

They were successful in co-operating towards the launching of Non-Aligned Movement at the International level, Sri Lanka gave full support to Indian action for the liberation of Goa, Daman and Diu from Portuguese possession and it even strongly pleaded the Indian case in the Security Council of the U.N. Nehru's death, on 27th May, 1964, was officially mourned in Sri Lanka and May, 28th was declared a public holiday. Sirimavo Bhandaranaike came to New Delhi to attend the funeral. In 1964, Sirimavo-Shastri Pact on Indo-Ceylon problem was made and this came to be a big breakthrough in the bilateral relations of the two countries.

The Improvement in Indo-Sri Lankan Relations: In 1965, political environment in Sri Lanka again underwent a change when Dudley Senanayaka formed a National Government in Sri Lanka. This change also proved more helpful to India because in his bid to check the Sri Lankan till towards China, as appeared during Sirimavo's regime. Mr. Senanayaka decided to improve relations, not only with the West but also with India. Similarly, during the second tenure of Sirimavo as the Prime Minister in the United Front Government in Sri Lanka (1970-77) important and meaningful efforts were made by both sides to maintain and develop the bilateral relations between India-Sri Lanka. The efforts, produced agreements on Boundary Demarcation and Kachhativu island, India-Sri Lanka Pacts on the issue of the citizenship and repatriation of stateless people of Indian origin in Sri Lanka, led to the strengthening of bilateral trade and economic links. This healthy trend continued till recently. In fact with the emergence of J.R. Jayewardene (UNP) as the leader of Government in Sri Lanka there appeared a welcome change in the psychological environment that governed the relations between India and Sri Lanka. There appeared even a maturer understanding between the leaders of the two countries and they started maintaining high-level contacts for improving Indo-Sri Lanka co-operation in various spheres. No doubt there continued to be differences over such issues as Indo-Sri Lanka problem. Trade imbalances and Balance of Payment problem, but through a better understanding of each other's view point India and Sri Lanka always tried to resolve these problems. The level of understanding between New Delhi and Colombo that has been increased after Prime Minister Rajiv Gandhi's initiative and his June 1985 Summit meeting with President Jayewardene, can surely help the two countries to resolve their differences, and to buildup a stronger and maturer friendly co-operation between the two countries.

IV. Major Issues and Problems

1. The Dispute: In March, 1956, India extended the limits of its territorial sea (Maritime belt) to six nautical miles and in November, 1956, the limit of conservation zones in the contiguous zone areas of India to a distance of 100 nautical miles. The Indian actions were regarded by Sri Lanka as harmful for its interests. Consequently, the Government of Sri Lanka also, in 1957, extended its territorial sea up to six nautical miles and the conservation zone to a distance of 100 nautical miles within the contiguous zone area. In September, 1967, India again extended the limits of it territorial seas to 12 nautical miles and Sri Lanka followed suit. As a result of these decisions, the maritime boundaries of the two countries came to overlapping each other. This increased the need to resolve the issue of maritime boundary demarcation.

2. The Island: Along with this issue, the question of ownership over the Kachhativu Island became a hot issue between the two countries. Kachhativu Island is an oval shaped island with a circumference of 3 miles. It is one mile in length from east to west and half-a-mile in breadth from north to south. Its area is about 280 acres and is about 10.5 miles from the nearest landfall in Sri Lanka and about 12.5 miles from the nearest Indian shore. It is a barren, uninhabited and cactus ridden place, which has been used since years by the fishermen as a resting place. It has no drinking water facilities and hence remains uninhabited. It has an ancient church of Saint Authoniarkoil on the northern coast. On the eve of an annual Christian function held every year in the month of March, it is visited by pilgrims from India and Sri Lanka.

3. The Dialogue and the Agreement: Both India and Sri Lanka claimed the island on the basis of the historical links, records and the location of the island. The Issue of Demarcation of Maritime Boundary involved the fate of this island also. When the negotiations over the maritime boundary were initiated the question of sovereignty over the Kachhativu Island was also taken up. After diplomatic and political negotiations lasting over nearly 6 years both the sides were in a position to sign a Maritime Boundary Agreement in 1974 followed by another agreement in 1976.

4. Maritime Boundary Agreements of 1974 and 1976: On 28th June, 1974, the international boundary between India and Sri Lanka in their historical waters in Palk Strait and Palk Bay was demarcated and the issue of over-lap in the territorial seas of the two countries in this region was resolved. It placed Kachhativu on the Sri Lankan side of the boundary. A boundary line was drawn falling one mile off the west-coast of Kachhativu. An important adjunct of this agreement was that each country was to be free to explore and exploit all petroleum and mineral deposits falling on its side of boundary, provision being made by the two countries to agree on the most effective method of exploration where petroleum or mineral deposits were found to extend from one side of the boundary to the other. "This agreement was made keeping an eye on Indo-Sri Lanka relations in the eighties particularly in the context of India's recent oil strike in this region."

The Maritime Agreement of 1976, extended this international boundary in the Gulf of Mannar and the Bay of Bengal and laid down sovereign right and exclusive jurisdiction over the continental shelves and exclusive economic zones as well as over their resources, falling on either side of the boundary line. "The signing of these two agreements," observes Shelton Kodikara, "must be regarded as a historic landmark in Indo-Lanka relations. They were the culmination of hard negotiations, between the two countries and are full of implications for the future, as being instruments which could pave the way for joint exploration and exploitation of sea bed resources in the territorial and exclusive economic zones." Indeed with the demarcation of maritime boundary between the two countries and the settlement of the dispute over Kachhativu, Indo-Sri Lanka relations attained a new high. However, still at times, the island becomes the object of concern for India due to several unhealthy incidents involving Sri Lankan naval patrols and Indian fishermen.

Issue of Citizenship: The issue of citizenship of the stateless persons has been a major thorny irritant in Indo-Sri Lanka relations. The existence of Tamil problem in Sri Lanka has made it even more complicated and difficult. Though two agreements were made in 1964 and 1974, the issue still continues to be there as an irritant in the relations between the two countries. Even during periods of good co-operation at bilateral and international level this issue had been source of strain and tension.

Initially, this issue involved a dispute over the political status or settlements of around one million people of Indian origin, mostly Tamils in Sri Lanka, residing largely in the northern and eastern parts of the island. Large scale immigration of Indians to Sri Lanka began in the 19th century, especially during the coffee boon. The need for rubber plantation in 1920s further led to an increased immigration of Indians into Sri Lanka and their number came to be around 1 million. A large number of these immigrants have been living in Sri Lanka for more than one generation. However, they have been maintaining their traditional cultural links with India. They have maintained Tamil as their mother tongue and have not come forward to mix with the Sinhalese. This makes them susceptible persons, who are regarded as persons not willing to join the national mainstream, and who are desirous of securing a dismemberment of Sri Lanka.

During the British rule in Sri Lanka, they were treated as British subjects and enjoyed almost equal rights with other people of Sri Lanka. However, no attempt was made, either by them or by the government, to secure Sri Lankan citizenship. In 1948 and 1949 Sri Lanka passed two Citizenship Acts. The net effect of these acts was that most of the people of Indian origin came to be debarred from Sri Lankan citizenship. They even could not claim Indian or Pakistani citizenships because of the new citizenship acts that had been passed by these two states. Hence, they became "Stateless persons of Indian origin in Sri Lanka." This causes serious concern in both Indian and Sri Lankan circles. Consequently, efforts were initiated to resolve the problem through bilateral negotiations, which in January, 1954, led to a general broad agreement — The Nehru-Kotelawala Pact. By this pact it was agreed that those persons (stateless), who were not able to be registered as Sri Lankan citizens could apply for Indian citizenship and if they fulfilled the conditions laid down in the Indian Citizenship Act, they could be registered as citizens of India. In October 1954, it was agreed that those, who were in employment were not to be disturbed until they attained the age of retirement.

Under the Nehra-Kotelawala Pact, 1,34,188 such persons got the citizenship of Sri Lanka and 53,085 persons became Indian citizens. But the bulk of such persons failed to get registered as citizens of either India or Sri Lanka, and hence remained stateless. India and Sri Lanka as such got negated in fresh negotiations for settling the issue of citizenship of such persons.

After protracted negotiations lasting for over 9 years, a major breakthrough was achieved in 1964. It was the Indo-Ceylon Agreement or the Shastri-Sirimavo Pact signed on 30th October 1984, between the Prime Ministers of India and Sri Lanka — Mr. Lal Bahadur Shastri and Sirimavo Bhandarnaike. The pact stipulated that over a period of 15 years, the Indian and Sri Lankan Governments would together confer citizenship on 82,500 out of a total of 9,75,000 stateless persons. Sri Lanka agreed to grant citizenship to 3,00,000 and India to do the same in respect of 5,25,000 stateless persons. Natural increase in the stipulated numbers for repatriation to India and grant of Ceylon citizenship, respectively, were also covered by the agreement. Further, it was agreed that the repatriates were to be permitted to transfer all their assets. The 1,50,000 persons not covered by this agreement were to the subject of further negotiations.

The issue was discussed when Mrs. Indira Gandhi visited Colombo in April 1973. But the final agreement to share equally the remaining 1,50,000 stateless persons was reached at the time of Mrs. Bhandarnaike's visit to Delhi in January 1974. In this way Indo-Ceylon, problem was subjected to 3 bilateral agreements in 20 years — 1954 Nehru-Kotlewala Pact, 1964 Shastri-Sirimavo Agreement, and 1974 Indira-Sirimavo Agreement. These bold attempts were made to resolve the ticklish problem between the two neighbours.

However, the process of implementation of these agreements has been rather slow, chiefly because of administrative delays in clearing papers and settling financial claims by the Government of Sri Lanka. Besides this, Prof. S.C. Gangal has listed the following three reasons behind the slow progress towards repatriation of emigrants:

(*i*) Sri Lanka Government's awareness about usefulness of the highly skilled Tamil workers on the tea and rubber plantations;

(*ii*) The heavy financial implications of having to settle the financial claims of intending emigrants, and

(*iii*) In some cases even some repatriates have secured rights and have been rather unwilling to leave their homes and hearths in Sri Lanka and to leap, as it were, into the unknown by emigrating to India.

Additional Problems, however, arose due to the differences over the fate of Shastri-Sirimavo Pact, and the recent strains over the issue of Tamil problem in Sri Lanka. The Shastri-Sirimavo Pact was signed for a 15 years period and as such is now stands lapsed. India is of the opinion that the pact has ceased to be operative now and consequently the stateless persons still living in Sri Lanka should be the responsibility of Sri Lanka because that country has been their homeland for the last 4 or 5 generation. In July, 1982, External Affairs Minister, Narasimha

Rao told the Rajya Sabha that the 1964 Pact was no more operative and India has no proposal to seek formal talks on this issue. Sri Lanka, on the other hand, maintained that this pact was still operative and India must share the burden of the stateless persons with Sri Lanka. Sri Lanka wanted a new pact. In February, 1982, President J.R. Jayawardene observed, "India and Sri Lanka should discuss the question of stateless people. We want to settle it once for all. My Government would like India to take back all those who became Indian citizens under Indo-Sri Lanka agreement, Sri Lanka for its part would do likewise.

Indo-Sri Lankan Accord on Stateless Persons in Sri Lanka: On January 16, 1986, India and Sri Lanka agreed to resolve, once for all, the problems of stateless persons of Indian origin in Sri Lanka. It was agreed that India will proceed with the process of conferring citizenship on 85,000 people of Indian origin, who applied for Indian citizenship prior to October 30, 1981, and Sri Lanka will simultaneously take necessary legislative and executive action to grant Sri Lankan citizenship to all the remaining persons of Indian origin, estimated to be 4,69,000 and their natural increase, including those who have already been given Sri Lankan citizenship. This agreement has finally clinched the issue of stateless persons of Indian origin in Sri Lanka.

Because of these differences, Indo-Sri Lanka problem continues to be a big problem. The recent controversy regarding India's expression of concern for the Tamils of Sri Lanka, has further affected the environment of Indo-Sri Lanka relations. It is bound to give a set-back to the efforts to settle the thorny issue of stateless persons. India expressed its concern with the fate of Tamils, purely on humanitarian grounds and did not in any way wish to interfere with the internal affairs of Sri Lanka. The Government of Sri Lanka and the press there has played this up for diverting the attention of its people from the grim domestic situation. *The Tribune* in its Editorial: A Needless Irritant, (25th July, 1983) observed, "Sri Lanka is making a mountain of a molehill by its "over-reaction" to Indian Government's mildly expressed concern for the safety of the people of Indian Origin..." This development has further made the Indo-Sri Lanka problem more difficult. A few months ago President Jayawardene declared that his Government was considering the grant of 'civic rights' to state-less, but the Sinhalese pressure and the recent developments in Sri Lanka have prevented him from taking any effective steps. The problem as such is bound to remain an irritant in Indo-Sri Lanka relations in the coming years. However, since both the countries are committed to settle all their problems and disputes peacefully and through bilateral efforts, it is hoped that the two countries would continue to work for securing a mutually acceptable solution to this issue.

Trade Imbalances: The economic aspect of Indo-Sri Lanka relations is an important and significant aspect, India has been one of the Sri Lanka's largest trading partners, but the trade relations have not been always very smooth. The unpopularity of Indian businessmen and money lenders in Sri Lanka and the trade deficit and imbalances have been the major irritants. The similar export interests, as both the countries are engaged in the export of tea, coconut and rubber, have tended to make the two countries trade rivals in the world markets. Further, being a better developed and technologically advanced countries, India can export many things to Sri Lanka. Even today, it accounts for 10 per cent of Sri Lanka's total imports. As against this Sri Lanka has a very limited export potential and as such cannot sell much to India. The net result has been a trade imbalance between India and Sri Lanka.

Both the countries have been trying to restore the trade balance, but their efforts have failed to click positively. There exists a strong need for giving a facelift to Indo-Sri Lanka trade relations. India being a bigger and better developed country must take effective steps for developing trade with Sri Lanka and for restoring the balance. Joint industrial ventures on a buy-back basis, expansion of mutual trade and export sales to third countries, further utilisation of the existing facilities in the various fields of industrial and agricultural development, promotion of tourism etc., can be some of the measures which can help the achievement of the objective. Dr. Urmila Phadnis in one of her articles in India and Sri Lanka relations has suggested: "India's Sri Lanka policy should necessarily comprise aid policies to stimulate trade not only with India but also in the Asian region. It should provide for economic linkage between the two countries that would make for the maximum utilisation of resource endowments in the two countries. India should also take steps for liberalising the imports from Sri Lanka." There exists a strong need for strengthening Indo-Sri Lanka trade relations.

Indian Ocean as a Zone of Peace: Besides these major issues, reference must also be made to certain other issues which have been influencing the course of Indo-Sri Lanka relations. Both the countries are committed to secure Indian Ocean as a Zone of Peace (IOPZ, Indian Ocean Peace Zone). Sri Lanka was one of the first few countries who took the initiative in demanding both in the meetings of the Non-aligned countries, and in the United Nations, that the Indian Ocean should be made a zone of peace. However, since early 1980s it has been advocating that after the securing of IOPZ, no littoral state should increase its naval presence in the area. Apparently, this demand has its roots in the 'Fear of India' with which Sri Lanka has been living since its independence. Sri Lanka wants that after securing IOPZ no littoral state of Indian Ocean should increase its presence in this area. India stands committed to the objective of securing IOPZ, but is not willing to undertake any commitment involving the future security interests of India. It wants an un-conditional acceptance of IOPZ and the liquidation of super power military bases in the Indian Ocean. India wants Sri Lanka to collaborate fully for securing this objective. But Sri Lanka now appears to be not very enthusiastic about IOPZ.

V. Problems of Tamils Till 1989

The Tamil problem in Sri Lanka constitutes the biggest irritant in the contemporary phase of Indo-Sri Lankan relations. It is an internal problem of Sri Lanka but it has been source of big strains on Indo-Sri Lankan relations because of socio-political and geographic conditions that constitute the environment of the relations between these two countries. The Indian concern for Sri Lankan Tamils and Sri Lanka's allergy to the issue have been the two main factors which are conditioning the bilateral interactions during the current phase of their relations.

1. Origin: The Tamils comprise 12 per cent (2.7 million) of Sri Lanka's population, and as such constitute the largest minority of Sri Lanka. The Tamils are the descendants of South Indians and have common cultural and religious links with the Tamils of India. Tamil continues to be their mother tongue and they do not mix up with the Sinhalese, who constitute nearly 70 per cent of Sri Lanka's population. They are always eager to maintain their culture and tradition and believe that under the majority rule of Sinhalese in Sri Lanka, their rights, culture and language are not secure. Consequently, since the independence of Sri Lanka, more particularly since 1958. When 'Sinhala' the language of the Sinhalese was declared by Bhandarnaike's Government as the official language of Sri Lanka, they have been struggling to safeguard their rights. Some of them have been demanding, the establishment of an independent state of The Tamils—The Tamil Eelam or Eylom, or at least to grant provincial autonomy to the Tamils within the Sri Lanka Federation. They are not prepared to accept full-throated Sinhalese nationalism and domination of the political life of Sri Lanka. This demand is being strongly resisted by Sinhalese and the government of Sri Lanka. Not to speak of a separate state of the Tamils, the Sinhalese are not even prepared to discuss or tolerate the demand for regional autonomy within a federal framework. They are in no mood to accommodate the aspirations of the Tamils. Because of such strong differences between the Sinhalese and Tamils, there has been present the Tamil problem in Sri Lanka. The tensions between these two communities have at times led to the outbreak of communal riots in Sri Lanka.

The Tamils have organised themselves into Tamil United Liberation Front (TULF) and through it they are trying to achieve their objective. The failure to get an equitable share in the political and economic life of Sri Lanka, has been a source of frustration for TULF and recently it has strengthened its efforts to secure the rights and aspirations of the Tamils. This has invited very strong reaction from the Sinhalese and there have been incidents of communal riots in Sri Lanka. In 1958, 1977 and 1982 there were widespread communal riots in Sri Lanka involving the Sinhalese and the Tamils. In the August 1982 riots, thousands of Tamils became the victims of killing, arson, looting and robberies. The government of Sri Lanka has been taking steps to prevent riots and acts of violence against the Tamils but these have failed to be effective. The present government of Sri Lanka is very keen to restore confidence of the Sri Lankan Tamils, and is taking important steps for accepting their legitimate demands. The problem, however, continues to be there and latest call for Eelam given by the England-based Tamils of Sri Lanka, has given a new dimension to the problem. The Tamil Committee in London has given a call for putting in all efforts for securing Tamil Eelam — a separate state for the island's Tamils. Although the TULF has rejected the call, yet within Sri Lanka this development has again generated communal tension, riots and almost a civil war in Jaffna.

India's Interests: The government of India has been largely following the policy of keeping aloof from the Tamil problem because it considers it is a domestic affair of Sri Lanka. However, at times, certain members of the Indian Parliament, particularly belonging to the DMK and AIADMK have often expressed their concern at the ill-treatment and discrimination meted to the Tamils of Sri Lanka. The Tamils of South India have strong cultural and historical links and relations with the Tamils of Sri Lanka and this has, at times, prompted the leaders of DMK, AIADMK, and even some others to express sympathy for the Tamils of Sri Lanka. They have in past appealed to the government of India for taking up the Tamil problem with the government of Sri Lanka. This demand has never been accepted by the Government of India. Certain sections of Indian press have been quite vocal in expressing the view that the Sri Lankan Government must take steps to satisfy the aspirations of the minorities, particularly, the Tamil minority. The Government of Sri Lanka has always been opposed to the expression of such views in India. It has always regarded it as an interference in the internal affair of Sri Lanka. It has always taken strong exception to the sympathy expressed by the DMK and AIADMK leaders for the Sri Lankan Tamils. In 1967, when the DMK came into power in Tamil Nadu, Sri Lanka expressed apprehension of an invasion of Sri Lanka by Tamil Nadu. Indian Prime Minister had to give an assurance to Sri Lanka, it was inconceivable for one state in India to go against the policy of the Union Government. Since

Indian policy was a policy of peace, friendship, good neighbourly links and non-interference in the internal affairs of it neighbours, "Sri Lanka should have no fear of an invasion from India."

The Sri Lankan View: Despite the direct and open declaration of its stand that India regards Tamil problem as internal affairs of Sri Lanka, the government of Sri Lanka continues to suspect that the Tamil trouble is backed by Indian people, particularly by the South Indians. The expression of solidarity and friendship with the Indian Tamils by TULF and other groups of Sri Lankan Tamils strengthens this suspicion. Consequently, Indo-Sri Lanka relations continue to experience tensions and strains caused by the Tamil problem. After assuming office the Government of Jayawardene announced some important steps for resolving the Tamil problem which however failed to get materialised in practice. The ensuing month saw a fast deterioration in the internal conditions of Sri Lanka in July, 1983, widespread anti-Tamil riots broke out in Sri Lanka, the failure of Sri Lankan government to protect the life of the Tamils made the Tamil extremist groups very active, and they decided to resort to terrorist method for securing their rights which included the right of self-determination and statehood in Jaffna area. The situation became very grim when Sri Lankan government initiated military action against the Tamil terrorists and insurgents. The loss of life in Sri Lanka was huge, and India felt no hesitation in expressing concern over the tragic killing of the innocent Tamils in the name of killing the rebels and insurgents.

On July 19, 1983, the Sri Lankan High Commissioner in Delhi, Mr. Bernard Tilkaratna was summoned to the Indian External Affairs Ministry, and was told by secretary K.S. Vajpai that while India did not wish to interfere in Sri Lanka's internal affairs, it was following the developments in Jaffna and the Sri Lanka government's response to the situation. The Sri Lanka press quoted Vajpai as saying that "he was expressing the concern of the Indian government at the highest level... that developments in Sri Lanka would have possible repercussion in India.

The Sri Lankan press strongly reacted against this development. It condemned the Indian position as a clear case of interference in Sri Lanka's External Affairs. Under a lead story headlined "India fixes muscles over northern issue — Lanka's Sovereignty threatened," the press observed that India's sudden "expression of concern." amounted to a threat to Sri Lanka's sovereignty. A Sri Lankan paper; the *Sun* reacted very strongly against the "Shocking about turn by Indira Gandhi." It wrote, "has Indira lost her grip on India and India lost balance outlook in International affairs? Is her heart bleeding for the terrorists in Jaffna? Or is Trincomalee the apple of her eye?"

India strongly refuted the charge that it was interfering the internal affairs of Sri Lanka and reiterated its concern with the developments in Jaffna. While commenting upon reports from Colombo alleging Indian interference, a spokesman of the External Affairs Ministry observed, "There is no question of Indian interference in Sri Lankan affairs. However, India had to protect the interests of its nationals. The historical links between the two countries have left links which we value. We exchange views on matters of mutual interest in a spirit of friendship."

The Tamil problem generated big strains in Indo-Sri Lanka relations. India fully sympathises with the Tamils of Sri Lanka, but purely on humanitarian grounds. It fully respects both Indian Prime Minister and Foreign Minister have declared time and again the sovereignty and integrity of Sri Lanka. Yet India can't remain indifferent to the mass murder of and atrocities against the Tamil minority in Sri Lanka. After the discussion between President Jayawardene's special emissary and Indian leaders, the clouds of distrust appeared to have thinned. India agreed to provide help and assistance to Sri Lanka for settling the Tamil victims of the July 1983 riots. After a meeting with Tamil leaders, Mrs. Indira Gandhi even made an offer of Indian good offices for helping the resolution of conflict in Sri Lanka. India expressed its readiness to help Sri Lanka in overcoming its internal problems.

Tamil Problem and Indo-Sri Lanka Relations: However, the Indian offer was again misinterpreted by Sri Lankan leaders and they felt it amounted to an interference in the internal affairs of their country. The repeated Indian assurances that India was interested only because of humanitarian reasons and because a section of Indian people, the Tamils of India had natural sympathy and affinity with Sri Lankan Tamils failed to carry much conviction with the Sri Lankan authorities. The Tamil problem, as such, came to generate big tensions and strains in Indo-Sri Lankan relations. The outbreak of a virtual civil war cum — Tamil insurgent movement in the Northern parts of Sri Lanka. Particularly in Jaffna — the area closest to Indian land mass, made things worst. The atrocities let loose by the Sri Lankan military as a part of the drive against the insurgents, in practice against all the Sri Lankan Tamils, gave rise to increased Tamil guerrilla attacks and subversive activities. The situation became alarmingly bad. The fall out for India came, first, in the form of tension in the Palk Straits area, resulting into firing on Indian fishermen by Sri Lankan naval boats which trespassed into Indian waters, and secondly, in form of a large influx of Tamil refugees into India. The Indian decision to give shelter to these refugees was initiated by humanitarian grounds, but Sri Lankan authorities interpreted it as an Indian move to pave the way for its intervention in Sri Lanka. The memories of Bangladesh crises and its result started haunting Sri Lankan authorities and they started talking in terms of Indian designs on Sri Lanka. The decision of Sri Lankan Government to take Israeli help to crush the Tamil rebels was criticised by India as an attempt to involve other countries in the affairs of Sri Lanka, which in the long-run were bound to prove dangerous for the peace and stability of South Asia and Indian Ocean. All these developments made Indo-Sri Lankan relations highly tense and strained and these continued to drift dangerously till April/May 1985, when Prime Minister Rajiv Gandhi, through several wise and bold steps was successful on the one hand, in restoring some health to Indo-Sri Lankan relations and on the other hand, in helping the Sri Lankan Government and Tamil rebel groups to cease hostilities and start negotiating at Thimpu for a possible solution to the Tamil/Ethnic problem.

The strains which the Tamil problem was inflicting upon Indo-Sri Lankan relations, India's concern with the fate of Sri Lankan Tamils and India's desire for securing a more developed friendship and co-operation with the neighbouring countries, were the factors which influenced Prime Minister Rajiv Gandhi to initiate steps for helping the process of finding a solution to the Tamil problem and for arresting the harmful drift in Indo-Sri Lankan relations which were fast assuming alarming proportions. The increasing hostilities between Sri Lankan forces and Tamil militants and the consequent fall out on Indian in the form of the burden of sheltering and feeding Tamil refugees and tensions in Palk Strait further influenced action designed at checking the problem. India felt the necessity of countering the Sri Lankan charge that Tamil militants were having their bases in India by projecting India as a country determined to refrain from intervention in Sri Lanka and as nation prepared to help one of its small neighbours to overcome its domestic crisis and get away from the brink of a near certain civil war.

In line with the general policy of developing more friendly and co-operative efforts Prime Minister Rajiv Gandhi, while expressing concern over the hostile stand adopted by Sri Lanka (arrest of Indian fishermen) observed that India favours a political settlement of the issue. Initially, Sri Lanka continued to voice its suspicions about the role of India, however, after some time, Sri Lankan President Jayawardene realised the fact that Indian leadership was genuinely interested in helping his country to resolve the Tamil problem.

In pursuance of his policy of developing more friendly and co-operative relation with India's neighbour, Prime Minister Rajiv Gandhi, on March 24, 1985, sent Mr. Ramesh Bhandari, the new Foreign Secretary, to Colombo. Mr. Bhandari held talks with Mr. J.R. Jayawardene during his two days stay in Colombo which helped the emergence of a new understanding between the two countries. The talks were fruitful and it was admitted that these would help a peaceful resolution of the ethnic crisis in Sri Lanka. A notable result of Mr. Bhandari's visit was an agreement that "It is necessary as a first step to bring about a cessation of all acts of violence." Both the sides also agreed to take steps for improving communication and travel facilities and to maintain regular consultations at an official level on bilateral and regional matters between the two countries. The visit improved the climate of Indo-Sri Lankan relations and during the talks, spade work was done for a Summit meeting between Mr. Rajiv Gandhi and Mr. Jayawardene.

Indo-Sri Lankan Summit: President Jayawardene of Sri Lanka and Prime Minister Rajiv Gandhi held Summit meeting in New Delhi for two days, June 2nd and 3rd, 1985, and discussed bilateral relations in general and Sri Lanka's Tamil problem in particular. During the talks Prime Minister, Rajiv Gandhi once again explained India's stand on a political settlement of the ethnic problem. Mr. Jayawardene, rising above the policy to crack down the Tamil rebels in northern Sri Lanka, expressed his keenness for negotiated settlement.

In the joint press statement issued after the talks, both the sides agreed that immediate steps should be taken to diffuse the mounting tension in Sri Lanka and create a proper climate for progress towards a political settlement which would be acceptable to all concerned within the framework of the unity and integrity of Sri Lanka. Both sides also agreed that it was imperative that all forms of violence should cease. President Jayawardene also gave his assurance that every possible effort would be made to restore normalcy in the severely affected northern and eastern provinces of Sri Lanka to facilitate the early return of Sri Lankan Tamils, who had fled to India. He also promised that he would declare amnesty for Tamil militants, if they unconditionally surrendered their arms to the government. The Summit talks were "very cordial and frank, characterised by a sincere desire to co-operate in overcoming difficulties and evolving a durable political solution." The two leaders agreed further to remain in close touch with each other.

The new understanding between the two leaders was further extended by their joint visit to Dacca as a gesture of goodwill to, and for expressing sympathy with the cyclone-hit people of Bangladesh. This gesture symbolized the new drive for a greater understanding among the countries of South Asia.

The Summit talks, Indeed, paved the way for a fresh and bold Sri Lankan initiative for resolving the ethnic problem. The declaration of June 18, 1985 whereby Sri Lanka announced that an agreement between the government and five major Tamil groups—LTTE, EPRLF, TELU, FROS and PLOT, on "a cessation of hostile acts for 8 weeks has been reached." It was indeed a bold first step towards solving the seemingly intractable ethnic problem.

Truce, Thimpu Talks and India's Role: After the Summit, a Sri Lankan delegation headed by Hector Jayawardene, brother of the President, came to New Delhi in accordance with proposal for an expert level meeting between the two countries. The delegation had discussions with Indian constitutional experts which touched possible amendments in the Sri Lankan constitution for suitably accommodating certain demands of the Sri Lankan Tamils. It was during this visit of the Sri Lankan delegation that the announcement of an agreement between the Sri Lankan government and Tamil separatists groups was made. "By this agreement a cessation of hostile acts for 18 weeks and conducting of talks for resolving the ethnic problem were reached. It was a big Sri Lankan move to find a political settlement of the problem. Indian diplomacy played a useful role" in bringing the Sri Lankan government and the Tamil leaders closer and in securing a truce and the decision to hold talks at Thimpu for resolving the issue.

After this breakthrough in Sri Lanka, delegations of officials from Sri Lanka and India conferred in New Delhi on June, 28 and 29, as a part of preparation for the forthcoming talks between Sri Lankan government and the Tamil militants. The first phase of the Thimpu talks between them was held in July, 1985 and lasted for a week. This meeting was of an exploratory nature and both sides restated their view points. It was agreed that the second round of talks would be held in August, 1985.

After the first round of talks, India stepped up its efforts to make the second round a more rewarding session. Prime Minister Rajiv Gandhi sent a personal letter to President Jayawardene and urged him to come out with fresh proposals which could form a framework for a solution. The Foreign Secretary of India flew to Colombo to persuade Mr. Jayawardene to narrow down the differences in larger interest of finding a solution within the parameters of a united Sri Lanka.

In the second round of Thimpu talks between Sri Lankan government delegation, led by Mr. Hector Jayawardene and the Tamil groups delegation led by Mr. A. Amirthalingam, both sides attempted hard to narrow down the differences in their quest for a solution to the ethnic problem. However, the talks failed to proceed because of rigid attitudes of the Tamil militants.

New Sri Lankan Proposals: After the collapse of Thimpu talks, the government of Sri Lanka came out with a comprehensive and detailed set of proposals on August 31, 1985. Through these Sri Lanka express her willingness to establish provincial council in each province and for this agreed that India should indirectly hold the negotiations with the Tamils. It was further pointed out that Sri Lanka was prepared the delegate adequate powers to such councils and these would definitely to meet the Tamil demand for autonomy within Sri Lanka.

Throughout 1986, the Tamil problem continued to strain Indo-Sri-Lankan ties. The policy of the Sri Lankan government to talk of negotiated settlement and prepare for a military solution of the problem kept the Tamil problem hot. The hard line adopted by the Tamil militants further created an unhealthy environment in which India felt greatly disturbed. In early 1987, Sri Lankan government decided to step up the offensive against the Tamils on the ground that the Tamil were not respecting the ceasefire. The Tamil militants also increased their terrorist activities and in April, 1987 the Sri Lankan government inducted its army in a very big way to crush Tamil militancy. A near civil war resulted in and the situation became very ugly and grim. India wanted both sides to show restraint and asked the government of Sri Lankan to cease all hostilities and resume negotiations with the Tamil groups within the framework of the December 19, 1986 proposals for finding a peaceful solution to the Island's ethnic problem. But the Sri Lankan government decided to go ahead with the military offensive and instead sought the help and co-operation of "all nations big and small to preserve peace, law and order in the law-abinding a democratic nations." It also decided to take all measures to eliminate terrorists and terrorism. This policy decision flared up the Tamil problem and gave rise to possibility of "outside involvement" in India's neighbourhood. The government of India cautioned Sri Lanka against such a possibility but got an unsupportive reaction from the Island's government. The Indian desire to give humanitarian food aid to the Tamils was also criticised strongly by the Sri Lankan authorities. The ethnic problem in Sri Lanka virtually turned into a civil war. Sri Lankan troops started killing Tamils on a large scale and imposed widespread curfew in the areas in Jaffna. The people of Jaffna were subjected to all sorts of pressures and atrocities.

India's Relief Mission to Jaffna: When India failed to get a positive response from the Sri Lanka government towards her desire to send relief supplied to Jaffna, she decided to sent the relief supplied by boats and duly notified her intention to the Sri Lankans. The Sri Lankan government did not permit these boats to deliver the relief supplies to Tamils of Jaffna. Thereupon India decided to air drop the essential life securing supplies. In a swift and neat operation, the Indian Air Force carried out a mission probably un-precedented in relations between states when it flew into war-torn Jaffna peninsula of Sri Lanka on June 4, 1987 for providing relief to the suffering peoples of Jaffna. Five AN-32 transport aircrafts escorted by Four Mirage 2,000 accomplished the assigned task. This clearly gave a warning to the Sri Lankans that India was not prepared to be a helpless spectator of the mass killings being done by the Sri Lankan forces, and that it favours a non-military peaceful solution of ethnic crisis of Sri Lanka.

Though, initially Sri Lanka charged India of a naked violation of Sri Lankan independence, later on she realised the necessity and importance of India's relief supplies. On June 15, 1987, India and Sri Lanka reached an agreement on the procedure for dispatch of relief supplies from the government and people of India to Sri Lankan citizens on the Jaffna peninsula. This agreement paved the way for Sri Lanka's presence in the SAARC ministerial level meeting.

However, on July 12, 1987, Sri Lankan armed forces launched another massive offensive operation in the Mullaitivu district of Northern Sri Lanka, and got engaged in a serious battle with LTTE guerrilla units. The Tamil problem once again became very hot issue between India and Sri Lanka. Indian Prime Minister Rajiv Gandhi, once again called upon Sri Lankan government to come up with new autonomy proposals for the country's minority Tamils.

VI. India-Sri Lanka Pact

On July 29, 1987, India and Sri Lanka signed a historic pact which heralded a new era of their bilateral relations. It constituted a bold attempt on the part of both the countries to adopt a co-operative approach not only in regard to the limited issue of resolving the ethnic problem in Sri Lanka but also with regard to all-round relations between the two countries. The pact was described by Mr. Rajiv Gandhi as "big and unusual as such an accord for mutual and collective benefit has been signed perhaps for the first time in the history of international relations."

The Pact reads:

"Attaching utmost importance to nurturing, intensifying the strengthening of traditional friendship of India and Sri Lanka, and acknowledging the imperative need of resolving the ethnic problem of Sri Lanka and the consequent violence, and for the safety, well-being and prosperity of people belonging to all communities in Sri Lanka have this day entered into the following agreement to fulfil this objective...."

The pact reaffirmed a faith in a unity, sovereignty, territorial integrity, multi-ethnic and a multilingual plural society of Sri Lanka and recognised that each ethnic group has a distinct cultural and linguistic identify which is to be carefully nurtured. It accepted the need for organising the adjoining provinces to join to form one administrative unit with the exception of those areas whose people may, through a referendum, decide to remain out a separate units. It enumerated in detail the provision for holding the referendum for the constitution of provincial councils. It was further agreed that the Emergency in Jaffna area shall be lifted by August 15, 1987.

A very striking feature of the pact was the provision that the Government of India will underwrite and guarantee the accord and co-operate in the implementation of its provisions.... The role of India towards the implementation of the accord was described as under:

(*a*) India will take all necessary steps to ensure that Indian territory is not used for activities prejudicial to the unity, integrity and security of Sri Lanka.

(*b*) The Indian Navy/Coast Guards will co-operate with the Sri Lankan navy in preventing Tamil militant activity from affecting Sri Lanka.

(*c*) In the event that the government of Sri Lanka requests the government of India to afford military assistance to implement these proposals, the government of India will co-operate by giving to the government of Sri Lanka such military assistance as and when requested.

(*d*) The government of India will expedite repatriation from Sri Lanka of Indian citizens to India, who are resident there concurrently with the repatriation of Sri Lankan refugees front Tamil Nadu.

(*e*) The government of India and Sri Lanka will co-operate in ensuring the physical security and safety of all communities inhabiting the northern and eastern provinces.

These clauses made it the responsibility of India to ensure the implementation of the pact.

Further, it was agreed that a cessation of hostilities will come into force all over the Island within 24 hours of the signing of this pact. All arms held by the militants will be surrendered. The process of surrendering of arms and confining of security personal to the barracks will be completed within 72 hours of cessation of hostilities.

Praising the provisions of the accord, Prime Minister Rajiv Gandhi described it as momentous event in the history of the two countries. "It heralds peace. It is a compact in the cause of brotherhood. It promised national reconciliation in Sri Lanka. It has created conditions for the return of refugees. It has dispelled the clouds that had hovered over the relationship between Indian and Sri Lanka. Every agreement is an act of faith. Triumph needs unremitting toil and unflinching determination. In democracies, critics are often more vocal than supporters. It is up to us to defend this agreement and bring round its detractors."

In India, the accord was hailed as a big positive development, however, in Sri Lanka the Sinhalese extremists and Buddhist monks criticised the accord as total Sri Lankan sell out to Tamils through India. Some sections of Tamil militants, particularly, the LTTE led by the Mr. Prabhakaran, too expressed their reservations because the accord called for laying down the arms before the implementation of other provisions. Sri Lankan Prime Minister Premadasa and some of his Cabinet colleagues boycotted the visit of Indian Prime Minister and the signing of the accord. However, the accord received full praise from the international press. The two super powers lent their support to the accord. This accord deserves our praise for the elimination of the chances of foreign powers intervention in Sri Lanka crisis.

An anti-climax however, came when an attempt on the life of Mr. Rajiv Gandhi was made by a member of the naval honour guard of Sir Lankan Navy during the course of presenting a guard of honour to the Prime Minister of India. Fortunately, the Prime Minister Rajiv Gandhi was able to duck away the rifle butt attack and it could just hit his shoulder. Undauntedly, he went ahead with the ceremonies at the farewell function. The opposition to the accord was demonstrated by the Sri Lankan soldier but it did not make any big impact on Indo-Sri Lankan agreement to resolve the ethnic crisis on the basis of the provisions of the July, 29 pact. Addressing a massive public meeting on August 2, 1987, Mr. Rajiv Gandhi termed the accords as "a major land-mark in the past four decades of India's freedom." He categorically declared that no sympathy will be shown towards the opponents of the accord, whether the LTTE militants or others.

The accord made India a party to the Sri Lanka ethnic crisis. On the request of Sri Lankan President, Indian Peace Keeping Force (IPKF) was dispatched to Jaffna peninsula, and the process of surrender of arms got commenced on August 5, 1987 when the "commanders" and leaders of the LTTE group symbolically surrendered their arms. The "supreme commander" of the LTTE, Mr. Vellupillai Prabhakaran however, chose to abstain from the ceremony. Soon afterwards several LTTE militant groups got engaged in acts of terrorism, subversion and armed clashes with the IPKF since that time the role of IPKF has been increasing, necessitating increased strength and increased involvement in restoring normalisation in Northern Sri Lanka, for preventing LTTE militants to hold out their arms and strike against innocent citizens, to liquidate militant bases, and to restore peace in the war-torn Jaffna. By the mid-November 1987, the IPKF was successful in liquidating the LTTE strongholds and prevent the flow of arms into their hands. India has made it abundantly clear to LTTE that it must surrender all the arms and accept the Indo-Sri Lankan peace accord and only then the IPKF will stop its operations against them. IPKF now has got freed the areas from LTTE control and is engaged in restoring normalisation personnels of Indian administration, with the consent of the government of Sri Lanka have started administering the areas as an interim arrangement. LTTE resistance has been virtually eliminated. However, the chances of LTTE activities resorting to guerrilla tactics and keeping up tensions and terrorism are still there. Hence, the presence of IPKF in Sri Lanka is found to remain there for quite some time. Complete liquidation of LTTE appears to be an essential condition for the successful implementation of Indo-Sri Lankan accord.

The internal opposition in Sri Lanka to the accord too constitutes an important hindrance. The grenade attack on Sri Lankan cabinet the emergence of anti-government terrorists activities and the continued delay in implementing the other provisions constitute the other hindrances. Indo-Sri Lankan relations have assumed a unique shape. The accord has on the one hand, made Indian role in Sri Lankan security, unity and integrity a necessary, essential and legally justified condition, on the other hand, it has increased opposition and criticism of India's role by several sections of Sri Lankan people. India's role and responsibility as the sub-regional power had increased. It is bound to be a source of strain on Indian resources for several years to come. All this, however, cannot and should not be taken to mean that India should not have signed the accord. The regional and strategic compulsions have forced Indian to take up this role. What is needed is a determined and systematic drive to secure the goals of national interests in the region.

Issue of Withdrawal of IPKF: Sri Lankan President Mr. Premadasa had in his election manifesto advocated the view that after elections he would secure the withdrawal of IPKF from Sri Lanka. But till May, 1989, he preferred to keep silent over the issue.

However, during the process of negotiations with LTTE, Mr. Premadasa, apparently under pressure from the LTTE because it was itself finding the pressure of IPKF unbearable, came to believe that withdrawal of IPKF from Sri Lanka can help the resolution of ethnic conflict. Moreover, the internal pressure upon Sri Lankan Government resulting from the activities of JVP extremists also compelled Mr. Premadasa to divert the attention of the people by raising the IPKF issue on June 1, 1989, President Premadasa observed in one of his public meetings that the last soldier of IPKF would leave the Island by the end of July and that he would ask Indian Prime Minister, Rajiv Gandhi to complete the withdrawal before July 29, the second anniversary of the signing of the Indo-Sri Lankan Peace Accord.

Sri Lankan government has demanded the withdrawal of IPKF for pleasing the LTTE leaders because they were finding it difficult to operate in the presence of Indian soldiers. Sri Lankan Government this unilateral announcement closely follows the initiative to India—Sri Lankan Army in Eastern Province to jointly patrol the Muslim dominated areas along with IPKF.

President Premadasa's opposition to the presence of IPKF in Sri Lanka has been a well-known fact. He now wanted to project IPKF as an occupation force and not an force requisitioned by former Sri Lankan President Mr. Jayawardene as a part of the Indo-Sri Lankan Accord. IPKF was solicited by it for restoring peace and order in the strife-torn and violence infested Jaffna. It was also given the responsibility to liquidate Tamil militants, who were trying to sabotage the implementation of the Accord. IPKF was entrusted with the responsibility to ensure the installation of civil administration through the election of Provincial Councils. IPKF has been successful in achieving, to a large extent, all these objectives. Yet neither the devolution of adequate powers to the provincial councils as envisaged in the

Indo-Sri Lankan Accord, nor the complete liquidation of terrorism (LTTE) has been possible. Hence, the Indo-Sri Lankan Accord continues to 'hung in balance'.

India fully accepts and respects the unity, sovereignty and territorial integrity of Sri Lanka. In fact, the IPKF was sent to help Sri Lanka to maintain these objectives by accommodating the legitimate aspirations of the Tamils of Sri Lanka. IPKF was sent:

1. At the request of the Sri Lankan Government;
2. To secure the implementation of the Indo-Sri Lankan Accord, and
3. To help the restoration of peace, order and civil administration in Northern and Eastern Parts of Sri Lanka.

Mr. Premadasa's call for the withdrawal of IPKF is based on a narrow view of the situation and for limited political gains. He has cared to ignore that:

1. Withdrawal of IPKF, a big force, cannot be practically secured overnight;
2. Withdrawal of IPKF will once again lead to increased LTTE terrorism and a re-emergence of civil war among the Tamil groups, and
3. It would negate the good work done by IPKF despite heavy losses.

The process of IPKF withdrawal has already been at work for the last six months or so. Any undue haste can be dangerous. It should be completed slowly in line with the gradual improvement in the ground situation.

Mr. Premadasa's government, however, it not prepared to face the realities, on the contrary it is trying to project to project herself as a victim of Indian domination. His decision to boycott the SAARC meeting of the Foreign Ministers and the decision of the Sri Lankan Foreign Minister, Mr. Wijeratne to reject an Indian invitation to visit New Delhi for holding talks for ironing out differences tend to reflect an unjustified rigidity and petulance in the part of Sri Lanka.

The Indo-Sri Lanka discord over Indo-Sri Lanka Agreement continues. The deadline set by Sri Lankan President Premadasa for the withdrawal of IPKF from North-East Sri Lanka has passed. Indian has resumed the withdrawal of IPKF in parts, with effect from 29th July 1989. Sri Lanka Foreign Minister, Mr. Ranjan Wijeratne has returned to Sri Lanka after conducting talks with Indian Foreign Minister, Mr. P.V. Narasimha Rao. It was a follow up of the signing of a joint communiqué on 28th July 1989, between Indian High Commissioner Mr. L.L. Malhotra and Sri Lanka's Foreign Secretary, Mr. Bernard Tilkaratna, in the presence of President Premadasa. This development proved to be a turning point. After the long impasse created by Sri Lankan President, Mr. Premadasa in demanding a total withdrawal of IPKF by 20th July 1989.

From 29th July to 4th August 1989, week-long talks were held between India and Sri Lanka for resolving the difference over the issues of IPKF withdrawal and the devolution of powers to provincial councils in Sri Lanka, as were established under the Indo-Sri Lankan Accord.

While announcing that the talks had ended, and the Sri Lankan delegation was returning home, an official spokesman said that the Sri Lankan side was carrying back "ideas and specific suggestions" that had emerged during the discussions.

He said the delegation would convey these to President Premadasa so that both sides may decide "how to proceed further."

The spokesman declined to elaborate on the ideas and suggestions and said no time limit had been fixed for resuming the negotiations.

The discussions were cordial and frank "characterised by a constructive approach." There were large areas of understanding and a better appreciation of each other's concerns.

Informed sources said the Sri Lankan side was not very enthusiastic about the phased withdrawal of the IPKF and the two sides had come to a "close understanding" on the devolution of powers and the linked issue of safety and security of Tamils in the North-eastern province.

The Lankan delegation, led by Mr. Wijeratne, had a "very relaxed and friendly" luncheon meeting with External Affairs Minister, P.V. Narasimha Rao, leader of the Indian delegation.

Both sides agreed that issues involved should be looked at from long-term perspectives in the context of more than 2,000 years of relationship between the two countries and cultural ties.

During its stay, the Sri Lankan delegation had two rounds of discussions with Mr. Rajiv Gandhi lasting four and a half hours.

It also had a meeting with Defence Minister K.C. Pant and held detailed discussions with Mr. Narasimha Rao and officials.

The spokesman said India would be having consultations with North-eastern province Chief Minister A. Vardaraja Perumal, who had arrived in the Capital.

Thus while the crisis, resulting from the fixing of July 29, 1989, as the deadline for the withdrawal of IPKF has passed, Indo-Sri Lankan differences over the implementation of Indo-Sri Lanka Accord and the issue of safety of the Tamils in Sri Lanka continue to characterises their bi-lateral relations. The fall out for South Asia has come in the form of inability to hold SAARC Foreign Affairs Ministers meeting.

India fully understands that it is neither desirable nor possible, nor even desired to keep IPKF in Sri Lanka even for a day longer than what is absolutely essential. Indian government feels that a sudden withdrawal of IPKF would certainly terminate the gains that have been registered during the last 2 years and it would jeoparadise completely the Indo-Sri Lankan Accord. It would, once again, set the stage for the re-emergence of LTTE terrorism, and a civil war among the Tamil groups. The new Tamil leadership which is managing the Provincial Councils wants that IPKF should continue to play its full role till the full implementation of Accord.

The present Sri Lankan leadership must rise above narrow nationalism, must put an end to diplomatic discourtesies towards India and must realise the dangers involved in demanding the sudden and total withdrawal of IPKF. Sri Lanka is on the brink of a disaster. JVP extremism, transport strike, immature leadership,

LTTE terrorism, Sinhala militancy, and economic crisis are the disturbing realities of Sri Lankan environment. These cannot be solved by demanding or even securing the withdrawal of IPKF. On the contrary, it can worsen the situation. Sri Lanka must realise the sincerity of India towards, Sri Lanka, Pakistan, USA and China cannot be collectively or individually good alternatives to India. Pakistan and the USA are involved knee-deep in Afghanistan crisis. China is still struggling to read just after the Tiananman happenings. India has been consistently considerate and helpful to Sri Lanka. Anti-India stance cannot really help the Sri Lankan government to build self-confidence and sustain its power. Both India and Sri Lanka can, through diplomacy, negotiate and accord on IPKF withdrawal. Sri Lanka must realise that the 'ceasefire demanded by LTTE, is a demand made for escaping the pressure of IPKF, the ruling party in North-eastern Provincial Government, which has been playing a constructive role in ending the ethnic strife and in restoring peace, order, stability and development in the region'.

Critics of India's Sri Lankan policy must not forget that Indo-Sri Lankan Accord and the consequent presence of IPKF have been instrumental in ending the 'blood bath' that had been taking place prior to these two developments. India cannot remain an idle by-stander to what happens in its neighbourhood particularly when it involves the life and limb of the persons of Indian origin in Sri Lanka, who have close cultural and emotional links with the Indian Tamils. India cannot ignore the possibility of a Pakistani or American involvement in Sri Lanka.

Sri Lanka should not be allowed to blame India for its own failures and the inability to secure a full implementation of the Indo-Sri Lankan Accord. The present Sri Lankan leadership must rise above its jaundiced vision and realise the helpful, benevolent and restrained role of India since the emergence of Tamil problem.

6

Nepal

I. Determinants of Indo-Nepal Relations

According to Dr. M.S. Rajan "In language and religion, gods and goddesses, food and clothing the two countries, India and Nepal, have more in common with each other than with any third country of the world." This observation rightly reflects the strong bonds that bind India and Nepal. Both have been living as good and friendly neighbours and there never has been a war between them. Since its independence India has always been very keen to maintain and develop further, the friendship and co-operation with Nepal.

India and Nepal are tied by the silken bonds of geography, history and culture. Together these constitute the three determinants, or more realistically speaking, the conditioning factors of Indo-Nepalese relations.

Geographically, the two countries inevitably form one geographic unit. Each one can be regarded as a territorial extension of the other depending upon whether one surveys the sub-continent from the mountain end or the sea-end. With the existence of an open boundary between them, the people of the countries have developed almost a shared living in the border areas.

Historically, the two countries originated from the same source. Ruling dynasties of one have mingled with those of the other and have even ruled areas which now fall within the bonds of the other. In the past, people or one country migrated to the other either in search of livelihood or business or on a spiritual quest.

For the two countries, the geographical contiguity and common historical past have given rise to a similar culture. "In language and religion, gods and goddesses, food and clothing, writes M.S. Rajan "two countries have more in common with each other than with any third country of the world."

In one of his speeches before the Lok Sabha, Prime Minister Desai observed on 12th December 1977; "we are bound to Nepal by ties of geography and mutual economic interests, and by religion, social and cultural bonds between our two peoples in a unique fashion with no close parallel anywhere in the world."

Indeed the above three factors have been a source of strength and gratification for Indo-Nepalese relations. Both the countries have always accepted the need to develop friendship and co-operation on the basis of these links and the similarities in the goals of their national interests. Both accept that the security of one is linked with the strength and stability of the other. For India, Nepal's strength, stability, progress and friendship together constitute an essential healthy condition for its national interests in South Asia. Particularly after 1962, India has come to realise the importance of Nepal for the security of India's northern borders. The Chinese occupation of Tibet and the continued Chinese aggression of Indian borders, have made India realise the importance of Nepal as a front-line buffer state. India has open borders with Nepal and the latter's northern border runs along the Tibetan frontier, therefore, if Nepal falls under the influence of China or any inimical power. Indian security would get exposed to dangers. It is in this respect that Nepal occupies an important strategic position in India's security system. India has no eye over Nepal. What India wants is the stability of Nepal as a Non-aligned country with strengthened bonds of friendship and co-operation with India. India fully respects the sovereignty and independence of Nepal and regards Panchsheel, besides the common historical and cultural links, as the basis for Indo-Nepalese relations.

Nepal also realises the importance of its relations with India. No one can go to Nepal without passing through India. Being a land-locked country with little scope for trade on northern borders, Nepal finds its economic and trade interests linked with relations with India. The nature and extent of trade and transit facilities provided by India constitute a determining factor of Nepalese economic and trading interests. Further, Nepal is fully aware of the inter-dependence of the national security systems of South Asia. It realises the important link between its security and the security of India. The presence of Chinese in Tibet and the existence of a boundary dispute between its two big neighbours — India and China, have made Nepal highly conscious of its security and of the need to maintain friendly and good neighbourly relations with India and China. The existence of close cultural links with India gives strength to the development of friendship and co-operation with India. Consequently, both India and Nepal have been engaged in the process of building warm, friendly and highly co-operative relations between them.

The Irritants in Indo-Nepalese Relations: Unfortunately, however, the path of Indo-Nepal relations has not been very smooth. The existence of certain irritants has prevented the development of highly co-operative relations between the two countries. Their relations have been generally friendly and co-operative but neither fully smooth nor highly co-operative. These have been characterised by ups and downs. Even today the issue of Nepalese demand for being accepted as a zone of peace continues to be an irritating issue in Indo-Nepal relations. The following factors can be described as the factors which have negatively influenced the course of Indo-Nepal relations.

1. Nepal's Fears: Despite strong geographical, historical and cultural links, Nepal has been quite apprehensive about India's role in the region. Being a small state, it fears India. Although there has never been a war between the two countries, Nepal fears that India can attempt an intervention in Nepal for securing its interests *vis-a-vis* China. Further, Nepal has been living with the fear of Indian interference in its internal affairs. The origin and spread of democratic movement in Nepal was regarded as a fall out of Indian National Movement. After independence, India's supports for the liberal democratic movement in the kingdom gave additional strengthen to such Nepalese fears. The sense of dependence in India for conducting sea trade too has been a source of fear for Nepal. It believes that India can exert political and economic pressures in Nepal for securing certain goals. The accession of Sikkim to India has been a source of disturbance for Nepal. China and Pakistan have been trying hard to exploit such

Nepalese fears for securing their objectives which include the objective of preventing the development of highly friendly and co-operative relations between the two 'Hindu States'— India and Nepal. The recent explosions in Kathmandu have again aroused fears in Nepal that anti-Nepalese elements having bases in India are behind these explosion. However, there has been no substance in such a wild thinking. Thus, Nepal's fear of India has prevented the speedier development of Indo-Nepal friendship and co-operation.

2. India's Initial Lack of Interest in Nepal: During the initial years of its independence, Indian Foreign Policy did not give much importance to relations with Nepal. There were two factors at the back of this lack of Indian interests in Nepal.

(*i*) India felt too much sure about Nepalese friendship. It regarded the geographical, historical and cultural links that existed between India and Nepal as the solid foundations upon which the two countries were destined to maintain and develop their relations. The feeling that Foreign Policy of Nepal cannot but continue to look to its interests as interests dependent' upon relations with India, made India complacent about relations with Nepal.

(*ii*) Secondly, India's over involvement in global affairs resulted into a virtual neglect of relations with its small neighbours like Nepal. In the words of Dr. L.S. Baral, "For some years after independence, India's foreign policy was principally determined by the existence of a hostile Pakistan, the cold war between the United States and Soviet Union, centralisation of authority in China, China's occupation of Tibet, and the U.S.-led security alliance systems in the Third World." This involvement prevented India from giving due importance to Nepal. Even the Chinese march into Tibet did not lead to major Indian attempts at securing more co-operative relations with Nepal. Indian leaders, perhaps felt that Chinese action in Tibet would made Nepal fearful about Chinese role and this in turn would make it realise further the necessity of developing relations with India. Under the circumstances, Indian foreign policy assumed that Nepal would continue to be friendly state to India and that there was nothing much to be done for securing this objective. Nepal's friendship with India was regarded as a historical necessity. Nepal, however, felt dissatisfied with such on Indian attitude. Initially it accepted the position because of the lack of options. Later on however, when China started emerging as a major power in world politics, Nepal felt no hesitation in working for the securing of friendship and co-operation with China. It then chose to ignore India's concern and interests for safeguarding its own security and other interests. As such, we can say that to some extent, India, because of its lack of interest in Nepal, itself was responsible for making Nepal look for an alternative to India. Indo-Nepalese relations during 1947-55 periods were alternatively affected by the lack of Indian initiative in this direction. Later on, India tried hard to repair the damage but had to be content with partial success.

3. **The Thesis of 'Special Relations' with Nepal:** During the period 1947-55, Indian foreign policy was governed by the perception of the thesis for India's special relations with Nepal. On 6th December, 1950 Prime Minister Nehru, in his speech in the Parliament observed, "We recognise Nepal as an independent country and wish her well. But even a child knows that one cannot go to Nepal without passing through India. Therefore, no other country can have as intimate a relationship with Nepal as ours is. We would like every other country to appreciate the intimate geographical and cultural relationship that exists between India and Nepal". The statement clearly indicates the Indian thesis of 'Special relations with Nepal.' This view gave the impression that India regarded Nepal as an 'area of India's influence'. It was such a thinking and the perception of its security system on the basis of British legacy that made free India adopt the old British policy towards Nepal. Such a policy was manifest in the treaty that free India concluded with Nepal in 1950 and which

renewed much of the spirit and content of the old treaties. "Free India," writes L.S. Baral, "obviously regarded those treaties as the surest means of protecting its frontiers in the north... and of keeping the three Himalayan monarchies (Nepal, Sikkim and Bhutan) within the sphere of its influence, as in the past, even in the changed situation." Such an Indian view was regarded by Nepal as an attempt to follow a 'big brotherly attitude towards Nepal'. It signed treaty of peace and friendship with India but felt concerned about the provisions. Naturally then, when India developed big strains and conflict in relations with China, Nepal did not hesitate to develop relations with China and to attempt a balance between India and China. This change in Nepalese attitude became particularly visible after 1960 and brought with it strains in Indo-Nepal relations. India tried to correct the things by following a policy of appeasement towards Nepal, but the move failed to repair the damage. Thus, this thesis of 'special relations with Nepal' proved to be a harmful factor in Indo-Nepalese relations.

4. The China Factor: China emerged as a Communist power in 1949 and soon after this change initiated steps for increasing its power and influence. It lost no time in claiming Tibet and in attempting to increase its power in Asia. India felt alarmed. On the one hand, it started working for securing friendship with China and on the other hand, it decided to link Himalayan kingdom's within a close fold of her friendship. In the fifties, India tried to counteract the growing Chinese influence in Nepal through diplomacy and by asserting close historical cultivating relations with both China and India as a means for safeguarding its security and other interests.

In 1959, China established its full sovereignty over Tibet and it was the time when Sino-Indian conflict over the boundary issue developed into a boundary dispute. Nepal felt her security threatened by this development and therefore decided to project the independence of its foreign policy from Indian foreign policy perceptions by undertaking moves designed at the development of relations with China. China utilised this change in Nepal's attitude by developing trade and political relations with the kingdom. The 1962 Sino-Indian border war and the humiliation suffered by

India, made things further worst for India. A visible tilt towards China appeared in Nepalese foreign policy, China tried to consolidate its position in Nepal by supporting the monarchy and its Panchayat system, and by the use of aid and trade as means for developing Sino-Nepalese friendship and co-operation. In China Nepal saw an opportunity of finding a counterpoise to India. Even today, Nepal continues to think in terms of a balance between India and China. Its demand for being accepted as a "Zone of Peace' appears to be governed by such a consideration. India fully respects the right of Nepal to have friendship with all countries, including China. Nevertheless, it does not want that friendship with other countries should in any way limit Nepal's friendship and relations with India. Speaking at the banquet held in his honour by their Majesties the King and Queen of Nepal at Kathmandu on 11th June 1959, Prime Minister Nehru observed..."We should remember that the activities of our two countries, like our borders, are joined together and they act and react on each other. We cannot forget this aspect, as well as our old relations which flowed from this. This affinity has benefited both of us in the past and shall benefit us in future also. Without doubt, we should have friendly relations with other countries as well, but we should not forget that forming the basis of all our present relations is an older relationship which we cannot renounce." India as such views with concern any attempt that is made by Nepal for cultivating friendship and co-operation with China. The China factor still continues to be a major determinant of Indo-Nepalese relations. It has definitely checked the process of development of co-operation between India and Nepal.

5. Internal Politics of Nepal: During the period 1947-60, New Delhi's attitude towards Nepal was also conditioned by the considerations for strengthening of democratic process in Nepal. In fact in the initial stages India regarded the democratic movement in Nepal as a part of her national movement. Prime Minister Nehru wanted that Nepal's political system—a feudal system headed by Monarchy, should be made broad-based by involving the common people in the administration of Nepal. India felt that in order to be a stable and progressive state

Nepalese political system must be responsive and responsible to the people. Consequently, India did not hesitate to give moral support to anti-feudal, and anti-Rana forces in Nepal. It was such a thinking that made New Delhi accept the role of mediator in the conflict between the Ranas and King Tribhuwan. It was largely due to Indian efforts that the constitutional crisis in Nepal was resolved and King Tribhuwan was restored to the Nepalese throne. Such a policy however, produced a mixed reaction in Nepal.

On the one hand, the people of Nepal appreciated the restoration of King Tribhuwan to the throne to Nepal, but on the other hand, certain sections of press and public opinion in Nepal regarded this as an undesirable Indian interference in the internal affairs of Nepal. Many influential leaders of Nepal did not hesitate to express anti-Indian sentiments through press, party resolutions and public demonstrations in Nepal.

In 1955, King Mahendra acceded to Nepalese throne. He did not view with favour the democratic set up and hence, wanted to strengthen the role of monarchy in Nepal. But Indian diplomacy was successful in making him accept the value of parliamentary democracy and the need for Nepal to have a responsible and responsive system.

In 1959, elections were held in Nepal and for the first time parliamentary democracy was established in the Himalayan Kingdom. But this change could remain effective only till December 1960, when royal takeover of administration of Nepal was effected. To begin with, this move gave rise to an adverse reaction in India, but later on due to the growing Chinese menace all along the Himalayan borders, India decided to observe restraint and accept the change as an internal affair of Nepal. India successfully prevented the transformation of this reaction against the Royal take-over into an anti-system movement in Nepal. It tried to maintain and develop further its friendship and co-operation with Nepal. Through aid, trade, and declarations affirming respect for the sovereignty and integrity of Nepal, to have political system of their choice. It has refrained from helping or sheltering the anti-monarchical and pro-democratic forces of Nepal. It has been voicing concern for the safety and welfare of certain Nepalese leader but in the main, it has been refraining from any involvement or action that may be considered as an interference in Nepalese internal affairs. It has accepted the existing Panchayat system of Nepal as the popularly backed political system. As such, the nature of Nepalese political system has now ceased to be an irritant in Indo-Nepal relations.

The recent popular verdict in favour of the Panchayat system in Nepal and the new reforms introduced by King Birendra have further improved the conditions. India and Nepal now understand each other better. The Governments of the two countries have now exhibited successfully the strong determination to keep Indo-Nepal relations free from such tensions and strains as have their roots in the difference between the political systems of the two countries.

6. The Issue of 'Zone of Peace': Since 1975, Nepal has been trying to get recognition as a 'Zone of Peace'. Such a status, argues Nepal, is essential for meeting the security and developmental needs of Nepal. King Birendra, while announcing the proposal for making Nepal a peace zone, described it as a sheet anchor of Nepal's international policy more in the context of imperatives of peace and for her own development needs than as a counterpoise to regional tensions. He observed, "In essence, it is only an extension of Nepal's genuine desire to live in peace. The absence of peace will delay, make more difficult and even deform our development, just as a world without peace will jeopardise our traditional independence." Further, Nepal feels that such a status is essential for maintaining true non-alignment and for playing an increased role towards the securing of peace and progress. Consequently, Nepal wants that all countries should accept Nepal as a 'Zone of Peace'. It, particularly wants India to accept and support this proposal India, on the other hand, has not been quite willing to accept this proposal. It is believed that this proposal, if accepted, would involve certain limitations for Indian foreign policy in South Asia. India believes that Nepal does not really need such a status. With India, it has already a Treaty of Peace and Friendship and the acceptance of this proposal would tantamount to an abrogation of the Treaty. Nepal, however, continues to regard this proposal as a vital necessity for securing its national interest and world peace. The peace zone concept has already become a national aspiration in Nepal. It stands enshrined in the Constitution of Nepal. India's hesitation towards the acceptance of this proposal has been a source of irritation for Nepal India would have to take clear stand on this issue in the near future. Preferably, India should use diplomatic means for satisfying Nepalese desire in respect of this issue. A tacit recognition to this proposal can create a large amount of goodwill for India in Nepal.

II. The History of Indo-Nepal Relations Since 1947

The relations between India and Nepal are age-old and based on geography, religion, culture, customs and so many other things. The people of the two countries are like brothers and there exists a strong bond of love and affinity between them. However, despite all this, the political relations between the two countries, since 1947, have not been absolutely smooth. These have been characterised by ups and downs, sun-shine and shades, goodwill and tensions, and co-operation and differences over various issues.

Analysing the history of their bilateral relations L.S. Baral has observed: "Indo-Nepalese relations have passed through a number of distinct phases during the past three decades. At times they turned sour owing to factors, global as well as geopolitical." From 1947 to 1955, India, influenced by the considerations of her security and the British legacy, tried to maintain special relations with Nepal. It considered Nepal a special area of interest and influence for India. In 1947, India concluded a 'Stand Still Agreement' with Nepal. By it the two countries agreed to maintain the old Treaty of 1923, until the conclusion of a new treaty. By another Tripartite Agreement, India, Britain and Nepal agreed that 12 Battalions of Nepalese Gurkhas shall be employed by India and 8 Battalions by Britain. In July 1950, a new Treaty of Peace and Friendship between India and Nepal was concluded. By this treaty, both the countries affirmed their recognition of each other's sovereignty and independence and agreed to hold mutual consultations on matters relating to each other's national security. It was stated that "the two governments hereby undertake to inform each other of any serious friction or understanding with any neighbouring state." Further, that "neither country shall tolerate any threat to the security of other by a foreign aggression. To deal with such threats, the two governments shall consult with each other and devise effective counter measures." Alongwith the treaty, it was also agreed that Indian government shall establish military check posts on Nepal's northern borders.

All these measures were governed by the Indian desires to secure its as well as—Nepal's security. The security and defence of India and Nepal were considered to be interdependent, particularly after the emergence of China as a Communist power and after the march of Chinese troops into Tibet.

India fully respected the sovereignty of Nepal and wanted to see Nepal becoming prosperous. At the same time, it wanted that Nepalese political system should be made broad-based, responsible and responsive. It wanted a change from feudal system, as was being maintained by the Ranas' of Nepal, to a democratic system. The co-operation between the peoples of India and Nepal during the era of freedom struggle in India, made it natural for the Indians to expect the establishment of a democratic system in Nepal. Their sympathies, as such, were naturally with the Nepali Congress, which was struggling to secure better participation of the Nepalese in their political system. India, therefore, felt no hesitation in expressing its concern at the attempts which were being made by the Ranas to forcibly maintain their domination over the administration of Nepal. When the crisis in Nepal became worsened and King Tribhuwan was forced to take refuge in New Delhi, India had to act as the mediator. It was with the efforts of India that a political settlement was effected in Nepal and King Tribhuwan was restored to the Nepalese throne. At this time, India secured an assurance from the Government of Nepal that steps would be taken towards the introduction of democratic reforms in Nepal. Such an Indian role, received a mixed reaction in Nepal. Some regarded it as a welcome move which accepted the continuance of monarchy in Nepal, whereas others felt that it was a case unwanted big brotherly attitude of India towards Nepal.

It was only in the early sixties that India could finally assure Nepal that is fully accepts and respects the right of the Nepalese to have a political system of their own choice. The introduction of Partyless Panchayat System and certain other democratic reforms of King Mahendra, were accepted by India as a part of Nepal's domestic affairs. The China fact made India highly conscious of its relations with Nepal and it decided to keep away from all such factors as were likely to cause strains in Indo-Nepal relations.

For developing trade and economic links India in 1950, signed a Trade and Commerce Treaty with Nepal. Both the countries agreed to exchange Consulate Generals. Nepal agreed to import arms and ammunition from India. India agreed to provide aid and assistance for the economic development of Nepal.

In 1952, India favourably responded to Nepal's request for the services of some Indian civil servants and military personnel for helping Nepal to undertake administrative reforms and military reorganisation. It also undertook projects for improving Nepalese transport and communication systems. The construction of Tribhuwan Rajpath between Raxaul and Kathmandu was undertaken. India did everything to provide aid, advice and assistance to Nepal, because it fully realised the need to make Nepal economically stable. Under the Colombo Plan Agreement concluded in July 1954, India undertook to contribute ₹5 millions during the next four years towards the development of communications, irrigation projects and water supply schemes in Nepal. India took these and other measures for improving Indo-Nepalese relations.

Indo-Nepal Relations (1955 to 71): In the second phase of Indo-Nepal relations, the emergence of certain new developments made the course of friendship and co-operation between the two countries uneven and strained. In 1955, King Mahendra ascended the throne in Nepal and he was interested in developing Nepal's relations with other countries, particularly with China. He regarded the development of relations with China as a means to assert Nepal's independence and identity. He was unhappy with the nature of Nepal's relations with India. The outburst of occasional anti-India demonstrations in Kathmandu and repeated criticism of India's alleged big brotherly attitude towards Nepal. Further strengthened the King's faith in the need for cultivating relations with China.

The emergence of boundary dispute between India and China, in the post-1955 period, further made him conscious of Nepal's security needs *vis-a-vis* both India and China.

Under these circumstances, Indian diplomacy decided to impress upon the King, the need to strengthen the political base of Nepal and to work for the maintenance of peace and friendship with China. In 1959, Indian diplomacy achieved success in respect of the first objective but failed in respect of the second. Nepal got disturbed over the situation particularly when in 1959. Chinese successfully accomplished the task of making Tibet a part of China. This development further deteriorated Sino-Indian relations and both became open rivals. In respect of Nepal, both started competing for the development of friendship and co-operation. The establishment of parliamentary system in Nepal in 1959, came as a big relief and help to Indian efforts which were aimed at cementing Indo-Nepal ties. To assure Nepal, Prime Minister Nehru even declared that "any aggression on Bhutan or Nepal would be considered aggression on India." The Nepalese Prime Minister B.P. Koirala also indirectly accepted the view when he observed, "I take Mr. Nehru's statement as an expression of friendship that in case of aggression against Nepal, India would send help if such help is ever sought." Nepalese government also realised the danger of Chinese expansionism and felt more inclined to strengthen ties with India. It resisted all such Chinese moves — a non-aggression pact with Nepal, withdrawal of Indian technicians in Nepal, building of Nepal-China road etc., as were aimed at creating a wedge between Nepal and India. The conclusion of Trade and Transit Treaty further brought India and Nepal closer, and hence, between 1955-60 Indo-Nepal relations continued to be deeply cordial, friendly and co-operative. Nepalese King's desire for developing Sino-Nepal relations remained subdued.

However, the situation got a setback in December, 1960, when King Mahendra took over the administration of Nepal. Indo-Nepal relations developed a stress and strain partly due to the liquidation of the popular and representative government of Prime Minister B.P. Koirala, and partly due to the new foreign policy posture adopted by the King in the years that followed. Much to the disappointment of India, the Nepalese king decided to go ahead with the plans to develop friendship and co-operation with China. The Indian attempts to secure a favourable change through the use of economic and political pressures produced a reaction in the form of Nepalese attempts to use China as a counterpoise against India.

During the Sino-Indian War of 1962, Nepal maintained a neutral stand. The humiliating defeat suffered by India, made it necessary for the Indian government to abandon, the policy of putting pressure on Nepal. Instead, it brought into operation certain moves which were designed to win over Nepal through appeasement and concessions. An attempt was initiated for securing a readjustment of relations with Nepal. India started reaffirming its respect for the sovereignty and independence of Nepal. It now decided to abandon its policy of supporting any particular type of political system for Nepal and to give greater regard to Nepalese sensitivities. India further agreed to give more aid and economic concessions to Nepal. It decided to reconcile fully with the new Nepalese political system — Partyless Panchayat System, that had been introduced by the King.

In March, 1963, Mr. Lal Bahadur Shastri, the then Home Minister of India, paid a visit to Nepal and assured King Mahendra, India's deep feelings of friendship and regard for him and his Government. India through this visit, initiated 'friendship diplomacy' in Kathmandu and promised friendship and economic aid to Nepal. Obviously, this changed Indian policy towards Nepal was born out of the situation that had come to develop after the Chinese Aggression of 1962. Many visits were exchanged by dignitaries of the two countries in 1963 and 1964. These consistently emphasised the need to maintain and consolidate the age-old intimate friendship and it is between India and Nepal. The contacts between the leaders of the two countries and the new understanding that developed helped the two countries to re-rail Indo-Nepalese relations.

But the Indian policy of appeasement could not fully succeed in weaning Nepal away from its apparently increasing association with China. On the one hand, Nepal during this period tried to secure maximum gains out of relations with India and on the other hand, it kept up its policy of securing relations with China. It justified this policy on grounds of achieving a balance in bilateral relations with India and China. It used the situation for securing favourable concessions from both India and China. For satisfying China, Nepalese Prime Minister K.N. Bista, in 1969, came out with the demand for withdrawal of Indian military personnel and liaison group for Nepal and for satisfying India, he kept on toasting the traditional links between the two countries.

Indo-Nepal Relations during 1971-77: The changes that took place in the South Asian sub-continent during 1970-71, brought into existence an environment in which India found it possible to replace appeasement with a more assertive attitude towards Nepal. The Indo-Soviet Peace and Friendship Treaty, and India's role in the liberation of Bangladesh gave a big boost to Indian prestige in the region. The status of being the major power in South Asia gave India the much-needed base for securing its interest in South Asia. In respect of Nepal, India decided to advocate reciprocity as the basis for Indo-Nepal relations. It made it clear what while making foreign policy goals, Nepal should not be unmindful of Indian interests and that it should not expect India to keep on developing friendship with Nepal through unilateral concessions. India followed this up by taking a bold stand over the issue of renewal of Trade and Transit Treaty with Nepal that had become necessary due to expiry of the old treaty in November, 1970. It was only after protracted negotiations, that the Treaty was renewed in August 1971. Nepal failed to get all the desired concessions from India and this strongly indicated the change in India's attitude towards Nepal.

In 1974, Indo-Nepal relations got strained when, because of a fear of a possible fall out on its political system. Nepal reacted strongly to Sikkim's accession to India. The happiness expressed by Nepali leaders, particularly Koirala, added fuel to Nepalese fears. India exhibited full firmness in respect of Nepalese reactions. On the one hand, it assured Nepal that friendship and co-operation would be maintained, on the other hand, it declared the resolve the deal firmly with hostility from any quarter. It further assured Nepal and Nepali Congress shall in no case be permitted to use Indian territory for activities against the Royal regime. Despite these Indian moves, Nepal showed no intention to change its views and this forced India to summon its Ambassador to Kathmandu, Mr, M.N. Rasgotra for urgent consultation and stay in New Delhi for several weeks. India also decided to take a more firm stand over the issue of supply of petroleum, and oil to Nepal. This stiff Indian attitude paid dividends and there appeared a welcome change in Nepal's attitude. The visits of Nepalese Prime Minister, N.P. Rizal to New Delhi and of Indian Finance Minister, Y.B. Chavan to Nepal further proved helpful in removing misunderstandings. But India still decided to maintain firmness in relations with Nepal.

In 1975, India did not show any inclination towards the acceptance of King Birendra's proposal for the acceptance of Nepal as a Zone of Peace. Along with this, India, once again, did not hesitate to express sympathy with the demands of Nepali Congress which included the demand for the return of its leaders B.P. Koirala, Ganeshman Singh and their associates to Kathmandu, and for the restoration of democracy in Nepal. Further, India decided to place restrictions on the movements of Nepalese nationals in some specified areas in Indian territory, on the ground "that those areas being "protected' were out of bounds for nationals of other countries." All these moves were of the nature of rebuffs to Nepal and were aimed to making the Government of Nepal realise the consequences of overlooking the importance of relations with India. Thus during 1971-77, India maintained friendly relations with Nepal; but along with it an attempt was made to base these upon reciprocity. India abandoned its appeasement policy towards Nepal and instead tried to develop relations on the basis of mutuality of interests and needs. Its improved power position helped it to secure the desired change in Indo-Nepal relations.

Indo-Nepal Relations in 1977-79 (Janata Era): In March 1977, Janata Party government came to power in India: Prime Minister Desai and Foreign Minister Vajpayee together agreed to give a new strength to India's relations with its neighbours. Improvement of relations with India's neighbours was described as 'the top priority' by the new Government. It decided to initiate steps for resolving outstanding issues and differences with neighbouring countries. Realising the existence of close geographic, historic and cultural links with Nepal, the decision was taken to initiate immediate steps for resolving Indo-Nepal differences over various issues. The issue of a composite trade and transit treaty and of the restrictions placed on Nepalese nationals in certain specified areas of India needed immediate attention and the Janata government was quick to take up these issues with Nepal.

In Nepal, the emergence of Janata Party to power in India was regarded as a wide spread support for the victory of democracy. Further the close relations between some of the leaders of the Janata Party and some members of the Nepali Congress were known to Nepalese rulers. As such, they feared an increased Indian pressure for the rehabilitation of Koirala in Nepal and for the introduction of democratic reforms in the Kingdom. At the same time, the rulers of Nepal decided to explore the chances of improving Indo-Nepal relations through renewed active contacts with the new leaders of India. It was this decision which prompted King Birendra to stop over in New Delhi for a day on 2nd April 1977, and to establish direct contacts with Prime Minister Desai and Mr. Vajpayee, Nepalese Foreign Minister, Krishan Raj, who accompanied the King observed that "the purpose of the visit was to have mutual understanding of each other's problems and aspirations." Similar views were expressed by the Indian leaders.

The net results however, were not very happy because the Nepalese King and other leaders were greatly disturbed over the expression of concern and sympathy for Koirala by some members of Indian Parliament. In particular, they felt disturbed by the nature and tone of the words which were used to describe Koirala. Mr. Karpoori Thakur described Koirala as "the unquestioned people's leader of Nepal, who had been fighting for human rights and people's freedom in his country." Similar words were used by many other Janata MPs. The subsequent expression of sympathy and support for B.P. Koirala by Shri Jaya Parkash Narayan further agitated the minds of several Panchayat leaders of Nepal.

The adverse comments in certain sections of Indian Press over the political situation in Nepal added fuel to the fire. Nepalese leaders came out with severe criticism of Indian support for rebels like Koirala, and they once again started denouncing the Indian Press comments as "baseless, misleading and mischievous" which constituted an irresponsible and unfortunate attempt at an interference in the internal affairs of Nepal. This development inflicted further strains on Indo-Nepal relations. The state of these relations reflected a trend that was much against the proclaimed desire of the Janata government to secure an improvement in relations with Nepal. Two Janata leaders, Mr. Chanderashekhar and Mr. Karpoori Thakur paid a 3-day (27-29, April) visit to Nepal for pacifying the Panchayat leaders of Nepal. But the visit failed to produce any positive result.

It was in May, 1977, that Government of India, through its Foreign Minister, Mr. A.B. Vajpayee declared that the views expressed in certain sections of Indian Press, which was both free and democratic, were not the views of the Government. Mr. Vajpayee gave an assurance to Nepal that India in no way wanted to interfere with Nepalese internal affairs and that it was interested in maintaining good and friendly relations with all countries. Particularly with the countries in the neighbourhood of India, Vajpayee's statement was well-received in Nepal, but still Nepalese leaders and press, including Prime Minister Giri, kept up playing the alleged undesirable policies and attitude of India towards Nepal. Prime Minister Giri in a Press conference in Kathmandu on 24th May, came out with a tirade against India, the Janata leaders and the Indian Press. The Nepalese Press followed this up by reenacting its anti-Indian posture, and it came out with the charge that India was irresponsibly interfering with the internal affairs of Nepal. Even the repeated assurances given by Mr. Vajpayee failed to a carry conviction with the Nepal Press. In its official releases, however, the Government of Nepal continued to express the determination to develop relations with India and other countries on the basis of equality, non-interference in internal affairs of other countries and respect and understanding for each other's political systems and aspirations. India also continued to repeat the determination to continue to work for the development of healthy and good neighbourly relations with Nepal. Despite these official expressions of determination to maintain friendship and co-operation, the Indo-Nepal relations continued to drift in different directions.

The decision of the Government of Nepal to release Koirala on health grounds and the July 14th to 16th, 1977, visit of Vajpayee to Kathmandu were the two development which set into motion the process of attempting an improvements in Indo-Nepal relations. Vajpayee's visit was not only successfully in removing the misunderstanding but also it paved the way for reactivation of certain projects in Nepal which were yet to be completed by India. Vajpayee assured Nepal that India was keen to develop friendship and co-operation with Nepal. He reaffirmed India's complete faith in the Indo-Nepal Treaty of Peace and Friendship and expressed the willingness of his Government to discuss the proposal for constituting Nepal into a Zone of Peace. This visit helped the process of securing an understanding between India and Nepal. The chances for improving the ties between the two countries further brightened when, in August 1977, Prime Minister Desai informed the Nepalese Ambassador that India was willing to conclude two separate trade and transit treaties with Nepal. In Nepal, the replacement of the hardliner Tulsi Giri by Kirti Nidhi Bista as the new Prime Minister of Nepal, further facilitated the attempt to secure and improvement in relations, between the two countries.

From 9th December 1977, Prime Minister Desai paid a visit to Nepal and his visit helped the two countries to eliminate some of the controversies and to develop a clear understanding of each other's view points on various issues. After his visit, Prime Minister Desai, while speaking in Parliament, observed on December 12, 1977: "My visit, the discussions which I had, and the general atmosphere of warmth, cordiality leads me to believe that apprehension and misgivings about India's attitude have been removed. The relations have to be restored to one of trustful, as is appropriate between countries whose abiding compulsion must link them in peace and progress." The talks cleared the way for completing the Indian aided projects—Karnali, Pancheshwar, Devi Ghat projects etc., in Nepal. Further, both the sides agreed on the desirability of widening and intensifying the scope for co-operation in harnessing common rivers for mutual benefits such as irrigation, soil conservation, power production and navigation purposes. However, during the visit Prime Minister Desai categorically repeated the view that in the presence of the Treaty of Peace, Friendship between India and Nepal, there was little substance in the proposal for constituting Nepal into a Zone of Peace.

On 17th March 1978, India and Nepal signed two separate treaties one relating to trade and the other to transit facilities. These treaties helped the restoration of confidence in Indo-Nepal ties. The Treaty of Trade provided: "In order to assist in the industrialisation process of Nepal, the Government of India have agreed to enlarge the scope of preferences for Nepalese manufactured products in Indian markets. The two Governments have also agreed to incorporate necessary arrangements to maintain supplies of essential commodities needed by each other. In keeping with the efforts of the two countries to promote mutual trade, preferential treatment would be accorded to be primary products on reciprocal basis." The Treaty of Transit laid down the procedures to be followed for Nepal's traffic-in-transit through India. It threw open the use of overland routes for the export of Nepalese goods to Bangladesh. Further, it was agreed to check unauthorised trade the two sides also decided to hold regular consultations for facilitating effective and harmonious implementation of these treaties and agreements. By an agreement signed on 7th April 1978, India agreed to provide ₹12.45 crores (₹18.05 crores in Nepalese currency) for the renovation and extension of the Chandra Canal System, construction of a pumped canal from western Kosi Canal for the irrigation and construction and distribution system from western Kosi Canal in Nepal.

On 15th April, the Nepalese Prime Minister, Kirti Nidhi Bista came on an 11-day official visit to India. This visit further extended the area of understanding between New Delhi and Kathmandu. The visit gave strength to Indo-Nepal co-operation in the setting up of joint enterprises in Nepal. India agreed to charge only domestic prices for different varieties of coal exported to Nepal. However, Nepal failed to get Indian endorsement to the peace zone proposal.

By an agreement of 8th June 1978, India agreed to provide ₹320 millions aid for the construction of Devi Ghat hydro-electric project in Nepal. (This project now stands completed and was Commissioned on 22nd July, 1983) From 26th to 30th July 1978, a high powered multi-disciplinary Indian delegation of industrial experts visited Nepal and held discussion with Nepalese official. At the conclusion of the discussions, a Memorandum of Understanding on Industrial and Economic Co-operation was signed and it was agreed to develop trade and industrial co-operation for reducing the trade deficit between the two countries. Understanding regarding the use of Udaipur Cement Plant and development of paper and pulp industries were also reached. A project for manufacturing diesel pumping sets in Nepal and plan for promoting small scale and cottage industries were also accepted. India further agreed to share industrial and technological expertise with Nepal. These developments gave strength to the process of Indo-Nepal co-operation.

Thus, during Janata Party period, the initial lack of understanding of each other's view point was successfully overcome and replaced by good progress towards the securing of Indo-Nepal co-operation in various spheres. India was successful in establishing a new understanding with Nepal. Irritants like Nepal's proposal for a Zone of Peace and the issue of restrictions upon Nepalese nationals in certain areas of India etc. continued to remain unresolved. But despite these, the Janata government was, on the whole, quite successful in securing the progress of Indo-Nepal friendship and co-operation on the basis of "Beneficial Bilateralism."

Indo-Nepal Relations in 1980: After the return of Mrs. Indira Gandhi to power in January 1980, the process of development of Indo-Nepal friendship and co-operation continued to progress satisfactorily.

Mrs. Indira Gandhi was quite alert to the need for maintaining good neighbourly relations with Nepal. Despite some differences over certain issues, the Government and leaders in the two countries showed exemplary pragmatism and realism. The two countries were successful in maintaining and developing further bilateral trade and took steps to overcome trade imbalances and balance of payment problem. Both started co-operating in giving a meaningful start to the process of South Asian economic and trade co-operation, the chances of increased co-operation among the countries of South Asian region further brightened, after the August 1983, New Delhi Conference of the Foreign Ministers of the seven South Asian countries.

The regular contacts and direct communications between the leaders of the two countries helped the growth of understanding between the two countries. In November, 1980, Indian Foreign Minister Mr. Narasimha Rao visited Nepal and held important discussions on a number of subjects with the Prime Minister Surya Bahadur Thapa and the Panchayat Minister of Nepal. Mr. Navraj Subedi after the talks, Mr. Subedi observed: "Indo-Nepalese relations had been further strengthened in recent times by our mutual trust and common aspirations." Mr. Narasimha Rao also re-affirmed that, "India attached the highest importance to nurturing of friendly and co-operative relations with Nepal." In December 1981, President Neelam Sanjeeva Reddy paid a state visit to Nepal. Speaking at the civic reception accorded to him at Kathmandu, President Reddy observed: "Relations between India and Nepal have been historically built on the solid foundations of extensive people-to-people contacts which make for abiding understanding." The address presented to Mr. Reddy by Kathmandu Nagar Panchayat, among other things, said "For such close neighbours as Nepal and India which have many things into common, it becomes all the more indispensable to strengthen their relations and to co-operate in each other's socio-economic development efforts on the basis of the five principles of peaceful coexistence."

This realisation about the necessity of co-operation and friendship between Nepal and India indeed helped the two countries to overcome problems and resolve their differences and keep up the process of development of friendship and co-operation. Both have been able to maintain and develop further trade links and economic co-operation. India maintained its commitments regarding the completion of hydro electric projects in Nepal.

The Commissioning of the Devi Ghat Hydro electric project in July 1983 was in line with the Indian policy of helping Nepal in its struggle for economic and industrial development. By an agreement on May, 1982, India gave a number of trade and transit concessions to Nepal. It decided to provide insurance cover to Nepal-bound goods from Calcutta Port. It also agreed that the movement of Nepalese goods from one place to another in India would be made faster. It further agreed to abandon the practice of charging triple rent from Nepalese parties. The time period for removing goods from the port was increased to 45 days. Moreover, India decided to give another point for trans-shipment of Nepalese goods at Gorakhpur.

Prime Minister Mr. Rajiv Gandhi has stepped up the drive to secure more friendly and co-operative relations with this Himalayan Kingdom. New Delhi has shown full respect for the sovereignty, territorial integrity and stability of Nepal by giving due-importance to Nepal the emergence of SAARC has indeed helped and is bound to strengthen further the economic trade and cultural co-operation among the countries of South Asia in general and among India and Nepal in particular because of deep and historical ties between these two countries.

The King of Nepal's visits to India in 1986 has helped the two countries to review their relations. Difference over Zone of Peace status for Nepal continued to surround the talks. However, both the Nepalese King and Indian Prime Minister, did not allow this negative factor to adversely affect the course of growing Indo-Nepalese friendly co-operation in economic trade, cultural and technological spheres. Both accepted that the 'Panchsheel' spirit and five principles constituted the best basis for conducting their bilateral relations.

Thus, India and Nepal continue to fulfill their desire to increase bilateral co-operation and to strengthen the bonds of friendship. India fully respects the sovereignty of Nepal and deals with Nepal on an equal basis. Realising the strategic importance of Nepal, Indian foreign policy has now very actively engaged in the process of developing Indo-Nepal ties. Nepal also now realises better the importance of its relations with India. It has become confident that India does not want to interfere with the internal political affairs of Nepal. The development of trade links and economic relations have helped Nepal in achieving the objectives of its national policy. Both the countries are now working towards the further cementing of their relations. "In the current scheme of things," writes Dr. Bimal Prasad, "Nepal is likely to develop co-operative relations with India on the basis of co-equality, co-sharing, non-dominance and non-dictator." The only outstanding issue that needs careful handing is the Nepalese proposal for getting the status of a peace zone. Indian diplomacy must come forward to amicably sort out and settle the issue.

III. Proposal for a Peace Zone Status

For the last ten years Nepal's proposal for a 'Zone of Peace' (ZoP) has been the object of discussion in India. In the context of Indo-Nepal relations, as well as of regional balance of power, this proposal has been an important object of deep interest.

It was in late 1975, that the proposal was announced by king Birendra as "a sheet-anchor of Nepal's international policy move in the context of imperatives of peace for her own development needs than as a counterpoise to regional tension, although it positively contained the potentials of leading to the idea of a 'Zone of Peace' being established in the region and extending these from one to other parts of the world." It was stated that the proposal was not mooted out of fear from any country or quarter. In its essence it was described "as an extension of Nepal's genuine desire to live in peace, because the absence of peace will deny, make more difficult and even deform our development just as a world without peace, will jeopardise our traditional independence." After its advocacy by the king, the Nepalese leaderships has always been engaged in elucidating, clarifying and justifying it. They have used a number of concepts—panchsheel, geo-political realities of Nepal, world peace, regional peace and good neighbourliness towards all the neighbours etc., for securing support for this proposal.

The Main Features: A former Prime Minister to Nepal, Mr. Surya Bahadur Thapa made it clear that Nepal, after being accepted as a 'Zone of Peace' by all of her neighbours, would carry out the following commitments:

1. Nepal will adhere to the policy of peace, Non-alignment and peaceful coexistence and will constantly endeavour to develop friendly relations with all countries of the world, regardless of their social and political system and

particularly its neighbours on the basis of equality and respect for each other's independence and sovereignty.

2. Nepal will not resort to the use or threat of force in any way which might endanger the peace and security of other countries.
3. Nepal will seek peaceful settlement of all disputes between it, and other state or states.
4. Nepal will not interfere in the internal affairs of other states.
5. Nepal will not permit any activities on its soil that are hostile to other states, supporting this proposal and in reciprocity such states will not permit any activities hostile to Nepal.
6. Nepal will continue to honour the obligations of all the existing treaties which it has concluded with other countries so long as they remain valid.
7. In conformity, with its policy of peace and Non-alignment, Nepal will not enter into military alliances nor will it allow the establishment of any foreign military base on its soil. In reciprocity, other countries supporting this proposal will not enter into military alliance nor will they allow establishment of military base on their soil directed against Nepal.

On the basis of such an analysis, Nepalese leaders strongly advocate the need for accepting Nepal as a 'Zone of Peace'. The fact that this proposal now stands enshrined in the Constitution of Nepal testifies to the importance that Nepal attaches to the Peace Zone concept. In particular, it is very keen to secure Indian acceptance of this proposal. India, on the other hand, till today, has refrained from committing herself to support the proposal. The opinion in India still stands divided. Some observers regard the proposal as superfluous, idealistic and unhelpful for Indian interests, whereas others hold that India can earn Nepalese goodwill by accepting the proposal and in the process has nothing to lose. Sunanda K. Dutta-Ray in an article published in *Times of India* has explained why it might be politic for India to respond positively to Nepal's insistent demand to be recognised as 'Zone of Peace'.

The main reason for such a view being that Nepalese goodwill and friendship is essential for Indian security.

Similarly, Surendra Raj Sharma, in his article, Nepal's Peace, Zone Proposal (NPZP) (*Indian Express*, 4 February 1983), supported the need for acceptance of this proposal for India. He writes, "Nepal's peace zone proposal, to be precise, is the product of the peace-aspiring and high-toned mind of King Birendra. The peace zone concept is by now enshrined in the Constitution of Nepal and as such, symbolises the aspirations of the entire nation for the peace. And the acceptance, recognition and ratification of this particular proposal would create for India the amount of goodwill of the entire. Nepalese nation as no other human issue will, at least for the foreseeable future. This is an irreducible as also an irrefutable fact."

India's View of the Proposal: Government of India is as yet not prepared to express its views on the proposal and technically the proposal continues to be "under active consideration." It believes that the existence of the Indo-Nepalese Treaty of Peace and Friendship does not justify the need to accept the proposal. There exists a difference of opinion between in India and Nepal over the proposal. Rishikesh Shaha in his article: 'Nepal's Peace illusions Diplomacy instead of Declaration", holds that the differences revolve around three basic questions: (1) What is the geo-political reality? (2) Are the security interests of Nepal and India indeed bound up as recognised by the 1950 Treaty? (3) Will acceptance of the proposal perpetually free the region, or even Nepali territory alone from being the scene of armed conflict?

The Wayout: After analysing the proposal on the basis of these question, Rishikesh Shaha holds that the proposal has in-built illusion and its acceptance would demand many changes in the context of Indo-Nepal relations. It may lead to an end of the recruitment of Gurkha soldiers for the Indian and British army's as regulated by the Tripartite Agreement of 1947 and periodically amended. Mr. Shaha regards the 1950 Treaty as comparable with the Soviet Union's arrangement with Finland, Mongolia, and "a peace zone would call for changes and adjustments that will not be realistic or in India's interests." In fact, he sees the idea as an ineffective Palace Plan to insulate Nepal from regional pressures and feels that it distracts attention from more substantive matters of mutual interest. He further suggests that King Birendra can achieve more for his country through quite diplomacy than by trying to institutionalise a theoretical concept. However, realising the delicate and emotional nature of Indo-Nepal relations, he advocates the need for making Indian diplomacy more active for checking certain attempts that are being made by India's two adversaries and competitions — China and Pakistan, who have already accepted the proposal to project the idea that India has a vested interest in Nepal. India, as a major power of South Asia has the responsibility to help the realisation of the aspirations of small states like Nepal. This has to be done without sacrificing India's national interests. The way out can be a token diplomatic support to the proposal for satisfying the Nepalese aspirations. This appears to be the best available course. Nepal, though fully committed to the concept of ZOP, now realises India's position in a better way. SAARC spirit has helped the two countries develop further their friendly co-operation despite differences over ZOP issue.

7

Burma (Myanmar)

I. Background

Burma has two well-defined regions, Upper and Lower Burma, Lower Burma in the south comprises the deltas and plains of the Irrawaddy, the Sittang and the Lower Salween, the province of Arakan and the Tenasserim peninsula. Here are produced rice (prior to the Second World War, Burma was the world's largest exporter of rice), tin and lumber. Upper Burma is an entirely different country formed of narrow valleys and towering mountains. With the exception of tin and oil, most of Burma's mineral wealth is found in Upper Burma. Only coal is lacking to give Burma the common requisites of an industrial civilisation.

Burma is a complex of antitheses. A national unity and a tribalistic disunity; the cult of serenity and withdrawal and the cult of force and violence; the worship of absolute authority, together with an absence of social barriers; relaxed and easy personal relations, constantly exploding into tension; these are some of the attributes of this puzzling country. Burma has undergone invasion, colonial occupation, foreign economic exploitation, the ravages of a 20th century war, the intoxication of a Socialist-style democracy and the drab regimentation of military rule. Burma has survived all these experiences with the essence of its social and religious life unimpaired.

In studying the history of modern Burma two significant facts have to be noted. The economic exploitation of Burma by Indian capitalists and businessmen and the large emigration of Indians into Burma gave to Burmese nationalism a two-fold character, anti-imperialistic and anti-Indian. The second fact is that though Buddhism ceased to be the state religion after the British annexation of Burma, its influence on the country was tremendous. While in China leaders of public opinion prided themselves on the fact that they had no religion, in Burma nationalist leaders had to profess to be devout Buddhists to gain popular support. For instance, the Burmese nationalist leader Dr. Ba Maw, who was baptized as a Christian in his childhood, declared that he had returned to Buddhism when he became a leader. Again people resented attacks on Buddhism and Buddhist clergy, Thein Pe Myint, the author of a well-known novel 'The Modern Monk' was forced to apologise publicly for his anti-clericalism in 1945.

"During a long period of her history, Burma was influenced by two great civilisations, the Indian and the Chinese. Her early inhabitants migrated primarily from Eastern Tibet and Western China. To this racial tie with China was added an even stronger cultural bond with Indian through the conquest of Burma by Hinayana Buddhism. After the 13th century when the Mongols invaded the country, Burmese history was marked by successive periods of political disintegration interspersed with the rise of aggressive and strong military rulers whose conquests spread beyond the borders of present-day Burma. Thus, Burma neither Indian nor Chinese, partook of the culture and life of her neighbours. The majority of the people are the Burmese and the others are the Karens, the Tais or Shans and Indians.

II. History of Indo-Burmese Relations

Burma is an important state among South-East Asian states on India's eastern borders. It has a long land border with India. Arunachal Pradesh, Nagaland, Manipur, Mizoram and Assam are situated along Indo-Burma border. India and Burma have close maritime boundaries. None of the two states as such can remain unaffected and unconcerned with the security situation in the other. The emergence of Communist China as a major power in the neighbourhood has been an important factor in the foreign policies of the two countries.

Till 1937, Burma was a part of India. It was to serve and preserve better the imperial interests of the British Empire that on 1st April 1937, Burma was separated from India and made a separate state. During Second World War, Burma remained under Japanese occupation between 1942-44. After the War, there emerged a strong nationalist movement in Burma and the Burmese people successfully got their country free on 4th January 1948.

After becoming independent, Burma decided to base its foreign policy on the principles of Non-alignment and Peaceful co-existence and to fight the forces of imperialism, colonialism and expansionism. Burma even decided to sever its links with the Commonwealth. It also decided to support fully the national liberation movements in other Asian countries against imperialism and colonialism. These principles of Burmese Foreign Policy were similar to the foreign policy principles of India and hence in 1948, the two countries found it quite convenient to embark upon the path of developing friendly and co-operative relations between them. The historical, cultural and economic links further provided a helpful basis for the development of Indo-Burmese friendship and co-operation. In 1949, China emerged as a Communist power and Burma felt it necessary to keep both India and China at equidistance. When in late fifties, there developed border dispute between India and China, Burma decided to maintain this policy even more scrupulously. However, with the passage of time, Burma fully realised the importance of its relations with India. Presently, both India and Burma are having highly friendly and co-operative relations and there exists no dispute between them.

The history of Indo-Burma relations can be fruitfully traced since 1948 *i.e.*, the year in which Burma became an independent sovereign state. In 1948, when Portugal again attacked Indonesia, the Burmese Government called upon Prime Minister Nehru to try to convene a conference of Asian countries for expressing opposition to this aggression against Indonesia. Since that time both the countries have been co-operating for promoting unity among the Afro-Asian nations.

Immediately after independence, India came to face a serious food problem. In such a situation Burma readily came forward to supply large quantities of rice to India. In 1954, an agreement was concluded between the two countries under which India received additional one lakh tonnes of rice from Burma for overcoming the food shortage.

At the time of separation from India in 1947, Burma inherited a loan from India. The dispute over the question of repayment of this loan created some tensions in post-1948 period. Both sides conducted negotiations and through an agreement in 1954 they were successful in resolving the conflict. This agreement opened the way for the flow of Indian economic aid and loan to Burma. In October 1955, an agreement was signed, and by it India agreed to give a loan of ₹20 crores at 4 per cent interest to Burma. Despite opposition from certain political parties, the Government of India decided to give this loan to Burma. The opposition to grant of loan to Burma was not due to any ideological considerations. It was due to the fact that in mid-fifties India herself was facing financial difficulties and its economy was dependent upon the foreign aid that certain developed countries were giving to India. This clearly exhibited the Indian desire to help Burma in its struggle to achieve economic development. Since the time India and Burma have been maintaining economic and trade links which have in turn helped them to develop mutual friendship and co-operation.

In 1954, India propounded the five principles of peace and peaceful coexistence — The Panchsheel. Burma became one of the first few countries to give full support to this doctrine. It lost no time in signing it with India. At the Bandung Conference when the Panchsheel was discussed, Burma gave full support to the principle and it co-operated with India in securing its adoption by the conference.

India and Internal Problems of Burma: Soon after getting independence, Burma was involved in internal problems. The ruling party — The People's League, faced disunity. In it the communists were not in great numbers. When they failed to achieve their objectives, they indulged into strikes and started creating internal disturbances. Certain other elements — the Karen rebels, joined hand with them and the situation became really grim in mid-fifties. The Government of Burma felt great difficulties in dealing with the rebels. India, at this time decided to treat the matter as a purely internal affair of Burma and hence adopted a neutral attitude towards the problem.

But soon afterwards, a grave development took place which made the Burmese situation very serious. Nearly 10,000 Kuomintang military men fled China and entered Burma. By their presence in Burma there developed unrest in the public life of Burma, because these men started creating disturbances in the border areas. In 1953, Burma complained to the UN General Assembly that by entering into Burma these Kuomintang soldiers were committing an hostile act. It demanded that UNO should help Burma to throw out these soldiers. India gave full support to Burma over this demand and along with a nine other countries, it moved a resolution in the General Assembly. The resolution declared that for establishing peace in Burma, it is essential to throw the Kuomintang soldiers out of Burma. Indian support for Burma made things brighter for the development of more cordial relations between the two countries. Speaking in the Parliament on 17th March 1953, Prime Minister Nehru observed: "I should like to say that with Burma our relations are very friendly. The House knows that Burma has had to face great difficulties, and has still to face them. There is disorder in parts of Burma. In the North-East of Burma a tremendous problem has existed for sometime because of the so-called Kuomintang troops having come in, unwelcome as they were, and squatting and creating mischief there. Burma has had to face all these grave difficulties, and throughout this period our relations with Burma have hardly ever been quite so co-operative and friendly as they are now."

India has always supported the policies of the Government of Burma towards the issue of Communist rebel menace in certain areas of Burma. But, at the same time, it has always regarded it as a internal affair of Burma and has never tried to intervene in the conflict.

Sino-Burma Border Dispute and India: It was in early fifties that a border dispute emerged between China and Burma. In 1953, Prime Minister U. Nu of Burma, during his visit to Peking, discussed the issue, with Chinese leaders. He wanted to secure, through negotiation, a Sino-Burmese agreement on borders.

His attempt proved unsuccessful because of rigid Chinese attitude. China refused to accept a 15 miles long boundary in Burma's border as stood settled on the basis of MacMahon line. India felt concerned with the issue because of Chinese refusal to accept the MacMahon line. The Indian concern became bigger when there developed the Sino-India boundary dispute.

In the early sixties, with a view to isolate Burma from India, China decided to accommodate. Burma and invited General Ne Win, the new head of State of Burma to visit Peking and hold talks for settling the boundary dispute between the two countries. In January 1960, General Ne Win visited Peking (now Beijing) and on 28th January 1960, a friendship and Non-Aggression Treaty was signed between Burma and China. It was under this agreement that the border dispute between the two countries was resolved. Through this agreement, China tried to demonstrate its desire and ability to peacefully solve the border disputes with its neighbour and to show that Sino-Indian boundary dispute was evading solution because of 'India's rigid attitude'. The Sino-Burmese agreement was against India's interest because it ensured Burmese neutrality towards the Sino-Indian boundary dispute. In 1962, when China launched aggression against India, Burma maintained a neutral stand — a stand which definitely favoured China. India did not like the Sino-Burmese Friendship and Non-Aggression agreement but decided to prevent the Indo-Burmese relation from the possible ill-effects of this agreement.

Problem of Indian Nationals in Burma: The issue of the right of the Indian nationals, who had been living in Burma since many years, became an irritant in Indo-Burma relations in late fifties and early sixties. After the independence of Burma, there were about 8 lakh Indian nationals in Burma and they were controlling a large portion of the trade in Burma. They owned nearly 10 lakhs acres of land in Burma. In 1953, the Government of Burma nationalised this land. Of course it paid compensation to the Indian nationals, but India felt that the compensation was grossly inadequate. India, therefore, wanted to hold talks with the Burmese Government over the issue, but the latter felt no need to discuss an affair which was regarded as an internal affair of Burma. This issue brought strains for Indo-Burma relations. A possibility of more strained relations further developed in 1955, when the Government of Burma decided to place additional restrictions' both on the migration of Indian nationals to India and on the sending of money to India. The worst, however, came in 1962-63, when Burmese Government nationalised the industries and business owned by Indians. In this situation many Indian families had to migrate to India and this led to an increased burden on Indian resources. The Government of Burma still maintained that it was an internal affair of Burma to nationalise any industry and business, as such it expressed total opposition to the proposal for talks with India on this issue. The situation created bitterness, but both the countries, realising importance of bilateral co-operation and friendship, decided to take things easy. India, in particular, decided to ignore it. The China factor, rather growing Chinese menace in Indian borders, made it necessary for India to check the chances of increased bitterness in Indo-Burmese relations.

Indo-Burma Boundary Demarcation: Initially India and Burma had some differences over the issue of demarcation of borders. Today these differences stand mostly resolved and nearly 1,000 miles of Indo-Burma border stands demarcated. Both the sides are committed to settle and demarcate through negotiations, the remaining areas that still form the undemarcated borders between the two states.

Naga and Mizo Rebels and Indo-Burma Relations: Naga and Mizo rebels of India have, at times, made use of Burmese territories for organising anti-national and unlawful activities in NEFA and other Eastern states of India. The existence of thick and dense forests and a terrain which hinders access, has been exploited by these rebels for carrying out hostile acts. The Governments of India and Burma have always agreed upon the need to check the operation of rebels in these areas and have in the past collaborated to prevent the rebels from undertaking hostile activities. With the emergence of Bangladesh as a sovereign independent state and due to the effective steps taken by the Government of India, the rebel problem has ceased to be a big problem. India and Burma are today bound by an agreement under which Burma has accepted the responsibility to help India in liquidating the rebel bases in border areas. This has definitely helped the process of development of co-operative and friendly relations between India and Burma.

Presently, there exists no major problem between India and Burma and this makes it possible for us to predict that Indo-Burmese relations are bound to develop more friendship and co-operation in the years to come. Both the countries now fully realise the importance of their bilateral relations. Mr. A.B. Vajpayee once well-observed, "We have historic and cultural ties of longstanding with Burma which is a bridge between South and South East Asia." India and Burma won their freedoms almost simultaneously and both of them are among the founder members of the Non-aligned group. During the freedom struggle our paths converged at many points and it is not surprising that the national leadership of the two countries developed more or less the same world view as well as the same commitment to Asian solidarity. During the 38 years of their bilateral relations, both have been successful in keeping the relations friendly and co-operative. Both have developed a mature understanding of each other and are presently co-operating towards the achievement of a new international economic order. Burma has expressed its readiness to rejoin the Non-aligned Movement (NAM). It withdrew from NAM when Cuba became the Chairman of the Non-aligned. Burma felt that under a committed country like Cuba, NAM can neither fulfill the desired objectives nor play an effective role in world politics. Now, when India is the chairman of NAM, Burma has expressed its willingness to rejoin the movement.

It is indeed a healthy and welcome thinking and would surely give new strength not only to the Non-aligned Movement but also to the bilateral relations between India and Burma. However, the China factor, the desire to Burma to develop more co-operative relations with ASEAN and the Indo-Burmese differences over the Kampuchea issue and Afghanistan crisis need careful handling by India. The strong cultural and historical links with Burma must be used to meet this need. The new President of Burma, Mr. U San Uh and Prime Minister Maung Maung Kha, are fully alive to the need of maintaining good neighbourly and friendly relations with India. So is Mr. Rajiv Gandhi and the Government of India. Prime Minister Rajiv Gandhi's 1987 visit to Burma has strengthened the process of development of increased economic trade and technological co-operation between the two countries. It has encouraged Burma to think in favour of rejoining the NAM. This visit has further developed friendship and co-operation between India and Burma.

8
Bhutan

Bhutan is situated in the Eastern Himalayas, between 26°45′ and 28°N lat and between 89° and 92°E long, bordered on the North and East by Tibet and India, on the West and South by India. Before 1949, Indo-Bhutan relations were governed by the 1865 Treaty as amended by January 1910 Treaty. Under this Treaty, the British Government undertook to exercise no interference in the internal affairs of Bhutan, and the Bhutan Government agreed to be guided by the advice of the British Government in regard to its external relations.

After Independence, the Government of India concluded a fresh treaty with Bhutan on 8th August 1949. Under this treaty the Government of Bhutan agreed to be guided by the Government of India in regard to its external relations, and the Government of India undertook not to interfere in the internal administration of Bhutan. As a measure of goodwill towards Bhutan, India agreed to retrocede to Bhutan an area of about 232 sq.miles in the territory known as Dewangiri, which was annexed in 1865. India continues to pay a subsidy to Bhutan and its amount has been now increased to ₹500,000.

Bhutan is a sovereign state. India has been successful in assuring Bhutan that its sovereignty and internal autonomy stand fully acknowledged and respected by India. In 1971, India sponsored Bhutan for membership of the United Nations and this put to an end to all such suspicions that India has designs over Bhutan. Since this development Indo-Bhutan relations have become closer and maturer. Bhutan feels fully satisfied with its relations with India. It has successfully resisted the temptation of entering into diplomatic relations with other countries. In particular, it has been keeping away 'The China feelers'.

Bhutan fully realises that her security is closely linked with India. Her rulers have been wise enough to have a special treaty relationship with India. They know, opines T.N. Kaul, that if it comes to the crunch, India would defend their security because it is vital to her own. China does not seem to have reconciled herself to this special relationship but has not dared to violate it. She has thrown gentle feelers, followed by vague threats through Bhutanese graziers, cowherds and frontier guards, from time-to-time, but Bhutan has stood firmly by her Treaty with India. In 1975, when Sikkim became a part of the Indian Union, many countries, particularly, China, tried hard to impress upon Bhutan the need to secure Bhutan against possible Sikkim type Indian role in Bhutan. The ruler of Bhutan, King Jigme Singye Wangchuk, however, paid no heed to such propaganda and felt assured of India's respect for the sovereignty of Bhutan. India's decision to sponsor Bhutan's membership of the United Nations, was quoted as the clear proof of Indian good-will towards Bhutan. Now Bhutan has diplomatic relations with Bangladesh and Nepal and Consular relations with Singapore, Kuwait and Hong-Kong, Bhutan is a member of the World Bank.

India on her part has been fully alive to the developmental needs of Bhutan, and has always contributed generously towards the economic development of Bhutan. India has provided economic, material and technical help to Bhutan for developing transport, communication and industrial facilities in the small Himalayan Kingdom. India has built the beautiful 200-km. long mountain road from Phuntsoling in North Bengal to Thimpu, the capital of Bhutan and airstrips at Paro and Thimpu. In 1975, India undertook to meet the entire cost (estimated at ₹83 crones) of the ambitious Bhutanese hydro-electric projection the Chukha river and Punden Cement plan. Bhutan, on its part has always acknowledged and appreciated India's co-operation and has tried to maintain and develop cordial relations with India. There exists good neighbourliness between India and Bhutan, as King Wangchuk has on many occasions observed that "India is not only our close neighbour but our genuine friend." India is fully aware of the need to maintain and further strengthen friendship and co-operation with Bhutan. However, things should not be taken for granted. So far, Bhutan has followed a closer relationship with India because it accords with the security and national interest of both the countries. This close relation must be given more substance and strength on a reciprocal basis, through continued contacts, meetings and consultations at the highest levels. India should prevent Bhutan from succumbing to Chinese pressures and for this, it should more readily come forward to accommodate the needs and aspirations of Bhutan. The past history of co-operation must be used as a basis for strengthening the relationship in the times to come. T.N. Kaul, in his book *Diplomacy in Peace and War*, has beautifully analysed the Indo-Bhutan relations within the border context of India's policy towards its small neighbours. He writes: "We should avoid the mistakes as we made in Nepal and not take smaller countries for granted or act as their big brother. They are sensitive, even touchy, on small things, proud and easily hurt. We must respect their sensibilities, honour their national aspirations and win their trust and confidence. They are subject to many pulls and pressures, stresses and strains, internally and cannot bear these alone without understanding and respect of a friendly neighbour like India." "It is a matter of satisfaction that relations between India and Bhutan are friendly and are developing along the right lines. They could become a model relations between a big country and a small. We should make efforts, honestly and sincerely, towards this end..." "Bhutan has come of age and we can depend on the new king and his people to reciprocate our efforts in further strengthening friendly relations."

The holding of SAARC meeting in Thimpu as well as the Tamil-Sri Lankan talks at Thimpu, has infused a new confidence in Bhutan as a country with respect, prestige and role in international relations. Bhutan fully realises and appreciates India's efforts in securing her national interests without in any way injuring the prestige and status of Bhutan in international relations. Rajiv Gandhi's initiation to encourage and develop more nature and deep friendship and co-operation with India's neighbours has given further strength to the cause of Indo-Bhutanese highly friendly and co-operative relations. Bhutan also fully realises the fact that because of the topography and geo-politics of the area the security and progress of the kingdom stands related to the concept of special relations with India. Bilateral friendly co-operation between India and Bhutan, as well as co-operation as members of the SAARC has been developing in a very satisfactory and healthy manner.

9

India and SAARC

India has always been keen to develop beneficial bilateralism with all her neighbours as well as for developing institutionalised co-operation among the seven South Asian countries—India, Pakistan, Bangladesh, Sri Lanka, Nepal, Bhutan and Maldives. She even favours the inclusion of Afghanistan and Burma, in the South Asian framework.

India has played a very positive and constructive role in floating South Asian Association for Regional Co-operation (SAARC) and making it work as a dynamic association committed to consolidate and expand socio-economic-cultural co-operation among the South Asian countries.

As the Chairman of SAARC, (1986-87) India helped the SAARC not only to overcome its teething troubles but also to make it adopt new goals and programmes for increased co-operation among the members of SAARC.

The efforts of the countries of South Asia, since 1980, were successful in 1985, when the South Asian Association of Regional Co-operation was formally launched in December, 1985 with the specific aim of promoting regional economic co-operation among the member States—India, Pakistan, Bangladesh, Sri Lanka, Nepal, Bhutan and Maldives. It is modeled on the lines of ASEAN, and is designed to serve as an agency for institutionalise promoting economic and cultural co-operation among the members. Its aim is to promote regional economic co-operation for development.

SAARC is indeed, the culmination of the initiative taken by Bangladesh on May 2, 1980. But it was only in August 1983, that the Foreign Ministers of the seven member nations, meeting at Delhi, adopted the 'Declaration in South Asian Regional Co-operation. Bangladesh undertook a detailed analysis of the geopolitical and socio-economic situation of the region and its conclusions helped to pave the way for the formal launching of SAARC in the December 1985 at Dhaka and the first summit meeting of the leaders of the seven SAARC members were held.

Before the formal launching of SAARC, useful and productive ground-work was done by several meetings of the seven South Asian States. The working paper was prepared by Bangladesh which affirmed that, "Economic and technical co-operation on regional basis was accepted by all developing countries as a desirable and necessary strategy." It also identified eleven areas of possible co-operation among the South Asian states.

At this meeting it was agreed that there was every need for regional co-operation for development but asserted that it should not be a substitute for bilateral or multilateral co-operation. The meeting agreed to explore possibilities for co-operation in five areas *viz.*, agriculture, rural development, communication, meteorology and health and population activities. A coordination committee of the whole was set up to handle and process the information and data collected by the countries in respect of the assigned areas.

Meeting at Kathmandu: At this meeting the recommendations of the five study groups as well as the report of the co-ordination committee of the whole was endorsed. It also decided to institute studies in 3 other areas, *viz.*, Transport, Postal Services, and Scientific and Technological co-operation.

Meeting at Islamabad: This meeting reviewed the report of the study group which has constituted in 1981 at the Kathmandu meeting. It endorsed the report and decided to constitute new study groups on sports, arts and culture. A notable and important recommendation was made by this meeting regarding the holding of a ministerial level meeting of the South Asian States during May-September, 1983.

Dhaka Meeting: The meeting, with Bangladesh in the chair, was held at Dhaka in March 1983. It endorsed the recommendation made by the committee of the whole and recommended the adoption of integrated programme of action by the Foreign Ministers. For co-ordinating this action programme, it decided to set up a standing committee.

Meeting at New Delhi: In this meeting the Foreign Ministers signed a Declaration of South Asian Regional Co-operation and initialed the consensus that all the countries agreed to co-operate for achieving the shared aspirations of the people on South Asia regarding socio-economic development and accepted that regional co-operation for development was an imperative necessity. The Declaration of South Asian Co-operation listed the following objectives of the South Asian Regional Co-operation (SARC):

1. To promote welfare of the people of South Asia and improve quality of their life;
2. To accelerate economic growth, social progress and cultural development in the region and to provide all individuals the opportunity to live in dignity and to realise their full potential;
3. To promote and strengthen collective self-reliance among the countries of South Asia;
4. To contribute to mutual trust, understanding and appreciation of one another's problems;
5. To promote active collaboration and mutual assistance in the economic, social, cultural, technical and scientific fields;
6. To strengthen co-operation with other developing countries;
7. To strengthen co-operation among themselves in international forums on matters of common interest and
8. To co-operate with international and regional organisations with similar aims and purposes.

The Declaration further affirmed that co-operation in respect of the above-mentioned rights shall be based on the principles of sovereign equality, territorial integrity, political independence, non-interference in internal affairs of other states and mutual benefits (in fact upon the five principles of Panchsheel). The meeting further declared that regional co-operation shall not substitute but complement the bilateral and multilateral relations.

The Foreign Ministers meet took further steps towards the institutionalisation of SAARC; (Before December 1985 it was known as SARC and not SAARC). It decided to set up several committees.

1. Technical Committee: The committee consisting of representatives of all the member states for implementing, coordinating and monitoring of all the programmes in each area of co-operation.

2. Standing Committee: The committee consisting of the Foreign Secretaries of the member states. It was to co-ordinate and monitor South Asian regional co-operation with regard to:

(*a*) Approval of projects and programmes and modalities of their financing.

(*b*) Determine the intra-societal priorities and over all co-ordination of programmes of action.

(*c*) Mobilisation of regional and external resources.

(*d*) Identification of new areas of co-operation.

The standing committee was to ordinarily, meet at least once a year but more frequent meeting could be held if the members deemed it essential. The standing committee was provided necessary support services for the meeting of Foreign Ministers of the member countries. It was to do the spade work regarding the formulation of policies, programmes and projects, which were to be submitted to the Foreign Ministers for approval.

3. Action Committees: Such committees were to be set up for implementing projects involving more than two countries. Action Committees were to be set up only with the prior approval of the standing committee.

4. Decision Regarding Finances: It was agreed that finances for the co-operative programmes were to be raised through voluntary contributions. The technical committees were to make recommendations regarding the apportionment of the costs for the implementation of agreed programmes. The technical committees, while making such recommendations were to keep in view the following heads:

(*a*) The cost of travel and subsistence for participants in seminar workshops and training and other programmes shall be met by the respective governments and the cost of organising such activities were to be met by the host country or apportioned among the participants in proportion to the facilities availed of;

(*b*) The cost of subsistence for experts shall be met by the receiving countries and cost of travel and/or salary of the experts be paid for by the sending countries; or shared among the participant countries;

(*c*) Other costs, including the costs of preparation of studies shall be shared on a mutually agreed basis by the concerned states;

(*d*) In the case of long-term projects the technical committee to estimate the cost involved and make recommendations to the standing committee on the modalities for meeting the cost.

Besides these, the cost of the projects and programmes for which sufficient financial resources could not be mobilised within the region, external help could be procured from other regional or other appropriate sources with the approval of the standing committee.

New Delhi Meeting 1984: A meeting to discuss and reaffirm the commitment to South Asian Regional Co-operation was held at New Delhi on 27th February 1984. The meeting gave the call for developing friendly political relations along with the development of socio-economic-cultural co-operation among the South Asian countries.

Standing Committee Meeting at Male in February 1985: A meeting of the Standing Committee of the SARC was held at Male in February, 1985. This meeting recommended the establishment of a ministerial council of SARC countries for institutionalising their collective resolve to pursue mutual co-operation. The proposal was cleared by the Foreign Ministers and put up for adoption by the first summit of meeting of heads of States and Governments of South Asian countries to be held at Dhaka in December, 1985.

The First Summit Meeting of the SAARC: Before discussing the nature and scope of decisions taken at the Dhaka Summit of SAARC, it must be clarified that the initial name South Asian Regional Co-operation (SARC) was abandoned in favour of the name South Asian Association for Regional Co-operation (SAARC). This was done to specify that it was an association for the promotion of regional co-operation among the South Asian countries.

The Dhaka Summit was attended by all the seven heads of states and governments of South Asian countries *viz.*, Bangladesh, Bhutan, India, Maldives, Nepal, Pakistan and Sri Lanka. It adopted the declaration for the creation of SAARC with President H.M. Ershad of Bangladesh as its first chairman. The Declaration stated the objectives of the association and the principles on which these were to be pursued and secured. Development of social, economic, cultural, technical co-operation among the member countries was accepted as the objective, and the principles of sovereign equality, independence, integrity and non-interference were accepted as the guiding principles. It was stated that decisions at all levels shall be taken on the basis of consensus and that bilateral and contentious issues shall be excluded from the deliberations. It was further accepted that regional co-operation shall be complimentary and supplementary to bilateral and multilateral co-operation among the member states.

Regarding the organisational set up, the declaration stated that the heads of the states or governments shall meet annually and a Council of Ministers consisting of Foreign Ministers of the member states shall be constituted to formulate policies, to review the progress of the co-operation, to establish additional mechanisms and to decide on matters of general interest. This Council of Ministers shall be assisted by the Committee of the Foreign Secretaries of the member states. It also laid down the setting up of Technical Committee, comprising representatives of member states for implementing, co-ordinating and monitoring of programmes and Action Committee for implementation of projects involving more than two states. It was also affirmed that a

Secretariat for the association shall be established at an appropriate time.

Second Summit of the SAARC: On November 17, 1986, the Second Summit of the SAARC heads of State and Government opened on a note of optimism. It was attended by all the seven member states. It lasted for two days and reaffirmed the commitment of the members to expand and strengthen regional co-operation as well as to devise common policies and approaches for finding solutions to their common problems. Prime Minister of India, Mr. Rajiv Gandhi took over as the Chairman of SAARC (for 1986-87) from President H.M. Ershad of Bangladesh while taking over the Chairmanship, Mr. Rajiv Gandhi, reaffirmed the commitment of all the seven states to make SAARC a success.

This summit decided to set up technical committees on women's participation in developmental activities and for the implementation of measures to end drug abuse and drug-trafficking, thus formally bringing these two areas under the purview of SAARC. It also agreed in principle to expand the SAARC efforts at co-operation to five new fields, South Asian broadcasting programme, promotion of tourism, providing facilities to students and academicians and harnessing of the idealism of youth. The summit adopted a declaration on political and economic issues calling upon the member states not to allow their territories to be used for terrorist activities against other states. The SAARC leaders agreed to co-operate in combating and eliminating terrorism from the region. It gave a call to the great powers to take effective steps for securing an environment of peace and respect for International laws. It voiced grave concern over the escalation of the nuclear arms race and the failure of Reykjavik Summit between USA and USSR.

Referring to the global economic crisis, particularly the mounting debt burden of developing nations, the SAARC leaders agreed to regularly consult and co-operate at international conferences and institutions to achieve the objectives of enlarged concessional assistance. They also agreed to work together to achieve commodity price stabilisation and transfer of technology and to ensure that less developed SAARC countries received special treatment.

This summit took a major step towards institutionalising SAARC by establishing a permanent secretarial to co-ordinate the implementation of SAARC programmes. A Memorandum of Understanding was signed by SAARC Foreign Ministers listing the role, functions and finding of the Secretariat, which was to be established at Kathmandu. (The Secretariat has started functioning *w.e.f.* 16th January 1987 and is presently playing an important role in handling SAARC work). Mr. Abdul Ahsan of Bangladesh has been appointed the first Secretary General of the SAARC. He heads the Secretariat which has seven Directors of the ranks of counsellors, one from each of the member countries. The tenure of the Secretary General is two years and is non-renewable. The first Secretary General has, however, been allotted a tenure of two-and-a-half years in view of the preparatory work involved in connection with the establishment of the Secretariat. In future, the Secretary General will be appointed by the Council of Ministers on nomination by the member states on the basis of the principle of rotation in the alphabetical order—Bangladesh, Bhutan, India, Pakistan, Maldives, Nepal and Sri Lanka. The institutionalisation of SAARC can be described as an important success because without proper and efficient organisation no regional association can be expected to deliver the goods it is designed to deliver.

The Standing Committee of SAARC, in its New Delhi meeting held on 16-17 June 1987, has agreed to co-operate in the fight against terrorism. It has successfully reached a consensus about the nature of terrorism to be liquidated as well as the means to co-ordinate the efforts of the seven SAARC countries against terrorism. It is indeed a welcome agreement, it can go a long way to harmonies relations among the South Asian states.

In the June 19, 1987 meeting of the Foreign Ministers of the seven South Asian nations, concrete shape was given to five new programmes. It approved proposals for: (1) Combating the menace of terrorism in South Asia; (2) Building up of a South Asian food reserve; (3) Exchanging SAARC audio-visual programmes; (4) Organisation of tourism in the region, and (5) Establishment of a documentation centre and a youth volunteers programme.

Prime Minister Rajiv Gandhi in his inaugural address observed the need for adopting not only consolidation but also expansion and growth of SAARC spirit and co-operation on the objective. He described SAARC as an authentic expression of "our particular needs, our particular priorities and particular genius." "We have drawn upon our ancient traditions of conciliation, consensus and concord while responding to contemporary circumstances." For future co-operation two areas were identified: Role of women in development and the prevention of drag-trafficking and drug abuse.

SAARC-Third Summit: The Third Summit of the South Asian Association for Regional Co-operation was held at Kathmandu in November 1987. The Chairmanship passed on from India to Nepal. After reviewing the progress of SAARC under the chairmanship of India, the meeting decided to extend the co-operation to the suppression of terrorism, forming a South Asian food security reserve and adopting the Kathmandu Declaration, which called for efforts to intensify co-operative efforts in areas of trade, industry, disaster management and environment conservation.

Recognising the shared aspirations of the peoples of South Asia to communicate and co-operate with each other at people-to-people level, the Summit declaration called upon the SAARC to be increasingly oriented to the people's needs and aspirations with a view to bring about a qualitative improvement in the general atmosphere of the region and for strengthening peace, friendship and co-operation in the area.

The regional convention on terrorism was signed by the Foreign Ministers of the SAARC countries in the presence of their leaders. The member countries pledged to refrain from organising, instigating or participating in civil strife or terrorist acts in their areas. It was indeed, a major success of Indian diplomacy in SAARC.

The Summit initiated preliminary steps towards trade and industrial co-operation, protection of environment in the context of natural calamities, and establishment of a SAARC food security reserve. It was agreed that the food reserve will begin with a stock of 200,000 tonnes of wheat and rice and that India lone will contribute 15,200 tonnes of food grains to the reserve. Release of the food grains to a country in need, including the prices, terms and conditions of payment in kind or otherwise will be through direct negotiations between the member countries concerned, but they will at the same time inform the board of the deal.

The proposal for the establishment of such a food reserve was made by India; as such the establishment of the food reserve can be described as India's success.

The Summit also decided to commission a comprehensive study of the region's environment and the necessary measures for its protection and preservation. The decision to commission the study followed informal discussions among the SAARC leaders. It was agreed that the study will be handled by the SAARC Secretary General and that it will cover, in a well-planned and comprehensive framework, the causes and consequences of natural disasters.

The SAARC members also agreed to intensify their disaster management capabilities and expressed concern over the degradation of the environment which was "severely undermining the development process and prospects of the member countries."

The meeting expressed grave concern over the deteriorating international political environment and felt that it was mostly due to Super Power policies and practices of domination and intervention. It also recorded its voice in favour of the need for reducing the fast increasing military expenditure. The leaders observed that high defence spending was a major constraint on world development. They welcomed the new understanding between the two super powers in favour of eliminating from Europe the intermediary range nuclear missiles. It was hoped that this will be precursor of future accords in favour of nuclear disarmament and arms control. The leaders unanimously expressed their resolve to continue their efforts towards the creation of an international environment and opinion in favour of total nuclear disarmament. They expressed full support for the conclusion of a treaty prohibiting the vertical and horizontal proliferation of nuclear weapons.

India played an important role in the SAARC deliberations and decisions. The Pakistani attempt to frustrate the Afghanistan's efforts towards the joining of SAARC was successfully thwarted by India. The meet directed the Foreign Ministers Conference to examine the issue of new members. India's view that Pakistan's opposition to the policies of Government of Afghanistan cannot be allowed to come into the way of Afghanistan's sovereign right to seek the membership and join a regional association committed for the promotion of peace, security, stability and development in the region.

This SAARC Summit adopted a good basis for the successful operation of this regional association for development, when the seven South Asian leaders decided to measures for co-operation should be progressively carried out within a broad framework of a long-term perspective. In this context, they stressed the need for further consolidation and rationalisation of the on-going activities being pursued within the SAARC framework.

India, being the territorially biggest, population-wise the largest, development-wise technologically and industrially the most developed country of the South Asia, has played and continues to play a big role in the successful operationalisation of SAARC programmes for co-operation and development among the member states. India has accepted the SAARC as a voluntarily organised association of sovereign equal states for consolidating and expanding regional co-operation for development. India firmly believes that SAARC spirit can help the countries of South Asia to develop, and to resolve their bilateral issues outside the SAARC platform.

Ministerial Meet in August 1988: A two-day meeting of the Council of Ministers (Foreign Ministers) of SAARC was held on August 12-13, 1988. It welcomed the Pakistani offer to hold the 34th SAARC Summit meet in place of Sri Lanka which had expressed its inability to do so because of internal compulsion.

The meeting agreed that new members can be admitted to SAARC only if they accepted its objectives and principles, and only be a unanimous decision of the Heads of States and Government.

In a seven-page draft report, the Foreign Ministers welcomed the finalisation of the proposal on SAARC agricultural information centre to be established in Bangladesh. It suggested improvement in SAARC Audio-Visual Exchange (SAVE) programme, launched on November 2, 1987 and its extension to promote development communication programme in collaboration with World View International Foundation (WVIF) and other non-government agencies working in South Asia.

The meeting further agreed that the SAARC thrust should be for promoting co-operation in the spheres of production, trade, money and finance.

SAARC-Fourth Summit: The Fourth SAARC Summit was held on 29th December 1988 in Islamabad and all the seven Heads of States and Governments, attended the meeting. At this meeting the Chairmanship of SAARC passed from Nepal to Pakistan, and Prime Minister Ms. Benazir Bhutto became its chairperson. Ms. Benazir in her inaugural speech observed, "We should consider ways of limiting our arms expenditures and seek regional solutions for curbing the arms race and the danger of nuclear proliferation and war." She gave a call to vanquish the enemies-poverty, disease, slums and ignorance instead of spending heavy amounts on the defence front.

Mr. Rajiv Gandhi, who attended the conference, observed in his speech that "SAARC nations must try to come closer by allowing a free flow of information, a thrust towards trade and economic co-operation, positive action for environmental conservation and activities involving greater participation of the people." He regretted that "SAARC countries have not taken even one full step down the road towards regional co-operation of a kind which interferes with our people on development issues at the grassroots. If we play with shadows and allow ourselves to be overwhelmed by apprehensions, co-operation in development will remain a mirage."

The SAARC Summit pledged to stamp out terrorism and adopted the Pakistani sponsored initiative for a regional basic needs perspective plan 'SAARC 2000'. It envisages the pooling of resources of the SAARC states and utilising the same meeting the basic needs of the people of the region, particularly the needs for primary health care, removal of illiteracy, providing of shelter and clothing to the people. It also emphasises the need to undertake population planning for securing the above objectives.

The leaders decided to put in an all-out war against the drug menace which was posing a grave threat to political and social stability of the region.

A decision to issue 'SAARC Passport' to members of Parliament and Judges of the Supreme Courts of the South Asian countries enabling them to freely visit the seven countries was undertaken. It was decided to gradually extend the facility to new categories of people.

In the Fourth SAARC summit, Indian view point was accepted by all the countries in so far as a decision to extend SAARC co-operation to regional economic co-operation and free information flows, as recommended by Prime Minister, Rajiv Gandhi in his speech, was adopted.

However, India's role in SAARC is bound to remain limited because other countries, with the exceptions of Bhutan and Maldives, fear India and have bilateral disputes with India. Pakistan at the SAARC platform gave a call for limiting the arms race in South Asia, and yet it has been instrumental in generating an arms race by importing or getting high technology weapons from the United States in the name of parity or balance with India. India has a very long sea coast to protect, longest border with China, a country opposed to India's interests, and a big land border with Pakistan, Nepal, Bangladesh. As such its defence requirements are bigger than Pakistan and yet Pakistan wants parity with India. Indo-Pak conflict, despite the new hopes generated by Rajiv-Benazir is a reality of South Asia, Indo-Sri Lankan conflict over the withdrawal of IPKF from Sri Lanka, Indo-Nepalese differences may conflict over the trade and transit treaty. Indo-Bangladesh conflict over Farakka and Chakma Refugees issues, the continued problem of terrorist activities, smuggling and drug-pedalling etc., all combine to make SAARC environment unhealthy for the growth of regional co-operation. In July 1989, Sri Lankan boycott of SAARC Foreign Ministers' conference reflects the brittle nature of SAARC fabric. Sri Lanka has failed to realise the difference between bilateral relations and regional relations and this constitutes a danger signal for SAARC.

India's predicament regarding its role in SAARC results from the fact that if it decides to play a leadership role, it is charged of being a hegemonistic power, and if it keeps restraint and plays an equal role, the SAARC fails to function. Just as ASEAN countries have realised the natural leadership role of Indonesia in ASEAN, the SAARC countries must also accept India's role as the biggest and relatively most developed country of South Asia which alone can serve as the nucleus for the development of SAARC.

Index

N

O

P

Q

R

S

Y

Z